Towers and Colonnades:
the architecture of Cuthbert Brodrick

TOWERS
AND
COLONNADES

THE ARCHITECTURE OF
CUTHBERT BRODRICK

Derek Linstrum

LEEDS
THE LEEDS PHILOSOPHICAL AND LITERARY SOCIETY LTD
1999

This volume has been published in collaboration with the British Architectural Library Drawings Collection RIBA to coincide with an exhibition of Cuthbert Brodrick's work at the RIBA Heinz Gallery, London, from 23 January to 6 March 1999.

Proceedings of the Leeds Philosophical and Literary Society, Literary and Historical Section, Vol. xxv.

The Leeds Philosophical and Literary Society Ltd.,
City Museum,
Calverley Street,
Leeds LS1 3AA

Editor, Literary and Historical Section
IAN MOXON, M.A.
University of Leeds

British Library Cataloguing-in-Publication Data: a catalogue record for this book is available from the British Library.

ISBN 1 870737 11 3

Printed in Great Britain by W. S. Maney and Son Ltd., Leeds

Frontispiece. Cuthbert Brodrick *c.* 1870.

Contents

Figures

Figs. 19, 38, 44, 65, 67, 79, 105, and 107 first appeared in D.Linstrum, *West Yorkshire Architects and Architecture* (1978), published by Lund Humphries, and are reproduced by permission.

Figs. 8, 9, 10, 11, 12, 13, 14, 58, 86, 93, 106, 126, and 138 are taken from slides formerly in the library of the Leeds School of Architecture (now a department of the Faculty of Health and Environment, Leeds Metropolitan University).

Figs. 20, 22, 62, 75, 81, 114, 121, and 134 have been redrawn by Peter Dewes.

Figs. 18, 26, 32, 39, 41, 42, 43, 48, 49, 50, 68, 69, 70, 71, 102, 115, 116, 117, 123, 124, 125, 127, 128, 135, 137, 139, 145, 146, 147, and 148 have been taken or collected by the author.

Abbreviations

Linstrum, *WYAA*:   Derek Linstrum, *West Yorkshire Architects and Architecture* (London, 1978)

RIBA: British Architectural Library Drawings Collection, Royal Institute of British Architects

RIBA, *Catalogue*:   *Catalogue of the Drawings Collection of the Royal Institute of British Architects*, volume B (Farnborough, 1972), volume L–N (Farnborough, 1973), and volume O–R (Farnborough, 1976)

Prologue

1 George Dudley Harbron (1881–1953) was articled with Smith, Brodrick, and Lowther; from 1929 to 1949 he was in partnership in Hull with Allanson Hick (1898–1975). He was active in many local societies, but it was in writing that he found a congenial outlet. He contributed to *The Builder* and *The Architectural Review*, and wrote *Amphion; or, the Nineteenth Century* (London, 1930) and *The Conscious Stone: the life of Edward William Godwin* (London, 1949). For many years he took a leading part in architectural education in Hull. (Obituary: *The York and East Yorkshire Architectural Society Year Book 1953–54*, 46–47.)

2 Mr. John Soulsby, who had entered the office of Walker, Son, and Field (the last phase of the Hull practice which bore successively the following names: Smith and Brodrick; Smith, Brodrick, and Lowther; Brodrick and Lowther; Brodrick, Lowther, and Walker; Walker and Son; Walker, Son, and Field) as a pupil in 1933, remembers (1997) 'Dudley coming into the office at 77 Lowgate to see some of the drawings at the time he was preparing the article for the *Review*' (c. 1936). He also remembers that 'up what had been the servants' back stairs, I imagine, there was a largish room fitted up with wooden racks on which very dusty brown paper parcels, some big and heavy, housed I should say all the drawings [Brodrick] ever turned out. Also perspectives mounted on strainers lay about the room'. These would have included Cuthbert Brodrick's office drawings, which he left to his nephew, Frederick Stead Brodrick (1847–1927); Mr Soulsby particularly remembers the long drawings for the Custom House, Bombay. Through Harbron, a selection of these drawings was presented to the RIBA in 1940 by Trevor Field, the last remaining partner in the firm. Correspondence with Harbron about these drawings (1941 and 1946), referred to in the card index of the RIBA Drawings Collection, does not appear to have survived.

3 *The Architectural Review*, 79 (1936), 33–35.

4 Thomas Butler Wilson (1859–1942) set up in practice in Leeds and London in 1884, later taking Robert P. Oglesby into partnership. Several of their large houses were illustrated in professional journals. He wrote *Modern House Interiors* (London, 1897), as well as *Two Leeds Architects* (Leeds, 1937) which relied to a great extent on Harbron's article and brought an accusation of plagiarism. It is a useful book, but the facts are not always accurate and references are not given to support dates and facts. It formed the basis of a lecture which Wilson repeated many times.

5 A. Briggs, *Victorian Cities* (London, 1963), pp. 137–84.

'Cuthbert Brodrick, Town Hall, Leeds', an entry in a Leeds directory for 1856, was to become a nickname, but it succinctly describes the principal fact known to most people about the building's designer. It is almost as if he were the Mascagni or Charpentier of architecture, and the Town Hall the *Cavalleria Rusticana* or *Louise*; but there is more to Brodrick than that. He is, however, not an easy subject. There are virtually no family papers, since he had no direct or close family; no diaries; hardly any professional correspondence; and his sketchbooks have been lost. There are few portraits, and even the one document in the archives of the Royal Institute of British Architects, his application to become a Fellow, which could have provided helpful information, is unaccountably missing. All that we have is a group of beautifully rendered drawings (many of them failed entries in competitions), paragraphs in the mid-nineteenth-century architectural journals (in particular in *The Builder*), and a small number of executed works. Yet the finest of his buildings are of national, even international, importance.

As a consequence of this lack of information, very little has been written about him. In 1936 Dudley Harbron,[1] a Hull architect to whom we are indebted for salvaging the Brodrick drawings now in the Royal Institute of British Architects Drawings Collection,[2] wrote a short article about him in *The Architectural Review* under the curious title of 'Cuthbert Brodrick: or Cabbages at Salona'.[3] In 1937 a Leeds architect, Thomas Butler Wilson,[4] wrote a book, *Two Leeds Architects*, about Brodrick and George Corson. Evidently both Harbron and Wilson had access to some written or oral information and to more drawings; none of this material is any longer available. In 1963 Asa Briggs published *Victorian Cities*, in which the chapter, 'Leeds: a study in civic pride', is largely concerned with the building of the Town Hall as an aspect of social change.[5] Then there was nothing else until 1967 when the Institute of Advanced Architectural Studies, University of York, mounted an exhibition of Brodrick's drawings and I wrote an article about it in *Country Life*.[6] In 1970 I was invited by the Royal Society of Arts to deliver one of the Bossom Lectures, on the subject of Brodrick; this was published in 1971,[7] and it was the last published reference to him and his work, although there have been at least three university theses which have examined aspects of his buildings,[8] and Leeds Town Hall figured prominently in Colin Cunningham's *Victorian and Edwardian Town Halls*.[9]

Brodrick was a man of his time. When he was practising in the 50s and 60s, many members of his profession experienced a sense of failure in one important respect. 'The fact is, we have not yet an architecture of our own; and, in the way we are now going on, it will be long before we shall have it', wrote a critic in *The Builder* in 1862.[10] It was the age of styles and, although Brodrick was at heart a committed Classicist, he adopted others when he thought them appropriate or the occasion expedient. It was the age of the Victorian architectural competition, a mixed blessing from which he benefited in establishing himself at a relatively early age on the strength of winning the glittering prize of Leeds Town Hall, although later experiences were less auspicious and led to his withdrawal from the scene. It was the age of the emergence of the industrial towns as rivals to London in their architectural patronage, which was increasingly moving from the aristocracy to municipal committees and the middle classes, so that it could correctly be forecast that 'the archaeologist of a future age will look for the best specimens of the buildings of the present reign [in] some provincial towns'.[11] This was Brodrick's world; he experienced early success that put him in the company of leading metropolitan architects but which gradually turned to disappointment and abandonment of his profession.

Brodrick has always been something of a mystery, and now, almost a century after his death and nearly 130 years after he ceased practice, we are not likely to make any striking new discoveries about him. Anyone who tries to understand him has to deduce what can be gained from the buildings themselves and his unexecuted designs, placing him and them in their contemporary context. My Bossom Lecture was sub-titled 'an interpretation of a Victorian architect'; this monograph, so appropriately published by The Leeds Philosophical and Literary Society, is still an interpretation, but one based on additional research and a longer look at Brodrick's work.

Author's Acknowledgements

I am grateful to Ian Moxon, the editor of The Leeds Philosophical and Literary Society, for his enthusiastic support and careful editorial work, and to Dr. Terry Friedman, who read the draft typescript and made helpful suggestions for improvement. Peter Dewes kindly agreed to redraw the plans in a consistent format, sometimes from unclear sources which called for interpretation. Dr. David Neave and Dr. Susan Neave shared with me their knowledge of Brodrick's work in the East Riding, while Jon Burgess and Christine Leveson offered information about Lockwood and Mawson's work as well as Brodrick's. Brian and Dorothy Payne allowed me to quote from Dr. Heaton's diaries and letters which are in their possession, and I have had help in various ways from Susan Balderstone, William Connor, David Cookson, Colin Dews, Dr. Barbara English, John Goodchild, Bryan Perrett, John Soulsby, and John Thorp. I acknowledge the help I have received from several libraries, record offices, archives, and art galleries in Beverley, Bolton, Hull, Leeds, Manchester, and Scarborough, and their permission to reproduce drawings in their possession. Individual acknowledgements are given in the appropriate places. The staff in the Art Library in Leeds were always willing to bring me another pile of bound architectural journals, and those in the Local and Family History Library were unfailingly helpful, as were those in the West Yorkshire Archive Service (Leeds). I am grateful to the Victoria and

6 D. Linstrum, 'Architecture of Cuthbert Brodrick', *Country Life*, 141 (1967), 1379–81.

7 D. Linstrum, 'Cuthbert Brodrick: an interpretation of a Victorian architect', *The Journal of the Royal Society of Arts*, 119 (January 1971), 72–88.

8 D. Longmore, 'Cuthbert Brodrick's use of ornament', unpublished B.A. dissertation, University of Leeds (1975). D. N. K. Gaito, 'Cuthbert Brodrick of Leeds: a Victorian architect', unpublished M.A. dissertation, University of Sheffield (1976). C. Leveson, 'The work of Cuthbert Brodrick 1844–1869'. unpublished M.A. dissertation, De Montfort University (1995).

9 C. Cunningham, *Victorian and Edwardian Town Halls* (London, 1981).

10 *The Builder*, 20 (1862), 254.

11 T. W. Reid (ed.), *A Memoir of John Deakin Heaton, M.D., of Leeds* (London, 1883), p. 121.

Albert Museum, the National Monuments Record, the Richard Green Gallery, and the Toledo Museum of Art for their help with illustrations, as well as to those individuals who are acknowledged elsewhere. Special thanks are due to Charles Hind and his colleagues in the British Architectural Library, RIBA Drawings Collection, in whose keeping are the majority of Brodrick's drawings.

Editor's Acknowledgement

The publication of this volume has been assisted by the receipt of two substantial grants, one from the Marc Fitch Fund for help with the general costs of publication, the other from the Paul Mellon Centre for Studies in British Art to support in particular the costs of including coloured illustrations. On behalf of the Leeds Philosophical and Literary Society the editor records his thanks to both organizations for this generous help.

Early Years

Hull, or Kingston-upon-Hull to give the Yorkshire city its full official name, was described in the early-nineteenth century as being

situated at the confluence of the rivers Hull and Humber; the streets in the older part are narrow and incommodious; but in other parts of the town they are spacious and more regularly formed. The houses in general are built of brick; the streets are well paved with excellent durable stone, brought from Iceland as ballast in the ships employed in the whale fishery, and are lighted with gas by two companies; one for oil gas, established in 1821; the other for coal gas, in 1826.[1]

This was the town, one of the principal seaports in the United Kingdom, in which Cuthbert Brodrick, the future architect, was born on 1 December 1821.[2] He was the sixth son of John Brodrick and Hannah Foster, both of whom came from families associated with shipping on the east coast. They were married in December 1804 and produced ten children, seven boys and three girls, all of whom survived into adulthood. When Cuthbert was baptized at Holy Trinity, the impressive parish church in the Market Place in Hull, on 7 October 1822, the family home was in Summergangs, an area in Drypool parish on the east side of the River Hull; but by 1831 they were at 37 George Street, a street of brick-built Late Georgian houses in a good part of the town. John Brodrick was a well-to-do merchant and shipowner who, at various times up to 1857, owned one or more of a list of ten ships, mostly employed in the American passenger and emigrant trade, and in commerce with Baltic countries.[3] His office was at 21 High Street, in the heart of the town and the centre of mercantile life. In 1850 he was appointed by the government a member of the Local Marine Board.

There were trade and shipping connections between Hull and

Norway, Sweden, Holland, Hamburgh, France, Spain and America, to which it exports the manufactured goods and produce of the counties of York, Nottingham, Derby, Stafford, and Chester, with which it has greater facility of intercourse, by means of the Aire, Calder, Ouse, Trent, and other large rivers which fall into the Humber, and the numerous canals communicating with them . . . It carries on also a very extensive coasting trade in corn, wool, manufactured goods, and other articles of merchandise.[4]

Hull's standing as an international port was reflected in the quality of its architecture. Although Edward Baines wrote in his *History, Directory, and Gazetteer of the County of York* in 1823 that 'The public buildings . . . do not display any great degree of magnificence, nor many traces of antiquity', the town had been expanding and renovating itself in the Old Town district in the late-eighteenth and early-nineteenth centuries. Much of the building was anonymous, the work of builder/architects, with brick façades, sash windows, and Classical doorcases, but there was a high degree of good craftsmanship available for the wealthier merchants and

1 S. Lewis, *A Topographical Dictionary of England...*, 4 vols. (London, 1831), II, *s.n.* Kingston.

2 There are conflicting birth dates. Dudley Harbron, 'Cuthbert Brodrick: or Cabbages at Salona', *The Architectural Review*, 79 (1936), 33, gives it as 1821, and so does a French census return for 1876; T. B. Wilson, *Two Leeds Architects* (Leeds, 1937), p. 11, gives it as 1822, and so does the inscription on Brodrick's grave. Thanks to research by Mrs. J. J. Brodrick (*The Banyan Tree*, 41 (January 1990)) and Dr. Susan Neave, 1821 is confirmed as the correct date (Beverley, County Hall, East Riding of Yorkshire Council Archives and Records Service, PE 158/7, Register of Baptisms, Holy Trinity Church, Hull, 1 January 1813 – 31 December 1822). In brackets below the entry is written 'born Decr 1 1821'. This and other errors in Wilson's text make one cautious in using it.

3 *The Trade and Commerce of Hull: and its ships and shipowners, past and present*, 2nd edn. (Hull, 1878), pp. 110–11.

4 Lewis, op. cit. (note 1), II, *s.n.* Kingston.

1

shipowners. Despite the great destruction during the Second World War, there is still plenty of evidence of a sophisticated taste in architecture and decoration in the fine houses that remain.[5]

There were also some attractive opportunities for architects to add to the town's more ambitious buildings. Charles Mountain (c. 1743–1805)[6] was among the first Georgian architects of note in the town. Like many at that time, he had begun as a craftsman, in his case a plasterer, and then turned to building and architecture, following Palladian models and incorporating Adam-like decoration. Most of his work was domestic. George Pycock (c. 1749–99)[7] was another builder/architect who designed houses, but also the General Infirmary (1784). Joseph Hargrave (c. 1754–1802)[8] built the Charterhouse Hospital (1780). Then Charles Mountain junior (c. 1773–1839),[9] who had been practising in Lincoln, returned to Hull in 1805. His design for the Theatre Royal (1809–10) was conventional enough, but in most of his other buildings he introduced the Greek Revival to the town, as in the Trinity Hospital (1828) and the Public Rooms (1830–34). A much more interesting proposal for the latter, with a frontage of Corinthian giant-order columns set in front of a rusticated wall, was submitted by Richard Hey Sharp (1793–1853)[10] from York; it could almost have been the work of the young Brodrick, but he was then only nine years old. John Clark (c. 1799–1857)[11] of Leeds was another architect from outside the town who was attracted by the available commissions. He had brought a quality of Edinburgh's New Town to Leeds architecture, and in Hull he built the gigantic Greek Doric column to commemorate the famous Yorkshire member of parliament, William Wilberforce (1834). In 1834–35 Charles Mountain junior left Hull and moved first to Malton and then to Wakefield, leaving the way clear for a new man; he arrived in 1834 in the person of the young Henry Francis Lockwood (1811–78), who was to be the first architectural influence on the young Cuthbert Brodrick.

Lockwood came from a building-family background in Doncaster, and he was far removed from Charles Dickens's caricature of a provincial architect, Mr. Pecksniff, into whose hands the unfortunate Nicholas Nickleby fell. He had been articled in London to Peter Frederick Robinson (1776–1858),[12] who is best remembered today for his several publications of designs for villas, farm buildings, and lodges in various architectural styles, including a picturesque Tudor. Robinson had been an assistant to Henry Holland (1745–1806) after being articled to William Porden (1755–1822), which means that Lockwood had a good architectural pedigree through Robinson that covered both the Neoclassical and the Gothic styles. Robinson was also interested in old buildings; he read a paper to the recently formed Institute of British Architects in 1834 on 'The newly discovered crypt at York Minster', and he had been responsible for rebuilding parts of York Castle Gaol in a castellated style.[13] Lockwood, who had returned to his native Yorkshire in connection with this work while in Robinson's employ, wrote, jointly with Adolphus H. Cates, *The History and Antiquities of the Fortifications to the City of York* (1834). Interestingly, at the time when Lockwood was setting up his practice in Hull, Robinson had taken on three commissions in York; these

5 See I. and E. Hall, *Georgian Hull* (York, 1978/79).

6 H. Colvin, *A Biographical Dictionary of British Architects 1600–1840*, 3rd edn. (New Haven and London, 1995), pp. 670–71.

7 Colvin, op. cit. (note 6), p. 789.

8 Colvin, op. cit. (note 6), p. 460.

9 Colvin, op. cit. (note 6), p. 671.

10 Colvin, op. cit. (note 6), pp. 860–61. The design is in the Wakefield Museum, Gott Collection, vol. 7, fos. 1–7.

11 Colvin, op. cit. (note 6), pp. 249–50.

12 Colvin, op. cit. (note 6), pp. 826–29.

13 See Royal Commission on Historical Monuments (England), *An Inventory of the Historical Monuments in the City of York*, 5 vols. (1962–81), II (The Defences) (London, 1972), p. 66.

1. Kingston College, Hull (H. F. Lockwood 1837).

were the removal of eighteenth-century additions from, and the restoration of, Bootham Bar (1834), the City and County Bank, Parliament Street (1835), and De Grey House, St. Leonard's Place (1835). Could there have been a connection? Was Lockwood acting for Robinson from his York office? There is no confirmation, but it is not unlikely that there was such an arrangement.

However, what seems certain is that on 4 January 1837, when Cuthbert Brodrick was fifteen years old, he entered Lockwood's office as an articled pupil. What did that mean? According to advice to parents, published in 1842,

The youth desirous of becoming an Architect should be liberally educated, and in addition to the Latin language, he should be master of French and Italian; have some knowledge of mathematics, geometry and drawing. The premium required . . . is from two to five hundred pounds; the youth will also require a considerable sum for the purchase of books, instruments and drawing materials. He must, during his apprenticeship, learn to make architectural drawings from admeasurement, also to sketch picturesque buildings, columns, etc., he must be careful in observing the proceedings of workmen in every branch of business connected with buildings. When he is out of his pupilage, if he can afford it, he should spend a few months in Italy, to study the remains of the ancient masters, and the works of masters of a more recent date.[14]

Brodrick had been educated privately at first, but later he had attended Kingston College, Hull,[15] a private academy for sons of the well-to-do. At the time when Brodrick entered his office, Lockwood was designing a new building for the college, brick-built with stone dressings in the Tudor-Gothic style that was one of the possibilities in Robinson's published designs for houses. This was (and still is, although part has been demolished) a symmetrical building with a central hall flanked by a three-bay link to a twin-gabled house with bay windows at each end, a composition that was equally adaptable to a Classical interpretation. This would have

14 *The Complete Book of Trades or the Parents' Guide and Youth's Instructor*, quoted in F. Jenkins, *Architect and Patron* (Oxford, 1961), p. 160.

15 Wilson, op. cit. (note 2), p. 11.

been the largest commission in the office when Brodrick was introduced to architectural practice but, although Lockwood worked in a competent if unexciting manner in the Tudor-Gothic style on other buildings such as the vicarage of St. Andrew's church, Kirk Ella (1839), and Sculcoates Hospital (now Kingston General Hospital) (1843), he was essentially committed to Classicism. This preference must have been an influence on Brodrick. Apparently the young man was quick to show his talents as a draughtsman, and by the time he was seventeen he had been awarded a silver medal for his measured drawings of the splendidly elaborate fourteenth-century Percy Tomb in Beverley Minster, with its multiplicity of figures and pinnacles. He is said to have made measured drawings too of St. Mary's, Cottingham, and St. Augustine's, Hedon, two of the largest

4

4. The design for the Beverley and East Riding Public Rooms, Beverley (H. F. Lockwood 1839). This ambitious interior was 88 feet long, 53 feet wide, and 41 feet high.

16 RIBA, *Catalogue*, B, p. 111.

17 RIBA, *Catalogue*, B, p. 110.

18 J. J. Sheahan and T. Whellan, *History and Topography of the City of York; the Ainsty Wapentake; and the East Riding of Yorkshire*, 2 vols. (Beverley, 1855, 1856), II (1856), pp. 285–86. The building was known as the Beverley and East Riding Public Rooms, and still exists, though mutilated.

medieval churches in the Hull area. He was also a talented watercolourist, and two fine perspectives among the drawings that have survived from his office are presumably student exercises which also show a predilection for a different style. One is a view of the Pantheon in Rome in a theoretically restored state with figures in the pediment of the portico.[16] The other is of Karl Friedrich Schinkel's Neues Schauspielhaus in Berlin, apparently copied from the relevant plate in *Sammlung architectonischer Entwürfe*.[17] It is not difficult to understand why Brodrick chose these two buildings as exercises, presumably an early revelation of what was to become almost a mania for giant-order columns; but they are watercolours of a high quality and explain why he is said always to have made his own presentation drawings. Obviously he enjoyed it.

In 1839 Lockwood received two commissions which can be seen as crucial in Brodrick's maturing as a Classical architect. The first was in Beverley, where an Assembly Rooms had been built by public subscription in 1761–63 to a design by John Carr. Seventy years later additional accommodation was required for meetings and dinners of local associations, and Lockwood designed 'a very large lofty room',[18] which was built in 1840. A lithographic view of his proposal for the interior of this quite astonishing room was published in 1839. It was divided into bays with large lunette windows, and the vaulted ceiling had decorative plasterwork in the ribs and ceiling panels, all in a Late Classical French taste reminiscent of the work of Percier and Fontaine or of Louis-Pierre Baltard of the 1830s. It is not certain how much of this ambitious design was executed, but obviously it would have been known to Brodrick, who might even have worked on it. Its affinity with Leeds Town Hall is clear.

The second important commission in the Lockwood office at this time was the new Chapel for Trinity House, the most wealthy and ancient charity in Hull. It was a replacement for an earlier Chapel (1772) designed by Sir William Chambers, and it was built between 1839 and 1843. Externally the public west front is rendered and relatively austere with a projecting porch; the private east front, entered through Trinity House itself, is faced with stone and ornamented with Corinthian pilasters. Inside the centrally planned space with three Diocletian windows and a large window above the altar table rescued from Chambers's Chapel there is boldly detailed coffering in the cleverly managed vaulting. There is a half dome over the altar apse, and the fluently detailed capitals incorporate nautical motifs, anchors, shells, and dolphins. The Neoclassical concentration on architectural form is complemented by the use of marble for the columns — brown in the apse, white on the gallery columns, and mixed colours on the elaborate floor. There is a handsome pulpit with gilt-bronze mounts to complete this outstanding Late Georgian interior. These two designs, in Beverley and Hull, were

5. Trinity House Chapel, Hull (H. F. Lockwood 1839).

6. Trinity House Chapel, Hull; the capitals are variations on the Corinthian models and incorporate maritime allusions.

19 S. Redgrave, *A Dictionary of Artists of the English School* (London, 1878, facsimile edn. 1970), p. 9. See also D. Brooks, *Thomas Allom (1804–72)* (London, 1998).

20 *The Builder*, 30 (1872), 840.

21 H.-R. Hitchcock, *Early Victorian Architecture in Britain*, 2 vols. (London, 1954), I, pp. 340–41. One of the temple wings housed a Sunday School, the other the caretaker.

22 L. Hautecoeur, *Histoire de l'architecture classique en France*, 7 vols. (Paris, 1943–57), VII, pp. 191 ff.

obviously important in Brodrick's development, and one wonders what part he might have played in them.

One would also like to know more about the part played in the practice by Thomas Allom (1804–72), whose career had started by his being articled to Francis Goodwin (1784–1835); for a short period, approximately from 1841 to 1843, he was in partnership with Lockwood in Hull. Allom is remembered more today as an architectural and topographical illustrator than as a designer, and he contributed for publication many drawings of scenery and buildings. He did most of the drawings, for example, for *Lake and Mountain Scenery* (*c.* 1830) and *The British Switzerland* (1858), and he exhibited at the Royal Academy and other galleries. Samuel Redgrave wrote of his 'great skill in finishing architectural drawings', and that he 'drew and sketched with great facility'.[19] His obituarist wrote that 'he was frequently called upon to assist his professional brethren', and recalled 'the vigour and beauty of the drawings . . . of the new Houses of Parliament, . . . presented by [Sir Charles Barry] to the late Emperor Nicholas'.[20] Did Allom's 'charming pencil' also draw later for Lockwood or Brodrick? The three or four years when Allom was in partnership with Lockwood were formative in Brodrick's career, and one might assume that at least some of his talents as a draughtsman and watercolourist were developed by Allom's example and encouragement.

Allom was also successful in his architectural work. He was premiated in at least nine competitions, obtaining the first prize in four, including the William Brown Library and Museum, Liverpool (1856), which was built to his design; but, in an action not uncharacteristic of nineteenth-century competitions, it was turned over to the town surveyor for execution. He was awarded second prize in the Manchester Assize Courts competition (1859) and, according to his obituarist, Allom's friends insinuated that it was his plan that was carried out after Alfred Waterhouse had seen it.

The Trinity House Chapel was completed in 1843, by which time Brodrick would have been nearing the end of his articles and playing an active part in the office; there is no knowledge of whether Lockwood had other assistants at that time, apart from Allom. By then two Nonconformist places of worship had been on the drawing board since 1842. Albion Independent Congregational Chapel (destroyed 1941) was a Greek Doric templar design with a monumental hexastyle portico which continued the pattern set by Charles Mountain junior for public buildings in Hull; but a more interesting building was Great Thornton Street Chapel (burned 1907),[21] which one can see as the Classical version of the composition of the Tudor-Gothic Kingston College.

It was an unusual design for a chapel, with its octastyle Corinthian-temple portico flanked by Greek Doric colonnades and pavilions, the whole set on a high podium and a monumental flight of steps. It was in what one might call a European public-building form suitable for town halls, courts of justice, museums, and art galleries. Indeed, it was an almost standard model, especially in France, about which the French historian, Louis Hautecoeur, wrote with a bored expression of 'the same façades, the same Doric peristyles . . . the same windows';[22] but it was not

a common model for an English Nonconformist chapel. *The Illustrated London News* thought 'the design presents a striking improvement upon the general style and character of places of worship not belonging to the Established Church [showing] the great advance of refinement and taste in the Fine Arts observable among Dissenters'.[23] Did Allom play a significant part in its design? Was its character in any way due to Brodrick? Had he already shown an interest in French architecture, even if only through publications? Or was it Lockwood himself who was influenced by what had been happening in Paris and introduced Brodrick to it as a source of ideas for design? It is impossible to say, but the design for the Beverley and East Riding Public Rooms suggests the latter.

Having completed his articles with Lockwood and continued to work for him for a further year, Brodrick set off in May 1844 on the customary grand tour of Europe undertaken by young architects from well-to-do backgrounds. He was financed for a year by his father and, so far as one knows, he went alone. There are no diaries of his tour, and sketch books which apparently existed in the 1930s in whole or in part cannot now be found; but from a handful of photographs made from slides of some pages of these vanished records, and from other sources, it is possible to ascertain that he first visited Salisbury, Winchester, and London before crossing the Channel to France, where he went to Carentan, Bayeux, Caen, Rouen, Amiens, and St. Omer. To judge by those names, his chief interest would at first have been in Gothic architecture, but after his arrival in Paris in the autumn of 1844 he was recording Classical buildings, the Louvre and the Hôtel de Ville, the Panthéon and the Bourse. At that time Louis-Philippe, the 'citizen king', was still in power and had four more years to go before he was deposed, but things were just beginning to recover after a long period of economic stagnation following the

23 *The Illustrated London News*, 27 May 1843.

8–14. C. Brodrick: pages from the sketchbook of his 1844–45 European tour.

8. The portico of the Panthéon, Paris (J. G. Soufflot 1756–90).

9. The grande salle of the Bourse, Paris (A.-T. Brongniart 1808–25).

10. The doorway to a *palazzo* in the Via Quattro Fontane, Rome.

Napoleonic Wars. Paris, like the government, was on the eve of change when Brodrick first saw it.

Louis-Philippe's policy had been to complete the unfinished projects started by Napoleon, which meant that there was little change in architectural character from that of the empire. Of the emperor's favourite architect/decorators, Percier died in 1838, but Fontaine lived until 1853, while the doctrinaire ideals of Antoine-Chrysostome Quatremère de Quincy, secrétaire perpétuel de l'Académie des beaux-arts from 1816 to 1839, which were based on Roman architecture, continued to impose an official style on public buildings. Some new apartment buildings were beginning to show a greater amount of applied decoration on their Classical façades, but the only really important new building project was Henri Labrouste's Bibliothèque Sainte Geneviève, which was under construction when Brodrick was there in 1844. Whether he would have had an opportunity to see illustrations of the design at that time is not certain, but there can be little doubt that he knew the building when it was completed in 1850. However, in 1844 the city cannot have looked very different from when Charles Robert Cockerell, an architect with whom Brodrick had much in common, had been there twenty years earlier. His diary survives, and it is interesting that he noted certain buildings, such as the Bourse and the Halle au Blé, as did Brodrick. He wrote with appreciation, as one imagines Brodrick would have done, that

It must be owned that France has given the mode in arch[itecture] and fine arts in northern & western Europe. It is a greater centre than England can be from its geographical position. The love of imitation & ease procured to the mind by catching at what others have . . . produced has been inducem[en]t with other countries to adopt everything French.[24]

But Brodrick could not have realized how Parisian architecture was to influence his work.

24 Quoted in D. Watkin, *The Life and Work of C. R. Cockerell* (London, 1974), p. 89.

9

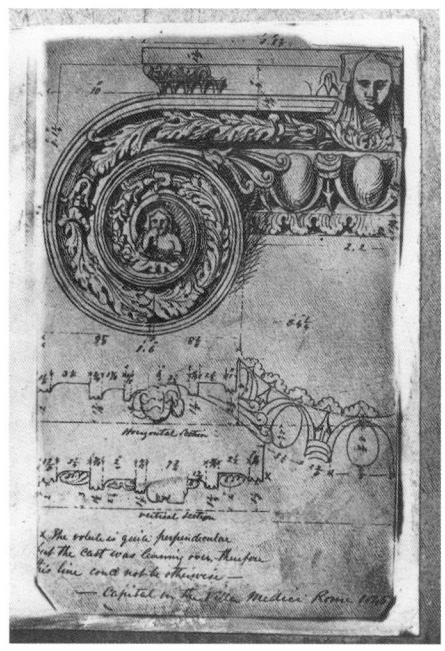 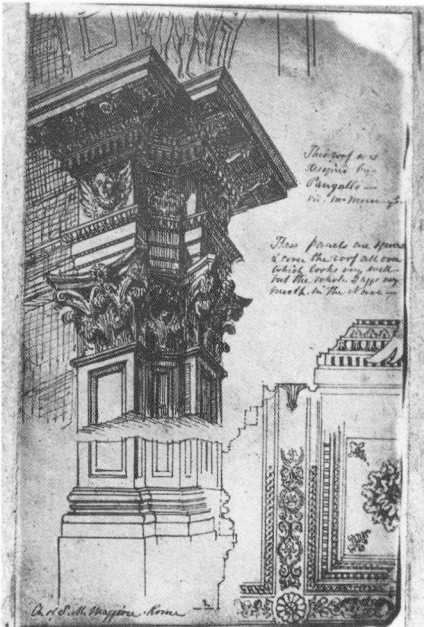 

11. A measured drawing of a capital in the Villa Medici, Rome. The sketch is annotated and dated 1845.

12. Details of the basilica of Santa Maria Maggiore, Rome, with a note to the effect that the roof was designed by Sangallo.

13. The staircase in the Palazzo dell'Università, Genoa (1623).

25 Wilson, op. cit. (note 2), p. 25.

26 *The Builder*, 4 (1846), 107.

After Paris he continued his journey to the architectural Mecca of Italy, where he visited Genoa, Verona, Vicenza, Venice, Florence, Siena and, finally, Rome. The only personal touch we have about this tour is that when he was in Rome in 1844 he made the acquaintance of Henry Garling, an architect who was almost exactly Brodrick's contemporary and was presumably on a similar tour.[25] They shared a taste for Parisian architecture and Garling was often to be submitting Second Empire designs (and sometimes winning) in the same competitions as Brodrick. Otherwise, from the scanty information we have, it appears that by this time Brodrick had developed an enthusiasm, not only for Paris, but also for Renaissance palaces and churches, and an unusual one for sculptured lions; he made drawings of Francesco Biggi's pair of animals at the bottom of the staircase in the Palazzo dell'Università in Genoa, and of Antonio Canova's famous recumbent lion on the tomb of Clement XIII in St. Peter's, Rome. They were to be useful later.

After this great experience, Hull must have seemed relatively dull when Brodrick returned in 1845. Lockwood evidently appreciated him and was anxious to have him back in the office. He offered the young man a partnership, and it could have been the firm of Lockwood and Brodrick rather than Lockwood and Mawson that was to play a leading architectural role in Bradford, Halifax, and Saltaire. But Brodrick declined the offer and set up in practice on his own account at 1 Savile Street, Hull. His first years as an independent architect were, on the whole and not unusually, uneventful; but he was fortunate in 1846 to obtain a commission when the directors of the Hull General Cemetery announced that they were 'ready to receive designs for laying out and ornamenting their grounds, and for a suitable chapel, entrance lodges, &c. A premium of twenty guineas is offered for the design most approved of, and another of ten guineas for the next best'.[26] The grounds were laid out by John

14. One of the lions on Antonio Canova's monument to Pope Clement XIII in St. Peter's, Rome (1783–92).

Shields, and Brodrick was awarded the premium for the buildings, which comprised an octangular chapel and an entrance with three lodges, all in the Gothic style; the centre lodge was described as 'a very neat gothic structure, with three gables crowned with stone crosses, an open turret, and an oriel window. This lodge and the gate piers are ornamented with heads, crockets and finials';[27] but Brodrick's drawing suggested more ornamentation than appeared on the buildings when they were executed. A letter has survived in which he advocated the style he had chosen because of

its beauty, durability and economy of construction [which] fully merits that preference it is so rapidly attaining throughout Europe. The Chapter Houses attached to cathedral buildings which are used for a variety of purposes have occurred to me as being sufficiently and yet not too exclusively ecclesiastical and therefore peculiarly adapted as models for this description of buildings. In this style, therefore, I have founded my design.[28]

In 1848 there was a group of shops and offices, a sober but dignified design with repeated rows of semicircular-headed windows and a modillion cornice, at 4–6 Silver Street, built for the Hull Charterhouse, a client for which he also made a layout design for villas at Hessle in 1847. In a letter to the trustees Brodrick referred to 'nearly all the Houses [being] in couples. My reason for this, is, that it improves the prospect from each house and at the same time diminishes the expense of construction very materially. It is a plan that I have adopted near Liverpool'.[29] The latter has not been traced. Could these semi-detached villas have been built in Toxteth Park? Then there was the Royal Flower Pot Hotel in Whitefriargate, Hull; but Brodrick came second to Lockwood and his partner, William Mawson (1828–89), in a competition for Hull Corn Exchange which was for 'converting the present corn market into a fish market, and for erecting a corn exchange over the poultry and butter market'.[30] It was all small-town stuff, and before long Lockwood and Mawson were opening offices in Leeds and Bradford. It was a good move

27 J. J. Sheahan, *History of the Town and Port of Kingston-upon-Hull*, 2nd edn. (Hull, 1866), pp. 700–01; see Harbron, op. cit. (note 2), p. 34, plate 3.

28 Kingston-upon-Hull Record Office, DBC 1/279.

29 Kingston-upon-Hull Record Office, Charterhouse Records, TCCh/1/18.

30 *The Builder*, 4 (1846), 107.

11

15 and 16. Hull Royal Institution (C. Brodrick 1852): the Entrance Hall to the Museum of the Literary and Philosophical Society.

which was to bring them important commissions on a scale beyond anything they might have expected if they had remained in Hull. But if it seemed to leave Brodrick to assume a leading role in the East Riding, fate had something else in store for him and he was on the eve of a very different career which was to bring him national recognition. 1852 was a busy year for him and the most important in his career. His T-square must have been flying up and down the drawing-board in his Hull office or in the attic of the family home in George Street, where he worked at night, worrying his mother, who was concerned for his health.

Hull was well provided with libraries and a learned society. A Subscription Library had been established in 1775, although it was not until 1800 that Joseph Hargrave erected a building for it on Parliament Street. There was also the smaller Lyceum Library, with its building of 1807 in Charlotte Street. Then there was the Literary and Philosophical Society, which had been established in 1822

to promote literature, science and the arts, for the accomplishment of which public lectures are given, and original essays, &c. are read, and a museum is attached to the society. The museum is over the exchange; it contains an extensive collection of specimens of natural history and of the arts, and is an object of considerable curiosity to the visitor, and of information to the student.[31]

'Over the exchange' sounds inappropriate for a society with such aims, and in 1852, when Charles Frost was president of both the Literary and Philosophical Society and the Subscription Library, the two agreed to combine in erecting a new building, to be known as the Hull Institution, on a site in Albion Street, then one of the best parts of the Georgian town. On 8 November Brodrick was appointed architect with a fee of 5 per cent; presumably he had already submitted a design, since tenders for the work were received on 22 January 1853. The library's share was £5,800, and the society's £6,900; although there were some discussions

31 Sheahan, op. cit. (note 27), p. 462.

about making reductions,[32] few changes were made to the design, which was to establish a number of hallmarks of Brodrick's design repertoire.

The two joint clients were separately accommodated. The Subscription Library was entered through an 'elegant entrance hall . . . ornamented with four handsome columns and eighteen pilasters, painted to represent green marble, the caps being in white and gold', and the Reading Room had 'a kind of apse at one end, supported by pillars and pilasters'. The Literary and Philosophical Society's rooms were entered through

an Ionic arcade, ornamented with 22 columns and 14 pilasters: and lighted from the top by three circular domes. The columns, which are of wood, are excellent fac-similes of red granite; the capitals are white, and edged with gold; and the cornices are beautifully wrought out with appropriate and varied shades of colour. On either side of this beautiful corridor, and separated from it by the arches of the arcade, is an aisle, and the ceilings of the whole are coloured light ultramarine.[33]

There was a Ledoux-like austerity of form and lack of applied decoration in these interiors, which seems to be a development from the Trinity House Chapel; but one can already see Brodrick's love of columns and his interest in polychromatic decoration. It is interesting to note that the Ionic capitals in the arcade were unusual in their detailing, with double volutes and a moulded neck on the column; the latter is rarely seen, but it was used both externally and internally by Jacques Gondoin on his famous and much-admired École de Chirurgie in Paris (1769–74).

The main elevation of the Institution to Albion Street was, in effect, a Classical screen, 160 feet long, which had virtually no connection with what was happening in the well-proportioned, handsome, club-like rooms behind it. The building was, in fact, two unexpressed storeys in height. In composition it was a long colonnade, twelve feet in advance of the main frontage, terminating in pedimented pavilions, but all maintaining the same parapet line. Immediately below the architrave of the entablature was a band of coffered panels, while the doorways and windows were framed by pilasters decorated with incised Greek ornament. The whole sat on a base of vermiculated, rusticated stonework. On the parapet, in the centre of the building, was a sculptured group of Minerva, Science, and Art, the work of William Day Keyworth junior, a Hull-born sculptor.

The coupled Corinthian columns of the portico inevitably recall those of the east front of the Louvre in Paris, designed by Louis Le Vau and Claude Perrault in the 1660s; but that is a façade that has long appealed to architects. It was the source of Ange-Jacques Gabriel's twin buildings in the place Royale, or place de la Concorde as it became, dating from the 1750s. It was probably the model for Henry Holland's screen of the 1790s in front of Carlton House, which gave a Parisian look to the prince of Wales's London residence. Joseph Woods, the author of *Letters of an Architect*, who was of a generation nearer to Brodrick, wrote of 'the beauty of the east front', asking 'in what does this beauty consist, . . . [a question] very important to an architect, and such as he ought to apply to every fine building which he sees'.[34] Admiration for the building con-

32 The Proceedings of the Royal Institution Committee show that Brodrick was instructed to reduce the building by one eighth, and there was an attempt to persuade the contractors to reduce their tenders; but only slight reductions were agreed.

33 Sheahan, op. cit. (note 27), pp. 638–43. The Institution was demolished after being damaged in the Second World War.

34 J. Woods, *Letters of an Architect from France, Italy and Greece*, 2 vols. (London, 1828), I, p. 95.

13

17. C. Brodrick: Hull Royal Institution, the presentation perspective of the main elevation to Albion Street.

35 J. Belcher, *Essentials in Architecture* (London, 1907), p. 127.

36 J. J. Sheahan, *General and Concise History and Description of the Town and Port of Kingston-upon-Hull* (London, 1864), p. 85.

tinued despite changing tastes. John Belcher, who was studying in Paris in 1862–63, later wrote of the 'fine effects of light and shade [which] are added to the beauty and grandeur of the whole composition',[35] which became an inspirational element in late-nineteenth-century Baroque Revival architecture. Obviously, Brodrick was in good company in his choice of model, but he was working on a less monumental scale in Hull, combining, one might say, the Louvre and Great Thornton Street Chapel; yet this unlikely fusion succeeded. The Parisian connection did not go unremarked; it was referred to in 1864 in a description of the building,[36] and it is not impossible that Brodrick himself had spoken of it. He had nothing to be ashamed of, and Prince Albert had complimented him on his first major achievement when Queen Victoria and her consort visited the town in 1854 and the prefix 'Royal' was added to the Institution's title. Four years later the prince and the architect were to meet again at Leeds.

There are no extant drawings of the Louvre among the few that have survived in photographs of pages from Brodrick's sketchbooks; but obviously he must have made many more drawings on his continental tour. However, there is a sketch of the interior of the Bourse, and there can be little doubt that he admired this building as much as did Cockerell when he went to Paris in 1824 and praised the depth of the front portico, the 'beautiful staircase', and the main hall, as well as the construction of the

18. The Bourse, Paris; Brongniart's original rectangular building (1808–25) was extended with wings in 1903.

roof.[37] If only Brodrick had left a diary comparable with Cockerell's; but one can predict that he might have written very similar comments. The Bourse is the one monument envisaged in Napoleon I's dream of an improved Paris that was actually built. It was designed by Alexandre-Théodore Brongniart (1739–1813) in 1808 (but not completed until 1825) as a great cube surrounded by a Corinthian colonnade supporting an entablature, but otherwise it was undecorated externally. Inside, the top-lit great hall was designed as two storeys of round-headed arches with discs in the spandrels, and the same arches are repeated on the exterior in the bays between the columns. Everything is regularly spaced and repetitive, and here it is necessary to refer to a famous nineteenth-century textbook which almost certainly Brodrick would have known: J. N. L. Durand's *Précis des leçons d'architecture données a l'École polytechnique*,[38] which was first published in 1804 but re-issued several times up to 1840 and which became, as Henry-Russell Hitchcock wrote, 'a sort of bible of Romantic Classicism that retained international authority for a generation or more'. In it, Durand recommended loggias and colonnades rather than porticoes with pediments, towers to enrich the skyline, and an 'insistent repetition of elements, both horizontally and vertically';[39] a grid was the basis of a design, and columns or pilasters were placed on the interstices of the grid in a rational, if rather mechanical, system. Applied decoration was not to be encouraged. Durand also gave examples of gridded, colonnaded halls, vestibules, and galleries suitable for public buildings. It was a useful textbook for anyone designing a great municipal palace, which is what the ambitious young Brodrick elected to do in 1852; but, if he was indeed consulting Durand's book, his eye must have passed over the statement that 'the Orders do not in any way represent the essence of architecture . . . the pleasure derived from their use and from decoration is only a chimera, and the costs required, a kind of folly'.[40]

37 Watkin, op. cit. (note 24), pp. 495–96.

38 See S. Villari, *J. N. L. Durand (1760–1834): art and science of architecture* (New York, 1990).

39 H.-R. Hitchcock, *Architecture: nineteenth and twentieth centuries* (Harmondsworth, 1958), pp. 20–42.

40 Quoted in Villari, op. cit. (note 38), p. 67.

A Noble Municipal Palace

19. St. George's Hall, Bradford (Lockwood and Mawson 1851–53).

1 J. James, *Continuation and Additions to the History of Bradford and its Parish* (Bradford, 1866), pp. 123–25.

2 See Linstrum, *WYAA*, pp. 380–81, for a list of Lockwood and Mawson's work in West Yorkshire.

3 James, op. cit. (note 1), p. 125.

4 J. Ryley, *The Leeds Guide* (Leeds, 1806), pp. 61–62.

5 F. Beckwith, *Thomas Taylor, Regency Architect* (Leeds, 1949), p. 18.

6 See Linstrum, *WYAA*, p. 316.

7 See C. Webster, *R. D. Chantrell: his life and work in Leeds 1818–1847* (Leeds, 1992).

8 See Linstrum, *WYAA*, p. 332.

It was, ironically, a great day for Leeds when, in 1849, a group of shareholders was formed in Bradford to build a public hall. £16,000 was raised in £10 shares,[1] and in 1851 there was a competition, of which the winner was Brodrick's ex-employer, Henry Francis Lockwood, and his partner Richard Mawson, who were by then established at 43 Kirkgate in Bradford.[2] Their design owes much in its external character to St. George's Hall, Liverpool, which was still under construction at the time. There is a grand show of columns and pilasters on the three exposed façades, which are raised on a high rusticated basement with mask keystones, and there are richly carved garlands and flowers decorating the large console brackets between the mezzanine-level windows. The Hall itself, which was also named after St. George, was designed to take an audience of 3,328 (although 'on extraordinary occasions, very many more have found places within it'); it is not unlike a Late Georgian chapel with galleries, but decorated with applied 'foliage, flowers, fruit, musical instruments, emblems, and figures displayed in most harmonious colours and happy taste'. It is less sophisticated, but was probably less expensive, than Lockwood's design for the Beverley and East Riding Public Rooms, of twelve years earlier; but it was claimed there was 'probably not a building of the same character in the kingdom', and the opening musical festival 'at once gave Bradford an important position in the eyes of the musical world'.[3] The challenge was what was needed to stimulate Leeds, Bradford's traditional rival, to respond, both architecturally and musically.

In the early-nineteenth century there had been a good number of new public buildings in Leeds. In 1794 a Music Hall was opened in Albion Street; it was said to be 'exceedingly commodious, and furnished with great elegance'. It had an orchestra and a gallery, and 'a lofty coved ceiling from which several handsome glass chandeliers are suspended'.[4] Thomas Taylor (*c.* 1778–1826), who had worked in James Wyatt's office, had built a court house and prison with a Corinthian portico in 1813;[5] Francis Goodwin (1784–1835) had designed 'one of the principal ornaments of the town', the Central Market, in a Grecian style in 1824–27;[6] Robert Dennis Chantrell (1793–1872), a pupil of Sir John Soane, had built a Neoclassical hall for the Philosophical and Literary Society in 1819–20, public baths in 1819–20, and the South Market in 1823–24;[7] John Clark (*c.* 1799–1857), an Edinburgh-trained man, and perhaps the most accomplished of this generation of architects working in Leeds, had won a competition in 1825 with his design for the elegant Grecian Commercial Buildings, which was preferred to entries by Charles Barry, Anthony Salvin, Goodwin, Chantrell, and Taylor.[8] But by the 1850s prosperity had increased in Leeds, and so had its population, which had reached 172,258. It needed to assert itself architecturally on a scale greater than the group of Late Georgian buildings.

There was also a stimulus to erect a monument to Sir Robert Peel, a statesman revered by the Whigs and the Tories alike, especially in the industrial North, who had died as a result of a riding accident on 2 July 1850. A public meeting was called immediately 'to ascertain the feelings of the inhabitants as to the erection of a large public hall'[9] as a suitable commemoration, and it was recommended that in this case Bradford's lead should be followed and that the money should be raised in £10 shares. Leeds responded less enthusiastically to such an appeal, and it was then proposed in October that a town hall should be built and paid for out of the rates. A two-to-one vote of the town council in January 1851 confirmed the proposal, and a deputation from the newly appointed committee visited other towns, including Liverpool, where they could have seen the unfinished St. George's Hall, and Manchester, where they could have heard about the proposal to rebuild their Hall, which materialized two years later as the Free Trade Hall. In Leeds, a site on Park Lane, in a district that was still residential in character, was chosen and purchased in September. But who was to be the architect of what was already being seen as a building with a message? None of the Leeds architects would be appropriate.

A Leeds Improvement Society was founded in 1851 'to suggest and promote architectural and other public improvements in the town'. The society's secretary was Dr. John Deakin Heaton, who became a prime mover and speaker in support of the erection of a town hall. He visited the Continent and looked with envy on those 'famous old cities whose Town Halls are the permanent glory of the inhabitants and the standing wonder and delight of visitors from a distance'. He was visionary enough and undoubtedly sincere in his conviction that,

if a noble municipal palace that might fairly vie with some of the best Town Halls of the continent were to be erected in the middle of their hitherto squalid and unbeautiful town, it would become a practical admonition to the populace of the value of beauty and art, and in course of time men would learn to live up to it.

His was a moral argument as well as an aesthetic one, and he challenged the wealthy town to consider the proposal

in the most broad and liberal spirit, and . . . incur that which might even seem to some to be an extravagant expenditure, rather than fail in a duty which it owed to the rest of the community and to posterity.[10]

To the council's credit, it responded, even if cautiously at first, as when the mayor's foundation-laying speech included the telling comment that the Town Hall was to fulfil two functions: it was to be 'an ornamental building, and in order that the local or municipal business of the borough may be concentrated in one building, and therefore be done better and cheaper than it could be otherwise'.[11]

In June 1852, before Brodrick had been given the commission for the Hull Institution, a competition for the Leeds Town Hall was advertised. The brief was for a building type such as did not yet exist in England. There were moot halls, concert rooms, court houses and assembly rooms;

9 A. Briggs, *Victorian Cities* (London, 1963), p. 156.

10 T. W. Reid (ed.), *A Memoir of John Deakin Heaton, M.D., of Leeds* (London, 1883).

11 See J. Mayhall, *The Annals of Yorkshire, . . . ,* 2nd edn., 3 vols. (London, 1878), I, pp. 633–35, for an account of the ceremony.

but in the new building the functions of all were to be combined under one roof, along with municipal offices and a suite of reception rooms for the mayor. Even Liverpool's St. George's Hall, the latest model of civic pride, contained only a public hall, a small concert hall, and assize courts; but Leeds was ambitiously aiming to build a municipal palace for the sum of £35,000 — a figure that excited derision. The brief asked for accommodation for 8,000 in the hall (more than twice as many as Bradford could cram into St. George's Hall). Did the council think that such a sum would pay for the Baths of Caracalla or Westminster Hall?

The instructions to architects on this occasion are more formidable than inviting; in fact, amount almost to a direct *noli me tangere*, when the absurdly short time allowed for planning the works and preparing the numerous drawings required (only two months), and the mere remuneration which is all that is promised to the successful competitor, are taken into consideration. There is something staggering even in the very first article of instruction, since it asks for a hall for public meetings capable of containing no fewer than eight thousand persons standing! Its area, therefore, can hardly be at all less than 12,000 square feet; consequently were its breadth 60 feet its length must be 200 feet (unless galleries be admitted), dimensions nearly equal to those of Westminster Hall; and as, to be in tolerable proportion, its height could hardly be less than 50 feet, that single room alone would swallow up the whole of the sum named as that to which the estimates are expected to conform.[12]

One good thing was that the newly knighted Sir Charles Barry, the architect of the Houses of Parliament, was to be the assessor, and for once there were no complaints about the organization of the competition, whatever scoffing there might be about the council's ambition.

The 'Instructions to Architects' offered no advice about the style in which the building should be designed, but probably there was no thought that it would be anything but Classical. As for the presentation, 'All the Plans to be plain lines, drawn to an uniform scale of $\frac{1}{10}$ of an inch to a foot: the elevations to be tinted in sepia only. Coloured Drawings will not be considered'. Perhaps because of the none-too-generous prizes offered, '£200 . . . for the best set of Plans, £100 for the second best, and £50 for the third best'; perhaps because 'the Council will not bind themselves to employ the Architect whose Plan may obtain any of the premiums'; perhaps because of *The Builder*'s description of the competition as a '*noli me tangere*'; perhaps because of the innovative nature of the brief, there were fewer entries than expected. Only sixteen designs were received, but in this case that did not mean an acceptance of a lower standard.

Barry was enthusiastic about the design entered under the motto 'Honor alit Artes',[13] which was then revealed as the work of a young architect, 'a Mr. Cuthbert Broderick [*sic*] of Hull . . . Henceforth [his] name will not have to be prefaced by an "*a*", his reputation being now decidedly stamped', wrote a correspondent in *The Builder*.[14] The second prize was awarded to Lockwood and Mawson, and the third to a Wolverhampton firm, Young and Lovatt. It was probably a disappointment to the council that their Town Hall was not to be the work of a national architectural figure, such as Barry himself, and the latter was asked

12 *The Builder*, 10 (1852), 503.

13 The specification which accompanied the design is included as Appendix C.

14 *The Builder*, 11 (1853), 59.

whether he thought such a young man . . . might be entrusted with the construction of so large a building. [He replied that although] previous to the competition he was not aware that such an architect existed . . . he was fully satisfied that the Council might trust him with the most perfect safety . . . After what he had seen of the drawings, he felt sure there was sufficient talent and genius in the architect to carry out anything which an architect could be required to do.[15]

It was a generous action of Barry's to support Brodrick in this way, and, it was said, to have 'predicted that the new Town-hall would be the most perfect architectural gem outside London'.[16] Doubtless he could himself have been open to the suggestion that he might be appointed, as happened in the case of Halifax Town Hall in 1859 when he was asked to advise after designs had been made by Lockwood and Mawson, George Gilbert Scott, and the borough surveyor.[17] But, unlike most assessors, he

20. Leeds Town Hall (1852): the first plan (redrawn from an original in Leeds District Archives). 1. Entrance Hall; 2. Hall; 3. Court Room; 4. Retiring Room.

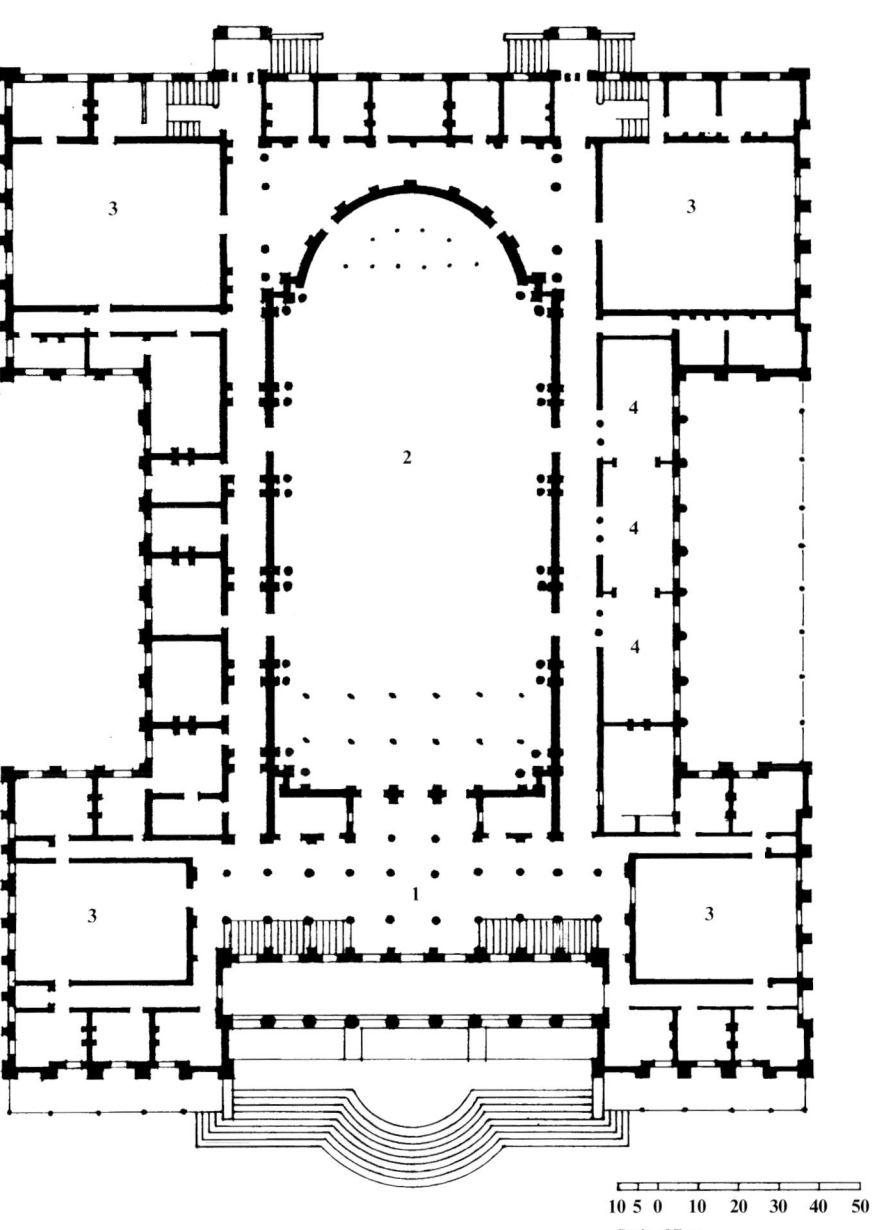

15 Briggs, op. cit. (note 9), p. 162.

16 *The Builder*, 11 (1853), 59.

17 See Linstrum, *WYAA*, pp. 344 ff. for an account of Halifax Town Hall.

10 5 0   10   20   30   40   50

Scale of Feet

21. C. Brodrick: an ambitious design for the main entrance hall and staircase. This had to be omitted when provision was made for the construction of a tower.

18 A complete edition of the prize-winning designs of the French Academy of Architecture was published in 1834; see also H. Rosenau, 'The engravings of the Grands Prix of the French Academy of Architecture', *Architectural History*, 3 (1960).

19 West Yorkshire Archive Service, Leeds District Archives: LC/Wks. Small Plans/A. The staircase was destroyed during Napoleon III's reign, but Brodrick could easily have seen it previously; in any case, the design had been published by Percier and Fontaine.

20 See A. Braham, *The Architecture of the French Enlightenment* (London, 1980), plate 180. The building dates from 1769–74. Brodrick's proposal is shown on the first-floor plan of his competition entry (West Yorkshire Archive Service, Leeds District Archives: LC/Wks/TH27).

21 *The Builder*, 11 (1853), 689–91.

22 *The Builder*, 11 (1853), 60. This is the only known reference to a glazed roof, which is not included in Brodrick's description of his design (see Appendix C, pp. 145–47).

23 Leeds Borough Council Minute, 21 February 1853. The council wanted to insert a clause in the contract which would hold Brodrick to the estimated cost, stipulating that he would get nothing if the final cost exceeded the budget. After resisting Brodrick agreed, provided it did not hold good if the cost was increased by means over which he had no control. Considering what the final cost was to be, and the extras incurred by changes directed or approved by the council, he was wise to make the proviso.

continued to show an interest in Brodrick and the progress of the Town Hall under construction. The clerk of works reported site visits on several occasions from the great man, whose son, the Revd. Alfred Barry, was the headmaster of Leeds Grammar School.

At the heart of Brodrick's plan, as it was in so many *esquisses* in the Prix de Rome competitions,[18] was the great basilican hall, of which Lockwood's design for the extension to the Beverley and East Riding Public Rooms (1839–40) seems such a remarkable and hitherto unnoticed precedent in its form and decoration. Like Harvey Lonsdale Elmes at Liverpool, Brodrick had gone to a Roman model for the most important element in the building. Around this he placed four courtrooms, one at each corner, linked by a corridor around the hall which gave access to ancillary rooms required by the members of the legal professions and the musicians. The main entrance was to be from the south, leading into a long hall, around 110 feet by 30, with two lines of columns, from which a monumental double staircase (possibly suggested by that constructed in the Louvre in 1806 by Percier and Fontaine when the Musée Napoléon was inaugurated)[19] ascended to an amphitheatrical council chamber (maybe another memory of Gondoin's École de Chirurgie).[20] This room was intended to balance the apse at the north end of the main hall and to be capable of being opened to the latter, theoretically making it possible to find room for 3,470 people sitting or 9,278 standing.

The whole plan was rational and Classical, and it probably attracted Barry because of its order and logic. It could have been based on principles expounded in Durand's publication referred to in the previous chapter. 'The plan is exceedingly good; the whole design highly creditable to Mr. Brodrick',[21] noted *The Builder* of the revised plan in which the single lines of rooms along the sides of the main hall were doubled, so making the building more of an enclosed rectangle on plan, but without sacrificing the colonnaded effect. One feature which did not survive is referred to in *The Builder*, which comments that in the first design there was 'an arched glass roof, evidently suggested by the Crystal Palace. To conceal the incongruity from the front view, Sir C. Barry proposes a cupola near the portico'.[22]

The contract was awarded to a Leeds builder, Samuel Atack, who signed an agreement for £41,835, which included a completion date for the building of 1 January 1856. In the event, both were hopelessly inaccurate. A great question at this stage, in 1853, was whether to build a tower. On 21 February the council had resolved 'that the altered design . . . now submitted by Mr. Brodrick be the design for the future Town Hall excepting the elevation of the tower, and that the sum voted for the erection of the said building be thirty-nine thousand pounds'.[23] This seems to indicate that Brodrick had already designed a tower, which was presumably the one shown on an engraving published in 1853. Evidently, if we may believe *The Builder*, Barry had recommended that a cupola or small tower should be built to divert attention from an arched glazed roof which showed above the parapet, but if that was the true origin, one can only comment that 'Tall oaks from little acorns grow'. Maybe Brodrick himself had prompted the idea and had been prepared with a design; but

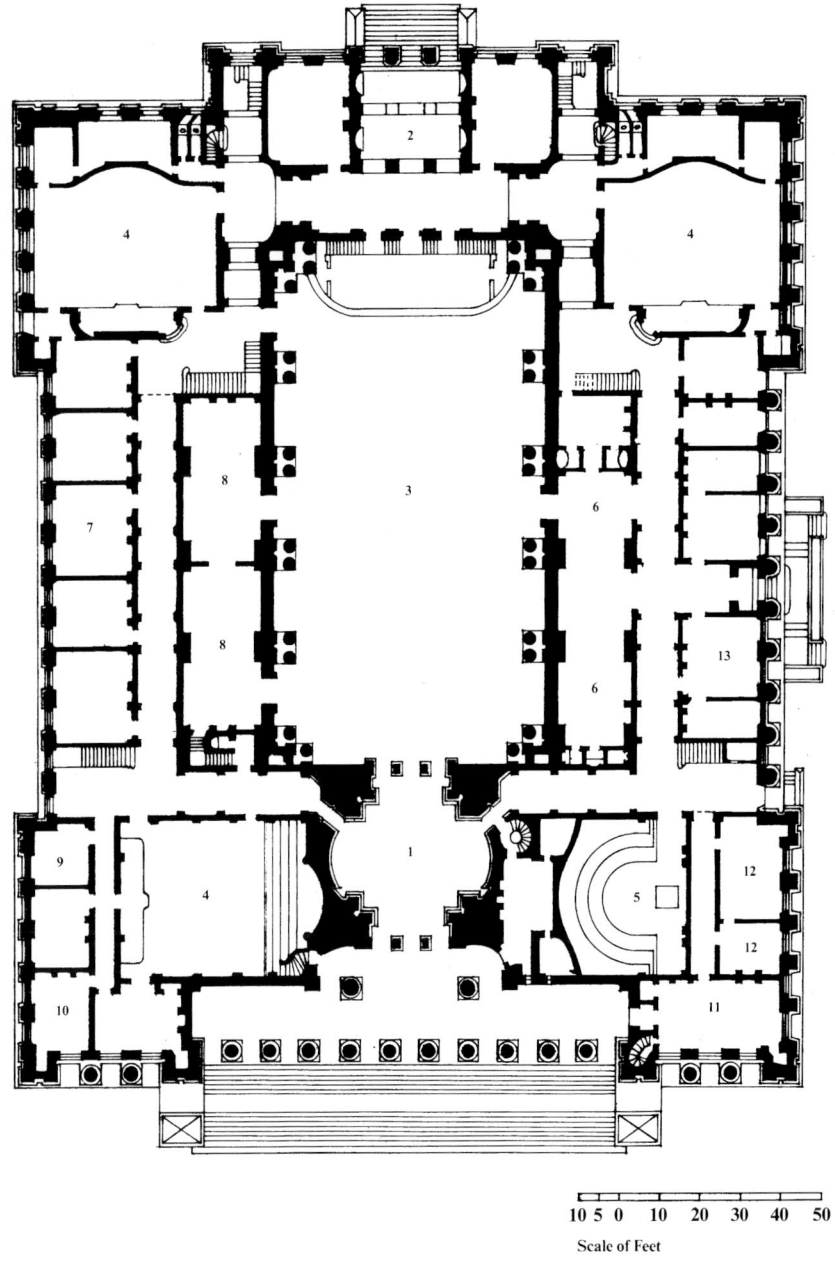

22. Leeds Town Hall (1853): the plan, as built (redrawn from *The Builder*, 11 (1853), 690). 1. South Vestibule; 2. North Vestibule; 3. Victoria Hall; 4. Court Room; 5. Council Chamber; 6. Retiring Room; 7. Barristers' Robing Room; 8. Refreshment Room; 9. Police Superintendent; 10. Magistrates' Robing Room; 11. Town Clerk; 12. Committee Room; 13. Treasurer.

10 5 0 10 20 30 40 50

Scale of Feet

certainly the image of an ideal town hall which Barry gave to the Halifax town council in 1859 included 'a Tower of commanding importance, having a clock which should be seen from all parts of the Town'.[24]

Brodrick's first design for a tower was much more than 'a cupola near the portico', and it was estimated to cost around an additional £6,000. Nothing happened, but the idea was raised again in September 1854, when Brodrick produced another design, this time estimated to cost £7,000; but once again there was a lack of support in the council, although it had been agreed in the previous February to alter the plan to make provision for a heavier superstructure. This meant the abandonment of the pillared entrance hall and the grand staircase (a great loss

24 R. de Z. Hall, *Halifax Town Hall* (Halifax, 1963), p. 43.

that was not compensated for by the mean substitute staircases) and the omission of the imaginative first-floor council chamber, which was brought down instead to the south-east corner. How then was the council's requirement about seating capacity to be answered?

There was a thought of constructing a large balcony at the south end of the hall in order to increase the accommodation; this is shown on the contract drawings, but in the event a small one, more a viewing platform than a balcony, was placed there, supported on huge consoles, and the five-bay basilican interior was constructed without such an intrusion, much to its gain architecturally. There was also a gain in the decision to increase the height of the domed vestibule. There was, however, still a need to find room for more people; large though the hall was, it would hardly take the 8,000 standers referred to in the brief. This was to remain a problem. There was an interesting later idea to place a small balcony in each of the side bays between the pairs of columns, once again supported

23. Leeds Town Hall: the 1853 design for the tower, including also views of some of the main rooms.

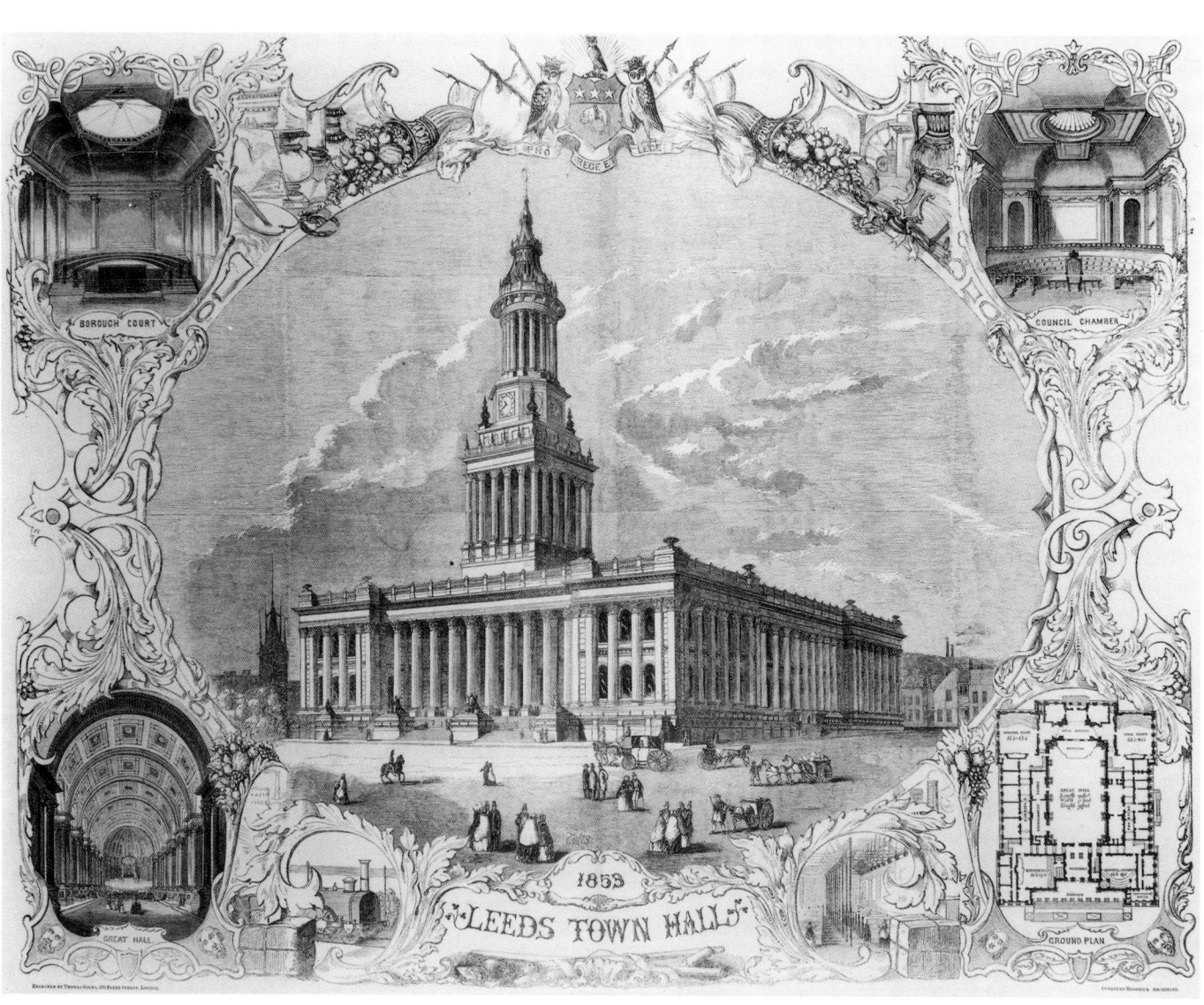

on large consoles and with a cast-iron front; but these remained on Brodrick's drawing-board.[25] The present balcony was added in 1890 to a design by W. H. Thorp.

But it was, of course, the external image of the Town Hall that was more affected by whether or not to have a tower. There were precedents for such an ornamental element in a public building. Liverpool Town Hall, which had been built as the Exchange in 1789–92 by John Foster from designs by James Wyatt, had acquired a domed tower in 1802, and the Royal Exchange in London had traditionally been distinguished by a tower; a wooden structure had been replaced by a stone one designed by George Smith in 1821, and Sir William Tite's new Exchange of 1841–44 has a tall tower rising above engaged columns and a broken entablature to a domed cupola above the clock. But what was a tower for? That, as well as the expense, was part of the argument. *The Builder*'s comment was:

Some have argued that the tower would be of 'no use'. The same *argument*, carried out, would reduce the building to four bare walls and a roof. A noble building is at one and the same time a symbol and an incitement; an evidence of the community erecting it, and an inducement to every member of the community to maintain that importance and exhibit that intelligence in his own proper person.[26]

Dr. Heaton, ever ready to speak out on behalf of the arts and civic propriety, gave his answer to the question of a tower's utility:

Were this a question to be decided on merely utilitarian grounds, I believe the tower must be condemned, for it is not my opinion that any of the possible uses suggested, to which such an erection might be applied, are of sufficient practical importance to warrant the expense of such a structure, were these the only or the chief consideration. But let us ask what is appropriate to a building for the purpose of the one in question, and what will be conducive to its dignity and beauty? And should we decide that a tower may be made and indeed is essential to fulfil these conditions, let us not, after having nobly determined on the expenditure of so large a sum upon the body of the work, grudge a few additional thousands to give this completion to the whole.[27]

25 An undated, unsigned drawing attributed to Brodrick, which shows this proposal, is in West Yorkshire Archive Service, Leeds District Archives: LC/Wks/ Drawer 30/Plan 28.

26 *The Builder*, 11 (1853), 690–91.

27 In a speech to the Philosophical and Literary Society; quoted in Briggs, op. cit (note 9), pp. 163–64. See the contract drawings in West Yorkshire Archive Service, Leeds District Archives: LC/Wks, Blue Portfolio 1–15, or the copies, LC/TC, Bin 42, 1–24.

25. Leeds Town Hall: the south elevation, a copy of one of the set of contract drawings.

28 Brongniart's Bourse was originally a perfect rectangle on plan. Wings were added to it in 1903; see M. Mosser, B. de Rochebouët, J.-M. Bruson (eds.), *Le Catalogue de l'exposition Alexandre-Théodore Brongniart (1739–1813): architecture et décor*, Musée Carnavalet 22 Avril–13 Juillet 1986 (Paris, 1986), pp. 160–61.

29 Boullée's design for the façade of the Bibliothèque Nationale, Paris, is for a colonnade of sixteen giant Corinthian columns; see Mosser, de Rochebouët, and Bruson (eds.), op. cit. (note 28), p. 148.

30 Braham, op. cit. (note 20), plate 191.

31 Braham, op. cit. (note 20), plate 313.

32 Braham, op. cit. (note 20), plate 329.

33 A. Drexler (ed.), *The Architecture of the École des Beaux-Arts* (London, 1977), p. 428.

34 Drexler (ed.), op. cit. (note 33), p. 349.

35 R. Middleton and D. Watkin, *Neoclassical and 19th-Century Architecture* (New York, 1980), plate 360.

Without a tower, the whole emphasis of the design would have been different. The building would have been a strongly horizontal rectangle surrounded by a screen of Corinthian columns and pilasters, with two storeys of semicircular-headed windows in the intercolumniations. It would have been very similar in concept to the Paris Bourse, even to the wide flights of steps and flanking podia which lead up to the main entrance.[28] Or, of course, the horizontality of St. George's Hall, Liverpool, is another example of how the Town Hall would have appeared without its famous vertical feature.

Both buildings, in Leeds and Liverpool, probably owed their origin, at least in part, to a French use of a giant order as a repeated element in a Classical screen. As Hitchcock noted, the lavish use of the Classical orders 'which goes back via J. N. L. Durand to E. L. Boullée in late-eighteenth-century France, doubtless influenced Cuthbert Brodrick . . . and the result is certainly magnificent'.[29] The eighteenth-century predilection for the Classical orders is illustrated in such buildings as the Grand Théâtre, Bordeaux (1773–80 Victor Louis),[30] the hôtel de Gallifet, Paris (1775 Étienne-François Legrand),[31] and the Grand Théâtre, Nantes (1784 Mathurin Crucy).[32] Louis Duc, the architect of the Palais de Justice in Paris (1840–79),[33] emphasized the French Beaux-Arts viewpoint when he asked: 'Without the Orders, what would our monuments be? Was it not the Order which, by its proportions ruled by those of man, became the unity and the measure of buildings?'[34] We can only assume that Brodrick's repetitious bay and column around the Town Hall would have found approval in nineteenth-century France. The Palais de Justice at Lyons, for example, built between 1835 and 1847 by Louis-Pierre Baltard,[35] has an impressive façade of twenty-four giant Corinthian columns which the historian, Louis Hautecoeur, called 'a memory of Palmyra and Baalbek' — an apt thought in interpreting Brodrick's columnar compositions. There is no evidence that his travels took him to the Eastern Mediterranean, but there were plenty of publications to refer to.

26. The Palais de Justice, Lyons (L.-P. Baltard 1835–47): an example of ideal public architecture according to the recommendations of A.-C. Quatremère de Quincy.

27. Thomas Cole: 'The Architect's Dream' (1840).

Obviously Brodrick shared Duc's opinion about the essential role of the Classical orders in architecture, so much so that it developed into a megalomania at times, putting one in mind of the fantasy painting, 'The Architect's Dream', by the American artist, Thomas Cole (1801–48).[36] In the foreground a bemused architect reclines on the top of an enormous Doric column, while behind him stretches out a long line of columns into the far distance. Or could Brodrick have known the apocalyptic scenes of John Martin's (1789–1854) imagination with their endless colonnades? On much stronger ground, a likely English influence on the design of the Town Hall elevations is Sir John Vanbrugh, the early-eighteenth-century architect who shared a taste for giant Classical orders in his heroic architecture, as in Blenheim Palace, Seaton Delaval, and Grimsthorpe. His garden front of Castle Howard, Yorkshire (1700–26), is also based on a repeated column bay with two storeys of semicircular-headed windows. It, too, has a domed tower. The description of Castle Howard by Joseph Gwilt in his popular *An Encyclopaedia of Architecture*, first published in 1842, could equally apply to the Town Hall: 'There is a portico in the centre, and a cupola of considerable height and magnitude. The galleries, or wings, are flanked by pavilions'.[37]

In March 1856 caution gave way to civic pride in the building that was visibly growing into something that could be seen to be the architectural symbol the council wanted, and £5,500 was voted for the erection of a tower. Brodrick's first idea, conceived in 1853 and illustrated in the published engraving, had been to erect a square colonnade, set back from the main colonnade on the south front. This part is reminiscent of James Pennethorne's 1838 unsuccessful design for the Royal Exchange, London.[38] On top of this colonnade, Brodrick proposed to erect a tall structure consisting of an octagonal base surmounted by an elongated rotunda and an elaborate Classical spire, adding column upon column to the massive composition with complete assurance.

36 Painted in 1840, now in the Toledo Museum of Art, Ohio.

37 J. Gwilt, *An Encyclopaedia of Architecture* (London, 1842), p. 217.

38 See G. Tyack, *Sir James Pennethorne and the Making of Victorian London* (Cambridge, 1992), plate 19.

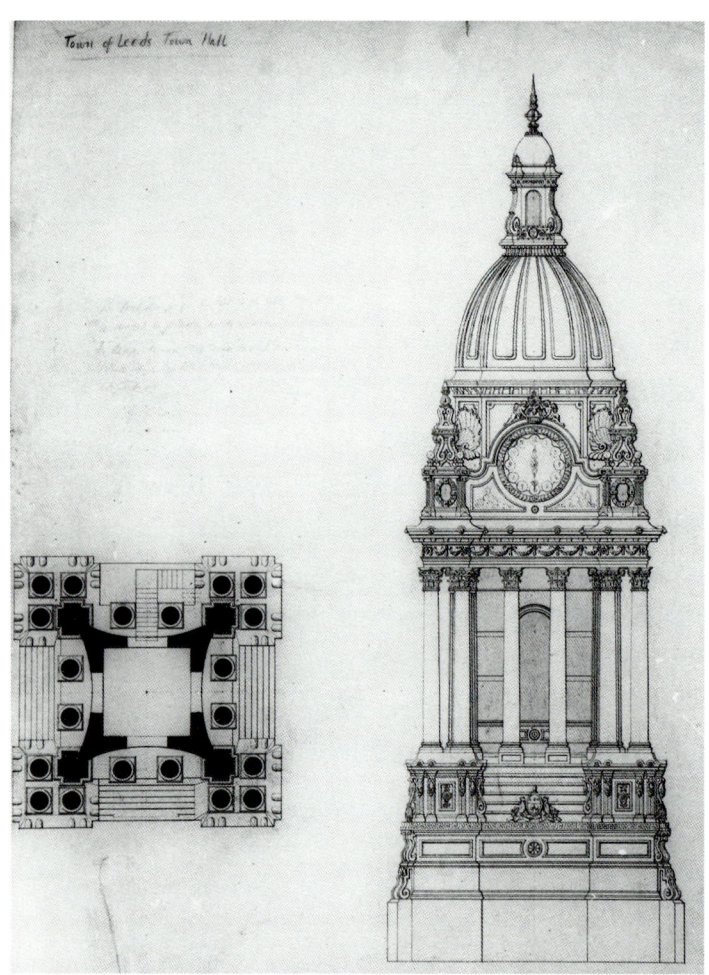

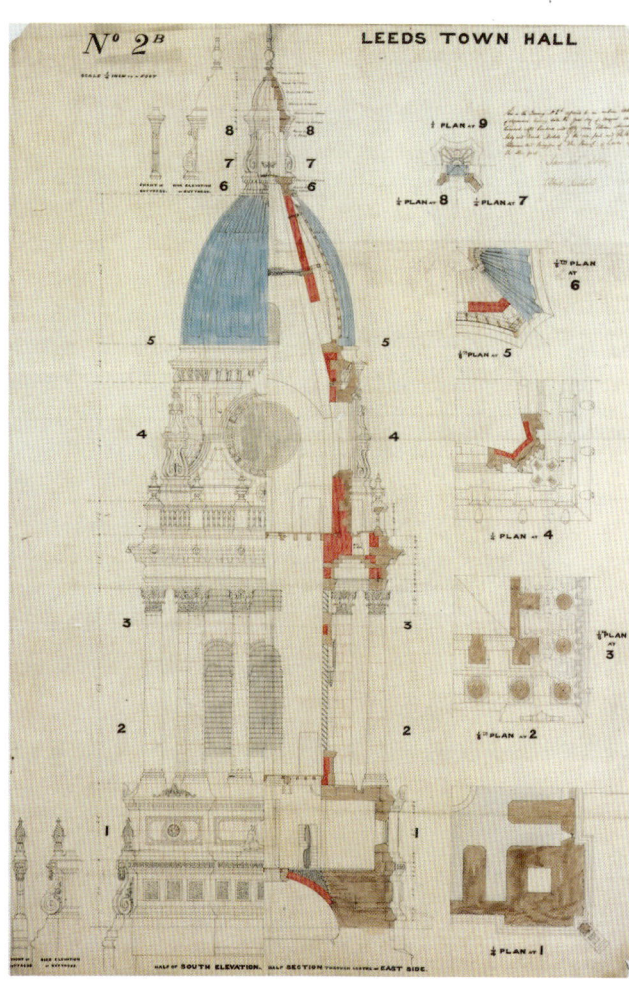

28. C. Brodrick: Leeds Town Hall. An early design for the domed tower. It was used as the basis of a plaster model made by (?)Barker.

29. C. Brodrick: Leeds Town Hall. A working drawing of the domed tower as executed.

30. Leeds Town Hall from the south-east.

39 E. T. Cook and A. Wedderburn (eds.), *The Works of John Ruskin*, 39 vols. (London, 1903–1912), XXXIV (1908), p. 725. The surprising aspect of the comment is that the critic, who is generally regarded as an apostle of Gothic Revivalism, apparently approved of the style in which the body of the Town Hall had been built.

40 J. Ruskin, *Lectures in Architecture and Painting delivered at Edinburgh . . . 1853 . . .* (London, 1854), p. vi.

Not everyone liked the idea of combining a colonnaded body and a huge tower. John Ruskin responded angrily in 1853 when asked to lecture in Leeds, saying he 'would do his best to crucify the snobs or charlatans in architecture who could put such an abortion as that tower upon a town hall of fair Roman composite architecture'.[39] On another occasion in the following year he wrote

I see that "The Builder" . . . has been endeavouring to inspire the citizens of Leeds with some pride . . . respecting their town-hall. The pride would be well, but I sincerely trust that the tower in question may not be built on the design there proposed.[40]

It was not, because by that time Brodrick had made an alternative design. While retaining the idea of a square colonnade, he crowned it with a dome that shows a family resemblance to Wren's pair on the Royal Hospital, Greenwich (*c.* 1704), especially in an alternative version of which a model was ordered. This had clustered columns at the corners of the colonnade, and recessed pairs in between; the latter were set against concave sides of the body of the tower. But the dome itself seems closer to that on Thomas Archer's St. Philip's Church (1709–25), now the Cathedral, Birmingham. Although other sources have been suggested, including a Northern Indian, it is perhaps most noteworthy that Brodrick

seems to have turned to English historical sources for the most conspicuous element in the building.

There were several different profiles of the dome, but the various versions all incorporated corner turrets composed of tiers of scrolls like little Baroque spires, set against the canted corners of the drum which are decorated with large shells. Above the four faces of the clock, which was designed by Edmund Beckett Denison[41] and for which the council agreed to pay £800, there is the lead-covered timber dome with eight concave sides, four wide and four narrow. The crowning detail is a cupola with concave sides, corner scrolls, and a little dome; it might almost have come from the Venetian church of Santa Maria della Salute, of which Brodrick had made a fine pen-and-wash drawing during his Continental tour.[42] Like the line of heavy vases he added along the balustrades of the building itself, after trying out full-size mock-ups *in situ* in May 1856, this tower seemed to be ushering in the later Baroque Revival, which only began officially in the 1880s; but in Brodrick's time art historians had not begun to use the adjective in its present-day sense. It was still a term of abuse such as Denison might have used when he spoke sarcastically of

the pomposity of the Italian style [that] was in accordance with the modern spirit of the age and of the municipal bodies who built Town halls . . . At Leeds . . . nothing could be contrived to relieve the monotony of the skyline but the imposition of a wonderful tower — a tower which, he ventured to say, would evoke the wonder of Sir Christopher Wren, or of the builder of Canterbury Cathedral.[43]

How does one assess the Town Hall in stylistic terms? In describing it as 'the most considerable English public monument built just after the mid century', Henry-Russell Hitchcock agrees that it 'recalls in its grandiose scale the English Baroque of Vanbrugh'. It is

no longer Romantic Classical, no longer Early Victorian; yet except for the rather clumsy originality of some of the detail and the varied outline of the tower . . . it is hard to say how or why it is so definitely High Victorian, and rather a masterpiece of High Victorian at that. Wallot in Berlin in the eighties approached Brodrick's mode of design in the Reichstag but had little of his command of scale or his almost Romantic Classical control of mass.[44]

It is, quite simply, unique.

A mark of recognition was accorded to Leeds in 1858 when, immediately after the first musical festival, the British Association for the Advancement of Science held its annual meeting in the town for the first time. It had been proposed on seven previous occasions, but it was only when 'the erection of a Town Hall, capable of containing a large assembly, commenced, that the project was renewed', and when 'there was no doubt in the mind of the Architect that the building might be completed' in time, that the invitation was accepted. The mayor and corporation placed the whole of the building at the disposal of the association, and it was reported that 'few towns in the kingdom could have provided [the necessary] accommodation under one roof'.[45]

That very roof was the subject of a talk by Brodrick to the assembled members of the association about its construction, which was unusual because of 'the absence of tie beams, which allows the ceiling being

41 Later Sir Edmund Beckett and then Lord Grimthorpe, he was well known for his designs for clocks and bells, including 'Big Ben', for his drastic restoration of St. Alban's Cathedral, and for his attacks on architects. The decision to install a clock and bell was taken in May 1857 after Denison had addressed the Leeds Philosophical and Literary Society on the subject of public clocks in December 1856.

42 This drawing cannot be found, but it was illustrated in D. Harbron, 'Cuthbert Brodrick: or Cabbages at Salona', *The Architectural Review*, 79 (1936), 33.

43 *The Builder*, 18 (1860), 119.

44 H.-R. Hitchcock, *Architecture: nineteenth and twentieth centuries* (Harmondsworth, 1958), p. 158.

45 British Association for the Advancement of Science, *Leeds Meeting, 1858. Report of the Local Committee . . .* (Leeds, 1859), p. 13.

46 C. Brodrick, 'On the roof of the new Town Hall at Leeds', *British Association Transactions*, (1858), 207–08. Evidently the use of laminated timber was not the first intention. The contract drawing in West Yorkshire Archive Service, Leeds District Archives (52 in Box 49–54), dated 1854, is a working drawing for wrought-iron ribs and cast-iron trusses. The contract drawing, no. IX (LC/TC, Bin 42), shows that originally Brodrick was proposing to construct flying buttresses to strengthen the outer walls of the Victoria Hall.

47 A. Young, *Travels in France during the Years 1787, 1788 & 1789*, ed. C. Maxwell (Cambridge, 1929), pp. 81–82.

48 M. K. Deming, *La Halle au Blé de Paris 1762–1813* (Brussels, 1984).

49 West Yorkshire Archive Service, Leeds District Archives, LC/TC, Bin 42, C: extracts from the journal of the clerk of works. James Donaldson was appointed clerk of works at the beginning of the contract and he remained until 20 February 1857. He left an invaluable almost day-by-day record of the works. Sir Joseph Paxton visited the building under construction on 4 December 1855 'and seemed much satisfied with everything'. Another visitor was Philip Charles Hardwick, who on 18 April 1855 'expressed himself much satisfied with the work generally'. Sir Charles Barry and his son were there three times one weekend in April 1855 on 13th, 14th, and 15th. It was then that Barry showed a great interest in the roof construction, discussing it with Brodrick, who immediately ordered a strengthening of the timbers.

50 Mayhall, op. cit. (note 11), I, p. 727.

51 Brodrick's design for the chandeliers is in West Yorkshire Archive Service, Leeds District Archives (TH 42), and three surviving examples are hanging in Leeds Civic Hall. A well-known watercolour by Owen Jones in the Victoria and Albert Museum shows the interior of Osler's London showroom in Oxford Street.

brought nearer to the exterior . . . than is usually the case'.[46] This was achieved by using semicircular laminated timber ribs formed of twelve 1½-inch planks, 9 inches wide, nailed together and fastened with wrought-iron bolts and straps. As a principle of construction, this method was used in the middle of the sixteenth century in France, and it was incorporated in the structure of the Venetian church of Santa Maria della Salute in the 1650s; but perhaps the most famous example was in the Halle au Blé in Paris in 1782–83, when Jacques-Guillaume Legrand and Jacques Molinos covered the 150-foot diameter courtyard with a great dome composed, as Arthur Young described it in 1787, 'upon a new principle of carpentry . . . it is as light as if suspended by the fairies'.[47] This was a building which must have fascinated Brodrick, although when he knew it the timber dome had been replaced with an iron one by François-Joseph Bélanger in 1803.[48]

This method of timber roof construction had, as Brodrick said, 'been adopted more frequently in France than in England'; in fact, Paxton's 1851 Great Exhibition Building and Cubitt's King's Cross Station were probably the only buildings in this country where it had been used, and in his address to the society Brodrick described the particular problems he had in the Town Hall because of the 'very elaborate plaster ceiling' attached to the roof timbers and the springing of the arched ribs being at a considerable distance from the ground. Sir Charles Barry seems to have been interested in this construction, and he paid a visit to the site to inspect.[49] Perhaps he expressed caution because, despite Brodrick's confidence that there had not been 'the least perceptible outward thrust or change of form since the ribs were put up', he doubled the number. The plaster ceiling is certainly elaborate:

The columns and pilasters support an enriched entablature . . . [from which] springs the fine circular ceiling, which is divided into five bays, corresponding with the columns, each bay being subdivided into five compound panels, highly ornamented with conventional foliage, in relief and coloured. The hall is lighted by ten semicircular windows immediately above the entablature, and at the springing of the ceiling. They are of very large dimensions and are mixed with stained glass by Messrs. Edmundson and Son, of Manchester. Above the windows are appropriate figures and ornaments in full relief by Mr. John Thomas, of London[50] . . . Projecting from the centres or key stones are ram's heads, from which are suspended ten magnificent cut glass chandeliers, made by Messrs. Osler, of Birmingham, especially for the hall.[51]

Evidently, whatever doubts about expenditure the council might have had in the early days, they were now determined that nothing was too good for their Town Hall. They exercised patronage on a hitherto unprecedented lavish municipal scale. The mayor's reception rooms were said to be 'splendidly furnished; the gilt chairs for the Royal Family on the occasion of the opening are kept here', and there were portraits of William Wilberforce, Charles James Fox, and a marble medallion of Napoleon III and Eugénie. Brodrick participated actively in all the details of decoration and furnishing in the public rooms, in which he did not repeat himself. Each had its own character, even the different court rooms. The Civil Court in the north-east corner of the building, with its pilasters and curving cast-iron-fronted gallery, was particularly

31. Leeds Town Hall: the Victoria Hall on 7 September 1858, with the royal party on the platform. This magnificent watercolour is not signed; it has generally been attributed to Brodrick himself, but, although he was an accomplished watercolourist, the outstanding quality of this work suggests that a professional perspectivist, possibly Thomas Allom, might have been involved.

32. Leeds Town Hall: the old Council Chamber (now known as the Albert Room).

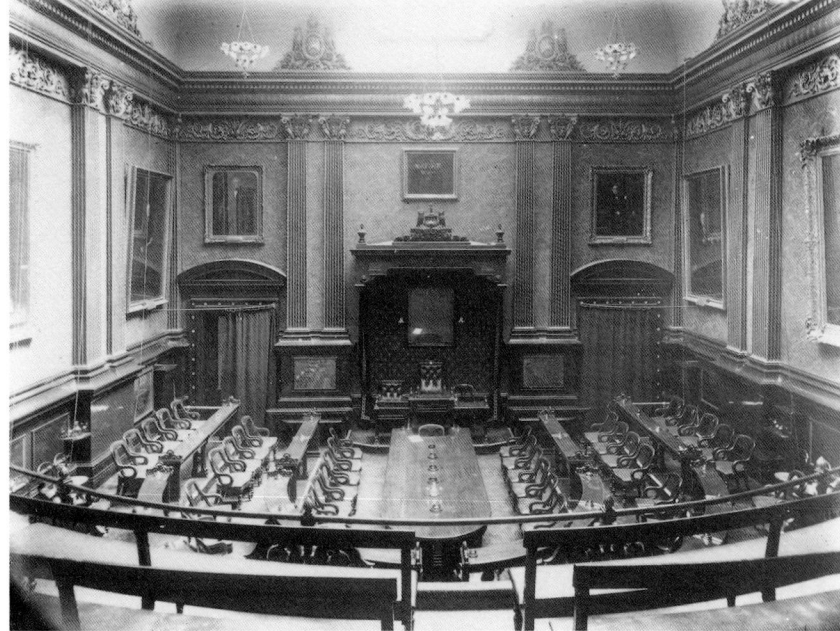

52 Now known as the Albert Room.

53 Ribart de Chamoust, *L'Ordre françois trouvé dans la nature* (Paris, 1783; reprinted 1967), p. ii.

54 T. Hamlin, *Benjamin Henry Latrobe* (New York, 1955), p. 270. Latrobe wrote to Thomas Jefferson in 1809 that 'This [corn cob] capital . . . obtained me more applause from the members of Congress than all the works of magnitude'.

55 R. and J. Adam, *The Works in Architecture of Robert and James Adam, esquires*, 3 vols. (London, 1773–1822, reprinted 1959), I (1773–78), plate 86.

impressive, although the richest effects were reserved for the Council Chamber in the south-east corner which, in addition to the coupled fluted pilasters and ornamented frieze, has an elaborate ceiling incorporating delicately painted glass panels and little domes. In this latter room, which is still largely intact,[52] although Brodrick's red morocco upholstered furnishings and the original gallery were removed in the 1930s, there is a characteristic example of a form of decoration within the Classical framework that evidently appealed to Brodrick.

Variations on the Corinthian or Composite orders had been invented by a number of architects but, in the opinion of Ribart de Chamoust who made his own contribution by devising 'l'ordre françois', in which the capital was based on natural forms representative of France, their efforts had been 'plus ou moins bizarres'.[53] In the early-nineteenth century Benjamin Latrobe invented capitals based on corn, tobacco, and cotton for the Capitol in Washington; in these the native plants replaced the Classical acanthus.[54] In England, Robert and James Adam created a 'Britannic order' for a proposed gateway to Carlton House, London; in this version a winged lion and unicorn replaced the traditional volutes and appeared to be flying out of the capital.[55] Such nationalist inventions remained curiosities, but both Lockwood and Brodrick obviously delighted in playing with the orders to introduce local references. Trinity House Chapel, Hull, has anchors, shells, and dolphins incorporated in the capitals, and in the Town Hall Brodrick devised decorative capitals expressive of the town's history. In the Vestibule and the Victoria Hall there are capitals of the giant-order columns which alternately display as a central element either a ram's head which symbolizes the golden fleece on which the prosperity of Leeds was based or the pinioned image of a Savile family owl which is part of the civic arms. The capitals in the Council Chamber are more ingenious and closer to the Adam example.

33. Leeds Town Hall: the entrance to the Victoria Hall from the Vestibule.

34. Leeds Town Hall: a detail of the decoration in the Vestibule.

Each has a pair of owls, each perching and facing outwards to left and right, above which the volutes branch out as if to protect the birds; but what could have become a distinctive 'Leeds order' had no successors and remains unique to the Town Hall.

In August 1858 the *Building News* was able to report that

the courts and the Council-chamber, as well as the Mayor's rooms, are in a forward state, and the large hall and the vestibule are nearly finished. The scaffolding, however, has not yet been removed, either in the hall or the vestibule, and it is difficult to anticipate the full effect of the decorations until that is done, but there is every reason to believe that they will excite general admiration, and be in every respect worthy of the reputation of Mr. Crace, by whom they have been designed and executed.[56]

The historical use of colour in architecture was a controversial but stimulating subject of discussion in France in the 1820s and 30s, but there was no great interest in England until 1854, when Owen Jones (1809–74) and Matthew Digby Wyatt (1820–77) designed the brilliantly polychromatic Greek Court in the Crystal Palace after its reconstruction at Sydenham. Then, in 1856, Jones published his classic *The Grammar of Ornament*, which contains one hundred chromolithographic plates of decoration

56 *Building News*, 4 (1858), 841–42.

35. Leeds Town Hall: a 'Leeds capital' in the old Council Chamber.

57 See M. Aldrich (cd.), *The Craces: royal decorators 1768–1899* (Brighton, 1990).

and colour from twenty countries and historical periods. It was a book to stimulate ideas about colour, and the Renaissance section must have interested Brodrick; the descriptions of the rooms in the Royal Institution and the Town Hall in Hull indicate how seriously he took the decoration of his buildings. But when it came to the colouring of Leeds Town Hall only the best possible advice was considered good enough and John Gregory Crace (1809–89) was brought in to execute the decoration at a cost of £1,600. He was the fourth generation of a remarkable family of decorators whose firm was founded in 1768 and worked at Windsor Castle, the Royal Pavilion at Brighton, Buckingham Palace, and great country houses from Chatsworth downward,[57] but Leeds seems to have been the only town in the whole country to employ the firm on its Town Hall.

Like Brodrick, Crace had travelled to the Continent as a young man, and he too had acquired a taste for French decorative art. Like Brodrick, he had admired the Paris Bourse, especially its 'very fair Ceiling', and after examining a good number of Parisian interiors he concluded that England lagged behind France in the excellence of its decorative art. Consequently he engaged a number of French artists to work for the firm. By the 50s, when Crace received the commission from Leeds, his

taste for what he called the 'old French style', by which he presumably meant the Rococo, had been modified by what he had seen in Munich of the decorated interiors of Leo von Klenze (1784–1864), with their deep colouring and stencilling, although he emphasized that strong colour did not necessarily mean the use of primary colours.

Strong colours were certainly used at Leeds, but only within an understanding of architectural form. Crace's son, John Dibblee Crace (1839–1919), the last generation in the family firm, referred explicitly and at length to the Town Hall in his *The Art of Colour Decoration* (1912) in the chapter on 'The Distribution of Values'. He took the Victoria Hall ('a large hall divided into bays by side columns, the arched roof being correspondingly divided') as an example to be analysed in detail for the relationship between colour and form so as to 'distribute our light and dark tones so that the eye will readily take in the structural forms'.[58] Unfortunately the elder Crace's admired work has been repainted several times, without paying attention to retaining its authenticity as part of the historic building; but it can be reconstructed in imagination (maybe, one day, in reality) from the description in the *Building News*.

The colour of the walls was 'a quiet green' relieved by marginal borders of fret ornament in a deeper tone of the same colour, outlined with maroon. The bold projecting columns are in imitation of Rosso Antico marble, the enriched capitals being of bronze and gold. On the upper fascia of the wall, in a line with the capitals are a series of appropriate inscriptions, in bold character on a deep violet ground margined with green, and relieved by coloured lines and ornaments.

These inscriptions, some in English and some in Latin, are generally indicative of civic virtues such as 'Weave Truth with Trust' and 'In Union

58 J. D. Crace, *The Art of Colour Decoration* (London, 1912), pp. 4–8. This Crace made a design for redecorating the Victoria Hall in 1894 (Victoria and Albert Museum, catalogued under E 1859–1912) which he reproduced as figure 2 in his book as an example for a detailed analysis of the distribution of colour values. It is believed that it was carried out, but there have been subsequent redecorations.

35

is Strength'. There must have been much discussion about the choice, especially about the Latin mottoes, although most would recognize that 'Labor Omnia Vincit' was part of Bradford's civic arms. On the semicircular frieze at the north end are the words 'Except the Lord build the House, they labour in Vain that build it'; and on the corresponding frieze at the opposite end, is the text 'Except the Lord keep the City, the Watchman waketh but in Vain'.

Under this frieze are a series of radiating panels, painted in appropriate ornament, and alternately bearing the arms of the town of Leeds, those of the clothworkers and those of the ironmongers; under these is an elegant light glass screen, framed in bronze and gold . . . Below the base line of the columns, the wall, forming a high dado, is in imitation of Verde antique and other rare marbles. The entablature above the columns is of a quiet stone colour relieved with gold and bronze, and the frieze is in imitation of the same red marble as the columns. The fine circular roof is divided into compartments; the main lines springing from the columns have leading ornaments and mouldings in bronze and gold. The general tone of the ceiling is a light neutral vellum colour with margins of citron and grey relieved in the grounds of the ornaments by maroon red or blue.[59]

An early perspective design of the interior of the Hall[60] shows that originally Brodrick intended to treat the large apse at the north end with pilasters on the wall and ribs on the half-dome. The organ case was to be a severely Neoclassical tripartite design, relatively small in scale; but it grew in size and elaboration until the final design dominated the apse so that there was no need for decoration other than 'the deep azure background [of the half-dome] powdered with stars'. The organ itself, designed by Henry Smart and William Spark, was one of the largest in Europe, with five manuals and pedals and a total of 6,500 pipes, and the swell box was the largest yet built by an English firm. Brodrick designed the monumental case which rises like the façade of a building with its strong vertical lines of burnished, diaper-patterned pipes, culminating in a rose-window effect crowned by the civic arms framed with garlands, while four gilded angels blow their trumpets. Surely they are playing an arrangement of Haydn's great chorus from *The Creation*, 'Achieved is the glorious work'.

The original brief had asked that the Great Hall (or Victoria Hall as it was named after the Queen had officially opened the building) should be 'designed principally for Public Meetings, but is to be so constructed as to be available for Lectures and Musical Entertainments'. After the opening, *The Builder* reported that acoustically it

must be regarded as eminently successful for musical effect. The notes, whether vocal or instrumental, seemed to acquire increased volume and freedom in the ample space, and are perfectly heard in every part of the room. But the resonance which enhances the effects of music is unfavourable for oratory.[61]

Edmund Beckett Denison thought both Liverpool and Leeds had great halls with lamentable acoustics. Moreover,

at Leeds there were under the same roof four smaller halls or courts, for the administration of justice; and so lamentably had the acoustic properties been neglected, that you could scarcely hear yourself speak in them — the speaker was, in fact, bewildered with the echo of his own voice.[62]

59 *Building News*, 4 (1858), 841–42. In 1878 the *Building News* reported that 'the whole of the interior of the Victoria Hall and vestibule of the Leeds Town Hall has been undergoing thorough repairs and re-decorations at the hands of Messrs. Roodhouse and Sons, upholsterers and decorators, of that town'. There is a detailed account of the colours used and reference is made to 'a novel feature . . . here introduced with marked success – the shafts of the columns, which are marbled a rich Rosso-antico, are varnished in the ordinary way, then felted down with ground pumice-stone and deadened, giving a semi-polished appearance without the harsh glare usually seen on polished or varnished work, and producing a wonderful stone-like effect' (*Building News*, 24 (1878), 228).

60 This design cannot now be found, but it was illustrated in Harbron, op. cit. (note 42), p. 34, plate 4.

61 *The Builder*, 16 (1858), 752.

62 *The Builder*, 17 (1859), 119.

37. C. Brodrick: Leeds Town Hall. The design for the organ case, as executed, except that the angelic trumpeters were augmented from two to four.

LEEDS TOWN HALL.

The criticism, especially of the acoustics in the Victoria Hall, has itself echoed down the years despite the prestige of the Triennial Music Festival and, more recently, the renown of the International Pianoforte Competition, which has brought the Town Hall into homes throughout the world on television screens. But Sir Charles Groves, a conductor who knew the building well, praised its 'reverberant acoustic, superb for big choral events. The details are as clear as anything, and there's a wonderful spaciousness. It is too reverberant for a solo piano. But if the sound doesn't come over in a piano concerto, it's the pianist's fault'.[63]

Nothing less than the angelic participation portrayed on the organ case could have matched the euphoria displayed in Leeds on 6 and 7 September 1858 when Queen Victoria arrived for the formal opening ceremony, making one of her rare visits to a northern industrial town. It is safe to say that the occasion has not been matched since, nor is likely to be, and the full eye-moistening account of the visit, when 'for a time, if only for a few hours, the borough became the seat of empire of the

63 W. Thomson with F. Waterman, *Piano Competition: the story of the Leeds* (London, 1990), p. 34.

38. Leeds Town Hall: a detail of the east front.

39. Leeds Town Hall: a detail of the west front with a sculpted mask by John Thomas.

38. Leeds Town Hall: a detail of the east front.

39. Leeds Town Hall: a detail of the west front with a sculpted mask by John Thomas.

greatest monarchy of the earth', is reproduced as Appendix E. It is true that the construction of the tower that had been so controversial was not complete; but that was a small detail which gave Prince Albert an opportunity to accompany Brodrick to the top of the structure where they 'entered freely into conversation on the subject of the building'. It was reported that the royal connoisseur had complimented the proud architect: 'When I first saw the building, Mr. Brodrick, I said to the Queen, "Magnificent! magnificent! beautiful proportion!" '. Brodrick was presented to the Queen in the Vestibule, where she was dwarfed by the mayor's gift to the corporation of

a splendid and admirable statue of the Queen, by [Matthew] Noble the sculptor . . . The statue is colossal, being eight feet six inches high, and is made of a block of Carrara marble of the very finest quality, spotless and pure. In front of the pedestal is the simple inscription "Queen Victoria, 1858". It cost the mayor a thousand guineas.[64]

There is no record of the Queen's words to Brodrick.

The progress of the building operations had not been without its troubles. The journal of James Donaldson, the clerk of works, is a continual story of visits to quarries in search of suitable stone; equally it records Brodrick's disappointment with the progress of the work, as well as his frequent dissatisfaction with the quality of the masonry.[65] One of the first entries writes of Brodrick's complaining there was 'not a sufficient number of through stones in the wall',[66] a constantly repeated comment in the early part of the contract. On one occasion Brodrick was so angry about 'the Rawden Hill stone being used for cornices . . . that he took a hammer and destroyed a cornice stone in order to prevent it being used in the building'.[67]

It was in the Town Hall that Brodrick first revealed his understanding of the local stone, from Bramley Fall, Calverley Wood, Pool Bank, and

64 Mayhall, op. cit. (note 11), I, p. 717. Originally the statue of Queen Victoria stood in the centre of the Vestibule, as it were at the heart of the empire which reached the four corners of the world named on the pendentives above; but it was moved to the eastern apse when a companion figure of Prince Albert was placed in the opposite apse.

65 See Briggs, op. cit. (note 9), pp. 165–69, and C. Cunningham, *Victorian and Edwardian Town Halls* (London, 1981), pp. 91–93.

66 West Yorkshire Archive Service, Leeds District Archives, loc. cit. (note 49), entry for 27 September 1853.

67 West Yorkshire Archive Service, Leeds District Archives, loc. cit. (note 49), entry for 10 March 1855.

40. 51 Market Place, Driffield: a minor example of Brodrick's individual detailing of masonry.

41. Leeds Town Hall: one of the four lions sculpted in Portland stone by William Day Keyworth.

68 *The Builder*, 14 (1856), 306.

69 West Yorkshire Archive Service, Leeds District Archives, loc. cit. (note 49), entry for 7 April 1856.

70 In 1858 *The Builder* reported (16 (1858), 380) that work had been suspended on the building of the tower because they had no stone and that it would not be completed before the opening. Also, Brodrick thought it desirable that sufficient time should be allowed for the foundation to consolidate. Apparently this hiatus lasted from May to October.

Rawden Hill, the tough material in which the large quartz grains glitter subtly when caught by the light. Fine detailing is impossible with this material, which is 'so destructive to edge-tools . . . [that] instead of the chisels cutting the stone, the stone cuts the chisels'.[68] Consequently, Brodrick's detailing is bold and simple, with deep horizontal rustication and vigorous vermiculation, surface texturing, and a minimum of carved decoration that is not unlike the work of da Vignola at, for example, Villa Farnese at Caprarola. Even the carving, as on the tower, is bold and virile, relying on clearly expressed and simplified forms for its effectiveness. This understanding of the quality of the local building material was one of Brodrick's strengths, and it helped to form a distinctive manner of design detailing and a recognizably individual architectural character which is just as apparent in the small three-bay bank in the Market Place, Driffield (1856), as it is in his major buildings.

The worsening relationship between Brodrick and the builder, Samuel Atack, who complained about the standard of workmanship required, was only exacerbated by disagreements between them about the certification of payments. The architect rightly withheld payment for unsatisfactory work, and there was a crisis in April 1856 when Donaldson reported that Atack 'has been over paid and Mr. B. will not certify any more money. Mr. B. and the Chairman gave strict & positive orders not to allow anything to be removed'.[69] Apparently the builder had started to take scaffolding away, and policemen were brought in to guard the site. Although the troubles were temporarily smoothed over, there was a final crisis at the beginning of 1857 when work stopped, and in March Atack was declared bankrupt. Other contractors were brought in to complete the work, but the delays caused by all these troubles, added to the difficulties in obtaining sufficient suitable stone, meant that the structure of the tower was incomplete on the great opening day of 7 September 1858.[70] However, this unfortunate fact was to some extent disguised by the

42–44. Three derivatives of Leeds Town Hall: 42. Bolton, Lancashire (W. Hill 1863); 43. Durban, Natal, South Africa (P. M. Dudgeon 1881–85); 44. Morley, Yorkshire (G. A. Fox 1895).

71 The lions were an addition to the design, probably inspired by those Brodrick had seen and drawn in Italy. Two were unveiled *in situ* on 15 February 1867, and the remaining pair on 7 June. Each is carved out of two pieces of Portland stone with zig-zag joints. The four cost £550. There was a fashion for lions at the time: others may be found guarding the Fitzwilliam Museum, Cambridge, St. George's Hall, Liverpool, the Institute, Saltaire, as well as the most famous ones in Trafalgar Square, London.

72 Cunningham, op. cit. (note 65), p. 19.

73 Reid (ed.), op. cit. (note 10), p. 121. The influence of the Town Hall on public buildings in other provincial towns and in English-speaking countries overseas would provide material for a separate chapter. The Australian examples are referred to later (see pp. 95–100); but there were several others. Philadelphia City Hall (J. McArthur jr. 1871–1901) can be seen as the ultimate expansion of the idea of a domed tower in the centre of a façade terminating in pavilions. Fuller and Laver's first design for the New York State Capitol featured a single giant order and there is a close resemblance between the tower and that of the Town Hall (see *The Builder*, 28 (1870), 426f.). The giant order was to remain a characteristic of public architecture in the USA well into the twentieth century, continuing the French model that had inspired Brodrick. In England, there were derivatives of Leeds Town Hall in Bolton (1866–73) and Portsmouth (1886–90), both the work of the Leeds architect, William Hill (see pp. 83–86), in Birkenhead (C. O. Ellison and Son 1883–87), in Dewsbury (H. Holtom and G. A. Fox 1888–89), and in Morley (G. A. Fox 1895). In South Africa, Durban Town Hall (P. M. Dudgeon 1881–85) is the most obviously indebted to Brodrick's original through Hill's close versions.

erection of a triumphal arch designed by Brodrick and placed at the end of East Parade so as to delay the royal party's view of the domeless tower's framework. No doubt they were too polite to mention it.

As for the cost, it had been escalating throughout the contract in a not unfamiliar fashion in the history of public buildings until eventually it totalled £122,000, almost four times the original amount, of which the architect's commission amounted to £3,685. Even so, before William Day Keyworth's four Portland stone lions had been placed in position to guard the main entrance,[71] it was recognized that the accommodation was inadequate for the municipal offices; in 1864 Brodrick produced a plan for additional ones on an adjacent site,[72] but nothing was done for another twelve years until there was a competition, in which a younger Leeds architect, George Corson (1829–1910), was the successful entrant.

Brodrick's Town Hall became a byword in the municipal world for costliness, but the council obtained the building it wanted to symbolize the town's prosperity and importance. It had strengthened the case for its nomination as an assize town, a claim boldly put forward in the loyal address to the Queen at the opening, although its nomination had to wait until 1864. Leeds was justly proud of its Town Hall; but what was its standing in the wider world? In his biography of Dr. Heaton, referring to the Leeds building, Wemyss Reid wrote that he could foresee a time 'when the archaeologist of a future age will look for the best specimens of the buildings of the present reign . . . [in] some provincial towns'.[73] The *Building News* offered some perceptive comments:

The erection of this building, one of a remarkable class, is not without its historical signification, for, like similar monuments of the middle ages, it shows not only the wealth to which the cities have attained, but the development of municipal institutions. There must be in any community the means for the aggregate expression of wealth; an autocrat will always provide palaces, garrisons and jails;

45. C. Brodrick: Leeds Town Hall from the south-east. The architect's watercolour (1854).

74 *Building News*, 4 (1858), 1289. Despite the praise lavished on the building, the writer followed the current regret that the age did not have an architecture of its own. 'While the surface is profusely covered with decoration, it is in the spirit of the age to remark that it is mechanical, patterned, and unmeaning, and, with the spirit of medieval performance, they look for the day when profusion may be expressed by profusion of invention, and when every detail may bear the touch of the master and not of the mould or the machine. The architect has felt this, but, limited in funds, he could not compass his desires, but inscriptions placed here and there appeal to the

a hierarchy temples and dwellings for its priesthood; and these are contributed by the associated taxation or offerings of the country, and may be concentrated in the capital or dispersed in solitudes which religion has hallowed; but unless the townspeople themselves have some organization, the resources of the cities will not be bestowed on civil edifices. Hence in many of our towns of later growth but of defective institutions . . . as in Leeds itself . . . these edifices are wanting, but the history of enfranchisement is recorded by the monuments of recent date. Thus our great towns have given expression not merely to the display of their prosperity, but their regard for the liberal arts, and have in their new buildings afforded a gratification to their own feelings, and offered objects for the admiration of posterity.

The Town Hall of Leeds is one of the gorgeous structures of the class. Profuse in its adornments, it represents an age in which wealth has passed beyond simple comfort to the enjoyment of luxury. It speaks of abundance, and displays it. Its clustered columns, its profusion of lights, its ribbed vault, bespeak the wealth of its builders, and it is made to minister to their recreation and indulgence.

The architect has undoubtedly achieved his aim, for he has given the people of Leeds a hall which tells of the luxury of kings.[74]

In the 1867 Paris Exposition, Brodrick exhibited his splendid water-colour of the Town Hall, which was then nearly ten years old. *The Builder* commented that it

says as much for classic study of architecture as we could well say, so long as Mr. Tite withholds his 'Royal Exchange', Mr. Scott his Whitehall Government Offices, and the Liverpool Hall of St. George by Mr. Elmes is out of the competition.[75]

The company is good. One hundred and thirty years later, in Vienna in the winter of 1996–97, the same watercolour was the only English representative of 'classic study of architecture', this time in the important Council of Europe exhibition, 'Der Traum von Glück: die Kunst des Historismus in Europa'[76] in the Künstlerhaus. The watercolour and the building's assessment have stood the test of time well.

mind better than the repeated paterae or alternating panels. When such a hall is filled with a moving throng, the organ inciting a thousand voices with the words of the poet and the tones of the composer, with life in its highest moments, why should art be dead and the building alone a sepulchre to the universal soul! Thus we look upon efforts like this remarkable one at Leeds as steps only in progress, leading us on to that time when architecture shall indeed flourish, and hand down distinctively to after ages our nation and our time.'

75 *The Builder*, 25 (1867), 421.

76 H. Fillitz and W. Telesko (eds.), *Der Traum vom Glück: die Kunst des Historismus in Europa*, 2 vols. (vol. I Beiträge, vol. II Katalog (of exhibition, 13 September 1996 – 6 January 1997, at the Künstlerhaus, Vienna)) (Vienna, 1996), p. 560, item 19. 19. There are, in fact, two copies of this perspective watercolour in the Leeds City Art Gallery. Both are apparently by the same hand, but only one is signed 'CB 1854'.

A French Interlude

There is a subtle but marked difference between the main body of the Town Hall, which is basically a strictly disciplined Classical building without ornament, and the tower, which is richly decorated and more Baroque in character. But there are other indications of a change in Brodrick's design vocabulary even on the colonnaded façades. There is the proud south entrance, rich in allegory, which incorporates John Thomas's great sculptured group of Leeds as it wished to be seen, 'fostering and encouraging the Arts and Sciences'. There are the monumental vases on the balustraded parapets, and the pedimented, garlanded ventilation towers, and there is even a difference between the delicately carved rosettes on the north front of the building and the bolder ones on the tower which became a hallmark of Brodrick's decorative detailing on his later buildings. What happened between 1852, when he made his first design for the building, and 1856, when the council agreed to build the final version of the tower? Almost certainly Brodrick paid more than one visit to France during those years.[1] In 1854 a tempting competition, open to the world, was announced. The town of Lille in the extreme north of the country was ambitious to have a cathedral. Contestants had twelve months (later extended to fifteen) in which to prepare their designs according to a detailed brief.

The style of the monument must recall the beautiful edifices, simple at once and imposing, of the first half of the thirteenth century. This church, of which the length is to be from 100 to 110 metres . . . must exhibit one or two towers, surmounted by spires, three deeply recessed portals, a nave and two aisles, single transepts, a choir, a sanctuary and apsidal chapels . . . the chapel at the extreme east end and to be dedicated to the Blessed Virgin, must have more importance given to it than the others.[2]

As for the materials, brick was to be used for the walls and vaulting, stone from Vergelet and Hordain for the mouldings and sculptures, and grit for the basements. The last material would have been very familiar to Brodrick, who entered the competition with an assurance strengthened by his success at Leeds. It can be reasonably assumed that he visited France to inspect the site, probably at the time he was considering the second design for the Town Hall tower. We know that William Burges, for example, paid three visits; one to reconnoitre, one to deliver his submission, and one to examine his rivals' designs.[3]

In 1855, still within the fifteen months allowed for submitting in the Lille competition, the Exposition universelle opened in Paris.[4] It was the major art event of the decade, intended to outdo the 1851 Exhibition in London, and it was such a success that a francophilia swept through the London art world; architecture, too, was influenced by what visitors to Paris could see in the city. If the art exhibited nothing else (and how could

1 T. B. Wilson, *Two Leeds Architects* (Leeds, 1937), p. 33: 'Not infrequently he made visits to Paris'.

2 *The Ecclesiologist*, 16 (N.S. 13) (1855), 2.

3 J. M. Crook, *William Burges and the High Victorian Dream* (London, 1981), p. 171.

4 See P. Mainardi, *Art and Politics of the Second Empire* (New Haven and London, 1987), pp. 33ff.

46. Leeds Town Hall: the south entrance. The allegorical group which represents Leeds 'in its commercial and industrial character, fostering and encouraging the Arts and Sciences'. The sculptor was John Thomas.

47. Leeds Town Hall: Baroque detailing on the base of the tower and one of the ventilating towers that Brodrick turned into ornamental features.

5 Mainardi, op. cit. (note 4), p. 69. The definition is by Adolphe Thiers.

one say that, considering that Ingres, Delacroix, and Courbet were the stars?), it established that the only way in which to describe the overall character of French art of the time was to use the convenient word 'eclectique', of which the definition was 'a taste which consists in combining the qualities of different schools into a harmonious ensemble'.[5] This was the mood within the Palais des Beaux-Arts, where part of the 1855 Exposition was being held. In architecture, too, there was much talk of eclecticism, both in France and England, and also of ornament which, although not a necessity, was considered 'an important auxiliary'.

44

48. The Bibliothèque Ste. Geneviève, Paris (H. Labrouste 1838–50).

49. The Bibliothèque Ste. Geneviève, Paris: a detail of the decoration on the façade.

50. The Palais de Justice, Paris: the façade to the Place Dauphine (L. Duc 1840–79).

51. The Pavillon Richelieu, the New Louvre, Paris (L. Visconti and H.-M. Lefuel 1852–80).

It is difficult to believe that the francophile Brodrick did not visit this important Exposition, especially as the Town Hall clerk of works's diary reveals that he was absent for the whole month of June. On the assumption that this was the case, what was happening in Paris? Three years earlier, in 1852, a coup d'état had put Louis-Napoléon on the throne as emperor of the French, and the lavish Second Empire life-style had been inaugurated. In 1853 the emperor had appointed Georges-Eugène Haussmann to transform the city and impose a pattern of boulevards, avenues, secondary streets, and intersections on the old fabric — a pattern

52 and 53. The New Louvre: details of the decorative masonry.

6 See P. de Moncan and C. Mahout, *Le Paris de Baron Haussmann* (Paris, 1991).

7 F. Loyer, *Paris, Nineteenth-Century Architecture and Urbanism* (New York, 1988), pp. 233–60.

8 P. Saddy, *Henri Labrouste, architecte, 1801–75* (Paris, 1977), pp. 37–60.

9 A. Drexler (ed.), *The Architecture of the École des Beaux-Arts* (London, 1977), pp. 428–49.

10 G. Bresc-Bautier, *The Architecture of the Louvre* (London, 1995), p. 218.

11 H.-R. Hitchcock, *Architecture: nineteenth and twentieth centuries* (Harmondsworth, 1958), pp. 158–59.

that was so coherent that it still serves today.[6] It linked the newly built or proposed railway stations, and it liberated selected historic buildings from their accretions, using them as visual foci. The new boulevards were lined with six-storey apartment buildings, richly ornamented stone structures in which the monumental character traditionally reserved for public buildings was transferred to domestic architecture.[7]

Of the public buildings Brodrick could have seen in 1855, one would have been Henri Labrouste's Bibliothèque Sainte-Geneviève,[8] which he had probably noted in the early stage of its construction when he was in Paris in 1844. It is not difficult to discern a kinship between some of his work and this austere building with its long line of arcuated windows and ornament that sinks back discreetly into the ashlar façade, which has an unbroken roofline. The library was finished in 1850, and four years later Labrouste was appointed architect of the Bibliothèque Impériale (later Nationale); but the famous reading room in the latter building was not started until 1860. However, in 1855 Louis Duc's additions to the Palais de Justice were under construction. There he illustrated the answer to his own question, 'Without the Orders, what would our monuments be?' On the western extension he used a giant Corinthian order, a central pavilion with a quadrangular dome, and a segmental pediment supported by caryatids. The strongly modelled façade overlooking the place Dauphine was treated with derivatives of Roman Doric columns as if they were a screen in front of the building.[9] The final *folie de grandeur* (but not completed until 1875) is a great monumental staircase guarded by lions.

The third prominent building that Brodrick would have seen in 1855 was the New Louvre, which was being built to link the old Louvre with the Tuileries Palace, where Napoleon III and Eugénie lived and held their court. This had been started by Louis Visconti in 1852, but he had died almost immediately and had been succeeded by Hector-Martin Lefuel, whose work became increasingly exuberant. On the façades he used motifs from the earlier phases of the building, 'such as oculi flanked by allegorical figures, caryatids, trophies in the attic stage, and female heads surrounded by hounds [but] he exaggerated the decorative effects, and encrusted his façades with luxuriant sculpture'.[10] As Hitchcock wrote,

When Brodrick designed his town hall very little was known in England of Visconti's project of 1852 for the New Louvre, and Lefuel had not yet begun to elaborate the design . . . But the wave of Second Empire influence arrived in England well before the Leeds Town Hall was finished. When the English swarmed to Paris to visit the International Exhibition of 1855 the character of the New Louvre became generally known to architects and to the interested public.[11]

These then were likely to have been among the new Parisian buildings which Brodrick would have noticed with great interest during the time the Leeds town council was making up its mind about spending more money on a tower, and reference will be made to them in subsequent chapters. But as the deliberations in Leeds were reaching a conclusion, so too were those in France about the design for the proposed cathedral in Lille. There were six judges, five of them French, and in March 1856 forty-one designs were put on exhibition in the Halle au Blé. Solemn High Mass preceded the first round of adjudication, which brought the number down to nineteen. Again the jury adjudicated, and on 13 April it was announced that the major prizes had gone to English architects, the first to William Burges and Henry Clutton, and the second to George Edmund Street.[12] The third went to a French architect, and among the silver medallists were three English entries, one of which had been entered under the hopeful nom-de-plume of 'Spes'.

A writer representing *The Ecclesiologist*, the dictatorial journal about all matters ecclesiastical and liturgical, went to see the entries and 'the gorgeous array of possible spires, and at least conceivable gables and crosses, breaking up the solid monotony of the ugly swamps and fens' surrounding Lille. The designs were still anonymous, but he commented about one:

So far as a popular verdict would decide the question, this design — apparently an English one — would be chosen for the first prize by the people of Lille; of whom an admiring crowd was always to be seen around it. And as usual the popular verdict would be unfair; for the author of this showy plan, though by no means a contemptible artist, has made his drawings *ad captandum*, and not in honest accordance with the conditions under which he was invited to compete . . . Nothing is easier than to design on paper such a reflex of Strasbourg as the pretentious west elevation before us, without the correction of the laborious detail and calculation required . . . by the Lille Commission . . . Then again, the style — developed Pointed — is not that prescribed by the regulations. An architect who thus ignores the terms upon which his competitors consent to contest the prize, is ineligible for anything more than a discriminating honourable mention. To this the author of *Spes* is undoubtedly intitled.[13]

The conditions of the competition had asked for one or two towers, and Brodrick, alias 'Spes', had chosen to have only one, three hundred feet high, an unusual feature in a French cathedral, though not uncommon in Belgium and the Netherlands, with which Lille is closely associated historically and geographically. Whatever criticisms the writer in *The Ecclesiologist* had, he had to admit that

the striking peculiarity of a single huge spire is certainly very effective, — richly pierced and well composed, and soaring above a grand horizontal line of open tracery which, however constructionally unreal, as masking nothing — is very charming in its airy gracefulness.

Was there a connection between this remarkable tower and spire and the first design for the Town Hall spire? True, one was Gothic and one Classical; but *eclecticisme* was in the air, and ten years later Brodrick was talking about making 'an attempt to combine Gothic outline with the Classic details';[14] one might suggest he was doing that in the 1850s, when one compares the two, tiered, elongated designs for Leeds and Lille.

In a later issue of *The Ecclesiologist*, after the awards had been announced, the writer agreed that Brodrick's design

deserves the rank assigned to it by the jury, who have shown the just discrimination for which we gave them credit . . . They commend the seductive grace of the perspectives; but observe that the conditions of the contest were not observed by this gentleman, and that his design . . . would have far surpassed the specified total cost of the undertaking.[15]

12 Crook, op. cit. (note 3), pp. 171–72.

13 *The Ecclesiologist*, 17 (N.S. 14) (1856), 96–97.

14 *The Bolton Chronicle*, 25 March 1865, p. 7.

15 *The Ecclesiologist*, 17 (N.S. 14) (1856), 165.

54. C. Brodrick: Lille Cathedral, the west front. Brodrick's competition entry received a silver medal and created much interest and admiration when it was exhibited (1854–56).

55. C. Brodrick: Lille Cathedral, the east front.

Accusations that Brodrick flagrantly ignored the conditions of the competition, including the stipulated cost, were to be repeated in later contests, but this award represented an important success for him on the international scene, especially for a man who had by this time declared himself a committed Classicist. He must have felt gratified when *The Builder* reported of his design that it would 'repay long attention'.[16] His interpretation of Classicism was broadening by 1856, and his growing disposition towards an increased richness of detail, such as was developing in Paris, became more noticeable, as in the work of several of his contemporaries; but what is unusual is that he not only followed Second Empire fashions but also looked to earlier Classical buildings as models. As for the Lille experience, he was proud of his success and displayed the silver medal on his chimney-piece; the framed drawings with their 'seductive grace' are said to have been hanging on the wall of the bedroom in which he died.

16 *The Builder*, 15 (1857), 70. The outcome of the contest was that the commission of seventeen citizens who had devised the terms of the competition rejected the jury's decision and employed a local man to prepare a design based on several of the winning ones. 'Intrigue has done its work', pronounced *The Ecclesiologist*.

The London Competitions

'Winning spurs in the architectural profession is like holding the belt of the Prize-ring and having to fight for its retention, at the cost of far more kicks than halfpence',[1] wrote a disillusioned correspondent to *The Builder* in 1867. The spurs were won by winning a competition, and there was no doubt that Brodrick had achieved his by triumphing in the Leeds Town Hall competition and being a prizewinner in the Lille Cathedral contest. They, particularly the former, had certainly put him on the map, apparently securely. When the Town Hall was complete and he had received encomiums from royalty and from his fellow professionals, he was still only in his mid-thirties, his spurs were sharp and burnished, and he ought to have been able to look forward to many more prestigious commissions. But his very success had stiffened the competition by pitting him against the best men in the profession, although the Leeds commission had proved that he deserved to be in such company. He took part in three of the most publicized competitions for public buildings in London: government offices in Whitehall, the Natural History Museum, and the National Gallery. On the whole, he acquitted himself well, but at times, in these and other competitions, he relied too much on repeating the formula of the Leeds building, which became for him a central *idée fixe* on which he essayed a number of variants while clinging to the assurance of his great success, both in composition and in style. 'His noble mass of columnar Neoclassicism was just about thirty years out of date', wrote Sir John Summerson of Brodrick's 1856 design for the War Office in Whitehall, emphasizing his affinity with earlier-nineteenth-century monumental buildings and, by implication, criticizing the Leeds Town Hall as out of date too.[2] More brutally, the *Building News* dismissed his 1866 proposal for the remodelling of the National Gallery in Trafalgar Square as being 'great in pillars. There are some thirty-six Corinthian shafts in the front elevation alone, and when we have said this, we have said nearly all that can be said of the design'.[3] But these three national contests illustrate the manoeuvring and abuses within the competition system. 'Where one might have expected [them] to be non-controversial — those organised by the Government — one finds the greatest confusion, almost invariably indecision, and the loudest complaints.'[4]

In 1856 the first commissioner of works, Sir Benjamin Hall, announced a competition, open to any architect from abroad as well as from the United Kingdom, for new buildings in Whitehall on the site between Downing Street and Charles Street.[5] There were three requirements: one was a master plan for the area, and the others were separate buildings for two government departments, those of the secretary of state for foreign affairs and the secretary of state for war. Strangely, a choice could be made by the competitor of what and which to submit, and there

1 *The Builder*, 25 (1867), 248.

2 J. Summerson, *Victorian Architecture: four studies in evaluation* (New York and London, 1970), p. 80. Summerson erroneously credits Brodrick with having been trained in Paris.

3 *Building News*, 14 (1867), 17.

4 J. Physick and M. Darby, *Marble Halls* (London, 1973), p. 17.

5 See M. H. Port, *Imperial London: civil government building in London 1850–1915* (New Haven and London, 1995), for many references to this competition.

was no need to design either of the buildings to suit a master plan. It was an ill-conceived competition from the beginning, especially when it became apparent that some entries were for one building which combined two departments, while others were for one or two separate buildings without an agreed context.

Nevertheless, the competition attracted attention as well as criticism. In March 1857 *The Builder* reported: 'We understand that 192 British competitors have sent in designs; those from abroad have yet to be received'.[6] In fact there were relatively few from overseas, partly because of the shortness of time (five months), and partly because of the requirement to use an unfamiliar scale of sixteen feet to an inch rather than the metric. *The Builder* also reported that 'some of the packages include drawings for the three competitions, some for two of them, so that the number of designs is of course greater than the number of competitors'. Among them were complete designs made by Brodrick for two buildings, for a combined one, for alternative exterior treatments, and for a master plan; obviously he wanted to win. The assessors, under Lord Stanhope's chairmanship, were the duke of Buccleuch, William Burn (the only architect), Sir William Stirling, David Roberts the painter, Lord Eversley, and the engineer, Isambard Kingdom Brunel. The choice of judges for competitions was often contentious, and on this occasion the *Building News* commented:

The profession and public — architects and amateurs — all ask what has any of these gentlemen ever done to prove his capacity for the office of judge in an architectural competition? and from no quarter can a satisfactory reply be obtained.[7]

The public response to the competition was surprising. 'Nothing so remarkable as the scene of Westminster Hall during the first three days of this week, has ever been known of by architects', commented *The Builder* in May 1857. Twenty-seven thousand people visited the display during that short time to look at the designs, although the editor was asked by a correspondent:

Pray put your head into Westminster Hall, and see the official doings there for the forthcoming Exhibition of Designs. The hall is being divided into small compartments, which [some] liken to sheep-pens, and some to eating-house boxes, but which will, I fear, considering the darkness of the Hall, prove very slaughter-houses to the unfortunate drawings which may be committed to them.[8]

Altogether there were 218 entries and nearly 2,000 drawings, including permutations of the three requirements, and the first reaction was that there was 'more of novelty and beauty than has been displayed in drawings for many years'.[9] *The Builder* euphorically declared that the exhibition would

leave lasting influences upon the architects who are so assiduously studying it, and the valuable results will be seen in our buildings as in the amenities of the profession for years to come.[10]

There was little secrecy about the identity of the competitors although the designs were submitted under noms-de-plume. Among the stylistically assorted Italianate, Gothic, and Second Empire proposals were

6 *The Builder*, 15 (1857), 178.

7 *Building News*, 3 (1857), 476.

8 *The Builder*, 15 (1857), 178.

9 *The Builder*, 15 (1857), 261.

10 *The Builder*, 15 (1857), 261.

56. C. Brodrick: the proposal for Block B, the War Office, in the Whitehall competition (1856–57).

VIEW of BLOCK B from PARLIAMENT St

57. C. Brodrick: Block C of the Whitehall competition entry (1856–57).

VIEW of BLOCK C from the RIVER

11 *The Builder*, 15 (1857), 169.

12 *Building News*, 3 (1857), 474. Presumably the drawings in the RIBA catalogue are only sketches for more finished presentation drawings which have not survived.

13 *The Builder*, 15 (1857), 269.

14 *The Builder*, 15 (1857), 437.

the excellent designs numbered 20, and marked 'Corona' [which] have strong points of resemblance to the town-hall at Leeds. Their merit is both in the plan, and the decorative treatment.[11]

It was also said that the whole entry was 'illustrated by a series of singularly beautiful drawings',[12] and the design was allowed to have 'great merit' although it was thought not to 'exhibit the character appropriate to government offices'.[13]

Looking at other designs, it would be difficult to identify what that character is, but evidently natural lighting to the offices, which was a current concern, was not a major consideration for Brodrick, alias 'Corona'. His designs were, indeed, very much indebted to Leeds Town Hall with their giant-order Corinthian screens, recessed porticoes without pediments, and their monumental trophies on the heavy attic balustrades. The plans do not seem to have survived, but the perspectives and elevations give the impression that the building is on an open site rather than in Whitehall. Nevertheless the jury awarded Brodrick fifth prize for the War Office; he was not placed in the Foreign Office section. The premium for the War Office went to Henry Garling, Brodrick's friend from their Rome meeting in 1844. His design was commented on for its strong resemblance to well-known buildings in Paris, no doubt having in mind the Hôtel de Ville, which was to be destroyed by the Commune in 1871.[14] Brodrick, like several other competitors, was also considering using a Parisian style with pavilion roofs, but evidently he preferred to be faithful to the style that had brought him success.

The prize for the winning entry for the Foreign Office went to Henry Edward Coe and Henry Hofland for a Second Empire design, but the thought of two Parisian-inspired buildings in the heart of London, and moreover for British government departments, was too much for *The Times*, which asked:

What do we want with the Hôtel de Ville from Paris on the edge of St. James's Park in order that a few hundred clerks may execute their daily tasks? The Colonies may be ruled from a building which is without the Pavillon de Flore at one extremity and the Pavillon Marsan at the other . . .

George Gilbert Scott, whose Gothic design for the Foreign Office had been placed third, then felt, as he said, 'at liberty to stir', with such effect that he was appointed architect in spite of all the recommendations of the assessors. It seemed as if the Gothic style was triumphing until the prime minister, Lord Palmerston, intervened in favour of the Italianate. Some parliamentary committee members, including Edward Akroyd, the Yorkshire industrialist MP and patron of Scott at Halifax, appealed to him to reverse his decision and allow Scott to design the building in his favourite Gothic, but the Italianate party rallied round Sir William Tite, who led a deputation of twenty stylistically committed architects, including Brodrick, to assure Palmerston that he had their support.[15] It is worth noting that Scott had recently written a criticism that would hardly have endeared him to Brodrick:

town halls are continually being erected in our provincial towns in styles as thoroughly unsuitable as can be conceived, and at a cost which would, in good hands and in a right style, have enabled them to vie with the glories of Brussels, Louvain or Ypres. Conceive for one moment what a glorious structure might have been erected at Leeds.[16]

By that malicious remark Scott meant, of course, in his good hands and in the Gothic style. But the Classical deputation to the prime minister invoked French architects in an unusual *entente cordiale*. Sydney Smirke told him:

During the last eight or nine years [French architects] had been enriching Paris with a mass of architectural magnificence, and yet not one public building has been there erected in the Gothic style. Nor was this owing to their not being conversant with that style . . . but by their totally abstaining from Gothic in their public works, they practically admitted its unfitness for them.

Doubtless Brodrick would have nodded approvingly, but the account in *The Builder* does not record any contribution from him to the meeting. The upshot of the famous 'Battle of the Styles' and 'the indignation felt by the majority of the competitors and of non-competing architects at the result' was that Palmerston assured the deputation that he 'knew of no style so suitable . . . as the Horizontal, or Classic, or Italian, or whatever names its branches might have gained . . . A public building ought to be handsome externally, while convenient in the interior; and the style which he preferred undeniably gave buildings which combined those

15 *The Builder*, 17 (1859), 562.

16 G. G. Scott, *Remarks on Secular and Domestic Architecture, Present and Future* (London, 1857), p. 201.

qualities . . . his mind was determined not to have Gothic, but Italian'. Perhaps he would have favoured Brodrick's design, but it was Scott's reluctantly Italianate Foreign Office that was the result, although he ignored Henry Cole's suggestion of copying Inigo Jones's unexecuted proposals for the Palace of Whitehall. The War Office was quietly forgotten for another time.

Brodrick's second experience of a national architectural competition followed in 1864 when the first commissioner for works, William Cowper (later Baron Mount-Temple), announced a contest for a new natural history and patents museum, which was to be built at South Kensington on the site of the demolished 1862 International Exhibition Building.[17] The intention was to relieve the pressure on space at the British Museum. There was to be

a general invitation to architects to submit a Block plan shewing an arrangement of the whole 17 acres in Museums, galleries and courts for the purposes of Science and Art, and also an Elevation of a plan in detail of that portion of the whole building which will be required to contain the Natural History Collections . . . and the collection of Models belonging to the Commissioners of Patents.

The financial incentive offered was premiums of £250, £150, and £100 (later increased to £400, £250, and £100). The whole business had been conceived without consulting the trustees of the museum, and not surprisingly the result of the competition was another fiasco.

The assessors were Lord Elcho, William Tite, David Roberts, James Pennethorne, and James Fergusson. There were thirty-three entries, a small number that probably reflected memories of the last competition. Captain Francis Fowke, the Royal Engineers designer of the 1862 International Exhibition Building and the Royal Albert Hall, was awarded the first premium for a multi-domed design of three linked buildings in an Italian Renaissance style which owed much to Bramante's unexecuted design for St. Peter's, Rome. Robert Kerr came second with a Second Empire design, and Brodrick was awarded the third premium of £100.[18] The main result was another blow to the architectural profession when it was announced that once again a military engineer had been preferred to an architect; but Henry Cole, secretary of the Science and Art Department, favoured the choice because he had more faith in the capability of Royal Engineers to put up better and cheaper buildings than architects could.

The *Building News* made some unexpected comments about the presentation of Brodrick's design. Considering the usual quality of his drawings, it is surprising to read that

it is much to be regretted that the author of this design, the outlines of which are very well drawn, should have failed in shading his elevation. In its present washed-out condition, few would be attracted by its appearance. Yet it has merits, and merits quite as great as many which are more effectively shown off. The absence of a perspective view is another drawback to its favour.[19]

Nevertheless, he was awarded the third prize, although what he submitted is something of a mystery. No drawings are known to have survived, unless some sketches in the RIBA Drawings Collection are related to this design. All that we have is a critical assessment in *The Builder*,[20] from

17 See Port, op. cit. (note 5), pp. 97ff., 173ff.; also *The Builder*, 22 (1864), 286ff., 505ff.

18 Port, op. cit. (note 5), p. 173.

19 *Building News*, 11 (1864), 313ff.

20 *The Builder*, 22 (1864), 346.

which to form an idea of what was entered under the nom-de-plume 'Pro Rege et Lege', which is the motto on the Leeds civic-arms. Evidently there was a central rotunda, 180 feet in diameter, surrounded by an ambulatory and covered with a dome that was pierced 'with some hundreds of openings'. This was to be the Patents Museum. The Natural History Museum was to be on the Exhibition Road side, subdivided into 'square spaces, nine of which in the centre, have each a circular lantern or domical light carried by arches and pendentives rising from slender piers'. This sounds reminiscent of Henri Labrouste's Bibliothèque Nationale (1860–67), and *The Builder* commented that the theatre in the north-east corner of the plan 'resembles one of Mons. Hittorff's circuses'.[21] Evidently this time Brodrick was attempting to win with an up-to-date Second Empire design. The Cromwell Road façade was to be flanked with pavilions, 'so as to give somewhat the effect of the new French Opera House', and all the pavilions 'are richly decorated and have attics with caryatides. There is some good rustication in the lower storey, where the windows are arch-headed, and there are festoons'. With a reference book of mid-nineteenth-century Parisian architecture, it would be possible to re-create the building's general appearance, and *The Builder* summed up the design as 'a compound of Florentine Italian and modern French . . . There is considerable merit about the decorative features . . . though many of them are more or less directly copied from models'. However, although *The Builder* was non-committal about the architectural character of the building, it was critical about structural aspects of the design; 'evidently, contrivance of the dome with reference to practicability could have formed no part of the competitor's labours'.

The museum trustees would have preferred to have Kerr's Second Empire design rather than Fowke's; but the first commissioner insisted on appointing the latter, who died shortly afterwards. In 1866 Alfred Waterhouse was brought in to execute Fowke's design, with which he found fault, and in 1871 he was able to substitute his own design, which is the familiar polychromatic, terracotta-faced, German Romanesque cathedral-like building in Cromwell Road. As for Brodrick, *The Builder* was to remember the outcome three years later when reviewing the National Gallery competition:

Mr. Brodrick's design is set off by two large and effective views; indeed the drawings are complete, and the design matured, as compared with his design on the last occasion of a competition of which the drawings were exhibited in the Royal Gallery; when he was so fortunate as to get the third premium for what could not have been executed in the way that the drawing showed the work.[22]

Brodrick's final attempt in a government competition followed within a year of the Natural History Museum episode. William Wilkins's National Gallery, which had been criticized, perhaps unduly, as inadequate architecturally ever since it was built in 1834–38, was also proving too small. There was talk of building a new one at South Kensington, even of encroaching on Kensington Palace to provide a site; but reason prevailed and the Gallery was allowed to remain in Trafalgar Square. The first commissioner for works, still Cowper, consulted James Fergusson, the architectural historian and critic, about the idea of holding a limited,

21 See T. von Joest, C. de Vaulchier, d'Uwe Westfehling, J.-M. Bruson (eds.), *L'Exposition Hittorff (1792–1867), un architecte du XIXᵉ siècle*, Musée Carnavalet 20 October 1986 – 4 January 1987 (Paris, 1986), pp. 171ff.

22 *The Builder*, 25 (1867), 42.

invited competition to find the right architect to consider how to expand the building by using land to the north, as well as how the Gallery might be improved. Fergusson was opposed to the idea of limitation because 'you virtually bind yourself to employ the successful candidate and I don't think there are half a dozen men in the profession I should like to see in such a position'. However, apparently Cowper could and he decided

to invite 5 or 6 architects to submit Designs for laying out the ground and for the elevation of the intended Buildings . . . I could not be expected . . . to engage that any one of these Architects will be employed . . . but I propose to remunerate each of the persons who send in Designs for the time and expense devoted to the preparation of them.

He proposed a remuneration of £200, which Sir William Tite complained 'would hardly pay for the paper and the framing and glazing of their drawings'.[23]

Invitations to six architects, Scott, E. M. Barry, Banks and Barry, Sir Matthew Digby Wyatt, George Edmund Street, and Brodrick, were sent out in February 1866. He was in good company, the best. Scott declined the invitation, probably because he had an intimation that a Classical design would be an obvious preference, and he had no wish 'to become the St. Paul of modern architects, to be subjected to any more perils and stripes than he has already received anent the Foreign Office'. The *Building News* then added:

It will be well if others follow his example. Nay, it might even be desirable for the sake of English art, supposing any such thing to exist, if some were to retire altogether.[24]

This spiteful outburst seems to have referred to Street, as well as to Francis Penrose, F. P. Cockerell, and Owen Jones, whose names had been added to the list along with those of James Gibson, Somers Clarke, and James Murray. Alternatives were requested: one was the extension of Wilkins's building; the other was its demolition and replacement, or its remodelling. This time the assessors were, once again, Lord Elcho and William Tite, to whom were added David Brandon, William Boxall and Richard Redgrave, William Russell, T. Gambier Parry, Lord Hardinge, and Beresford Hope.[25]

Almost all the designs submitted were, as predicted, Classical; but soon *The Builder* was reporting a rumour that the first commissioner was going to 'throw all the competitors overboard wholesale'. After asking for various clarifications, the assessors were told they were 'at liberty to refrain from recommending any of the competing designs for adoption'. Which they did, commenting only that Barry's was the best idea for a new gallery, and Murray's the best for altering the existing one. Brodrick and three other competitors had extended beyond the given site, while he and Cockerell had omitted to provide lavatories. Tite's helpful comment was that all the entries were 'drawings of eminent beauty and excellent as works of art', but not suitable for a national gallery. Representing the affronted competitors, Sir Matthew Digby Wyatt complained that, if they had not all believed that one of them would be selected to execute the

23 Port, op. cit. (note 5), p. 175; *The Builder*, 25 (1867), 24.

24 *Building News*, 14 (1867), 17.

25 *The Builder*, 25 (1867), 24.

58. C. Brodrick: a Second Empire design for the National Gallery, London.

59. C. Brodrick: a colonnaded design for the National Gallery.

26 Port, op. cit. (note 5), pp. 175ff.

27 RIBA, *Catalogue*, B, p. 110.

28 *The Builder*, 25 (1867), 41.

29 *Building News*, 14 (1867), 17.

30 A report by Brodrick to accompany his designs, 'The Enlargement of the National Gallery'. The proposed Gallery was part of his design no. 2 and is referred to on p. 6.

work, they would not have wasted their time upon the competition. After more than a year, Barry was appointed, but only for an extension to the north. After all, Wilkins's façade still overlooks Trafalgar Square.[26]

What were Brodrick's proposals? The plan is striking for its similarity to that of the Grand Hotel, Scarborough.[27] The design was made in the year the hotel was opened, and both are wedge-shaped in plan. The end of the Gallery opposite St. Martin-in-the-Fields was to have a large semi-circular bow like the hotel, and in the middle of the opposite end was to be a large octagonal room corresponding to the Ballroom. *The Builder* thought he 'displayed considerable ingenuity in planning', both in the scheme which added accommodation to the building, and in the one that was to be an extensive remodelling,[28] although the *Building News* complained that 'nearly the whole of the space is covered with buildings, so that neither light nor air worth mentioning is admitted into the interior of the site'.[29] Internally, Brodrick was proposing a rich Second Empire style of decoration. There was to be a monumental gallery which he likened to the Galerie des Batailles, Louis-Philippe's major addition at Versailles, 'with centre part of same resembling the "Salon carré" of the Louvre, and about the same dimensions'. This was to have columns, arches, enriched spandrels, and an arched ceiling, evidently still retaining something of the character of Leeds's Victoria Hall, with an added Gallic richness. He proposed to re-use the columns from Wilkins's portico, themselves re-used from the demolished Carlton House, in a new central vestibule with a grand 'Imperial' staircase and figures of 'Persians or Caryatides' in reveals.[30]

Some sketches suggest that Brodrick was trying out Second Empire ideas externally. There are various domes, one of which includes a procession of gilded, winged figures; but in the end he reverted to the familiar, and the National Gallery would have been the ultimate reworking of Leeds Town Hall and the War Office.

60–61. C. Brodrick; two of the various Neoclassical proposals for remodelling and extending the National Gallery, London (1866). The influence of Leeds Town Hall was still strong.

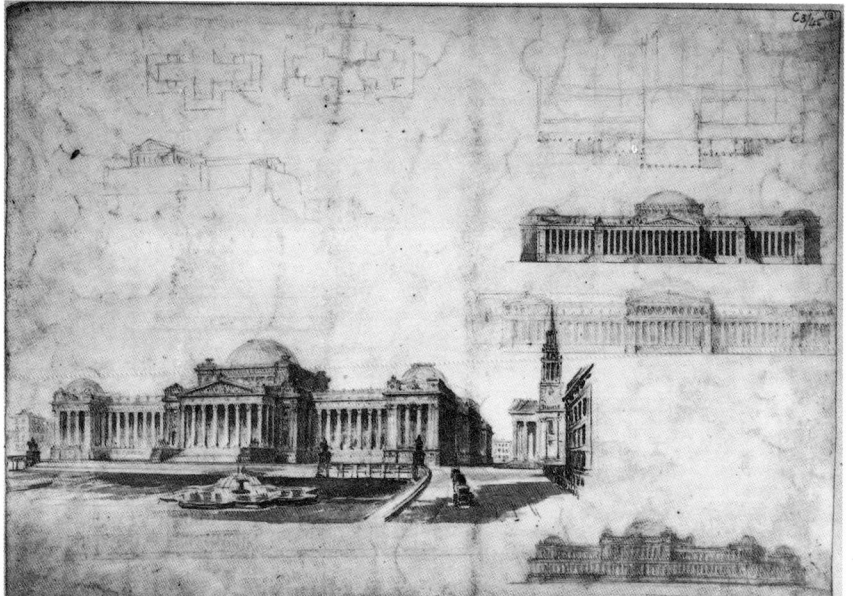

31 *Building News*, 14 (1867), 17.

32 RIBA, *Catalogue*, B, p. 109. There is also a similarity to James Pennethorne's competition design for the government offices in Whitehall (1855): see RIBA, *Catalogue*, O–R, p. 46. But to what extent might that have been influenced by Brodrick's Town Hall? (See G. Tyack, *Sir James Pennethorne and the Making of Victorian London* (Cambridge, 1992), plate 5.)

Mr. Brodrick is, as usual, great in pillars. There are some thirty-six Corinthian shafts in the front elevation alone, and when we have said this we have said nearly all that can be said of this design. Everyone who knows Mr. Brodrick's work at Leeds and elsewhere need scarcely be told that the composition is severe to a fault. Its great mistake is in the monotony which results from an excess of Corinthian pillars. The projecting portico shows no less than fourteen in a row, supporting a level entablature. The wings have each six shafts, and over the centre in line with the wings ten pillars appear, supporting the pediment which crowns the design.[31]

The idea of crowning the long, colonnaded building with a decastyle temple was probably a memory of Schinkel's Schauspielhaus, Berlin (1818–21), which had been the subject of one of Brodrick's student exercises.[32] Once again, he had gone back a generation to an already outmoded style with which he was obviously in sympathy; and, once again, he had failed to make a mark on London's architecture. If his design for the National Gallery had been built, its façade to Trafalgar Square would have had twice as many columns as Schinkel's Altes Museum, Berlin (1823–30), of which its author commented 'the site required a very monumental building'.[33] Evidently Brodrick had a similar thought. As for Lord Palmerston, he gave his opinion about government-sponsored competitions and their management in 1863 when he told MPs: 'If anybody will go to Liverpool, to Leeds, to Manchester, or to other great towns, he will see buildings of the most beautiful description erected, nor under the control of the Government, but by persons employed by the municipalities of the towns themselves'.[34]

33 Quoted in M. Snodin (ed.), *Karl Friedrich Schinkel: a universal man* (New Haven and London, 1991), p. 34.

34 *Hansard's Parliamentary Debates*, third series commencing with the accession of William IV, 26° & 27° Victoriae, 1863, CLXXI comprising the period from the twenty-ninth day of May 1863 to the thirtieth day of June 1863 (third volume of the session) (London, 1863), col. 207 (House of Commons, supply — Civil Service Estimates, supply considered in committee (2), 1 June 1863).

Successes at Home

When the fortunate young Brodrick was appointed architect for the Town Hall he needed an office in the town and took one at 30 Park Row, almost on the doorstep of the site for the building. Four years later he was at another address, 17 East Parade, which was even nearer, and then in 1863 he moved to 2 Park Place, a handsome terrace house in the town's grid layout of the 1760s. In the latter year he also opened a London office at 11 Buckingham Street, off the Strand. Wilson says that Brodrick had spacious offices and an extensive library,[1] but he does not say if these were in Leeds or London; probably the former. Evidently he was not interested in domesticity, at any rate when he was living in Leeds. He resided in untraced lodgings in Far Headingley and enjoyed the amenities of the Leeds Club, of which he became a member in 1853. There is no record of where he lived when in London; probably he joined a club there too.

Brodrick's excellence as a draughtsman has already been noted, and Wilson says he was the sole designer of his buildings. He made his own perspective drawings, and invariably smoked a cigar when colouring them.[2] Maybe that explains why he used the nom-de-plume 'Corona' on the entry for the War Office in 1857. Nevertheless, obviously he had assistants. Those known include John Simpson,[3] who is said to have helped with the entry for Lille Cathedral, Joseph Wright, who became a prolific designer of Methodist chapels in Hull and the East Riding,[4] and Irwin Cooke, who joined the office *c.* 1858 and was there for ten years; he inherited Brodrick's drawing instruments which were said to have been used in making the drawings for the Town Hall.[5] The eventual heir of all his books and drawings was his nephew, Fredrick Stead Brodrick (1847–1927), who was probably trained by his uncle, as was Walter John Brodrick (1847–67), another nephew. There was a 'Mr. Meade', who was in the London office; but nothing is known about who he was or what he did.[6] Indeed, like almost everything associated with Brodrick, there is a lack of information.

The town in which Brodrick had built his municipal palace was described in 1860, before the masonry had turned black, as 'a filthy and ill-contrived town', and many details were added to substantiate this verdict. 'Yet Leeds is wealthy and flourishing, and has spent money liberally and nobly.'[7] The writer in *The Builder* listed the new public buildings, of which the Borough Gaol at Armley was second in size to the Town Hall, but it was the latter to which another article in the same journal referred as having created a revolution. 'A building sufficiently good to please the Leeds people ten years ago will not pass muster now.'[8] By comparison with the grandeur of the Town Hall the other public buildings not only were inadequate but, more to the point of civic pride, they looked

1 T. B. Wilson, *Two Leeds Architects* (Leeds, 1937), p. 33.

2 Wilson, op. cit. (note 1), p. 33.

3 Linstrum, *WYAA*, p. 384.

4 Joseph Wright (1818–85) was born in North Cave. He is known to have designed at least thirty-four Methodist chapels between 1857 and 1877 (information from Colin Dews).

5 *The Yorkshire Post*, 4 March 1905. The drawing instruments are in Leeds, Abbey House Museum, Box 40, Store 2.

6 RIBA, *Catalogue*, B, p. 110.

7 *The Builder*, 18 (1860), 809.

8 *The Builder*, 18 (1860), 831.

insignificant. A new court house (1811–13 Thomas Taylor) had been viewed with pride when it was opened, but now it was fit only to be adapted for use as a post office.[9] In 1827 the foundation stone had been laid of a new corn exchange designed by Samuel Chapman (1799–?), a local architect whose father was head gardener at Harewood House. For more than thirty years this little pedimented Ionic building, which also contained shops and a tavern, had stood at Cross Parish at the north end of Briggate;[10] but that too was out of place in the prosperous town by the middle of the century, and now it was its turn to yield place to a grand successor, which would put in the shade such local competitors as Wakefield's impressive Greek Revival building (1836–37 William Moffat).[11]

In May 1860 *The Builder* reported a proposal 'to erect a new corn-exchange near the White Cloth Hall' in the traditional market area of the town. 'At a meeting, in the town-hall, of cornfactors and others, the markets committee exhibited a plan of the corn-exchange at Edinburgh' as an example of what might be built.[12] This was Italianate in style, the work of David Cousin, a pupil of the eminent William Henry Playfair. It was built around a large central space in which both the factors and the farmers transacted their business.

After the plan had been inspected, a great deal of discussion ensued, and a general opinion was entertained that it was desirable that the farmers and the factors should meet in the same building, but that there should be separate accommodation for each. A resolution to that effect was unanimously adopted [and] plans for the proposed building are about to be advertised for.

So they were, but a letter signed 'SCRU' appeared in *The Builder* in the following month complaining that not only were designs asked for but complete working drawings, specifications, and details 'sufficient to enable contractors to tender from'. The writer suggested that

the lucky author of the first prize will . . . have his hundred pounds handed over to him, and 'no further questions asked', as the custom is with fortunate finders of gentlemen's pocket-books, or ladies' pet-dogs

and he was also suspicious of the condition that 'if the cost of the selected plan, when contracted for, exceeds the architect's estimate, he will be held to have forfeited his claim to the premium'.[13] The dice seemed to be heavily loaded against the architects, but 'SCRU' and the other competitors were reassured by the borough engineer that it was the council's intention to instruct the successful architect to carry out the design as well as to receive the premium.[14] In August it was announced that the three prizes had been awarded to familiar names. Brodrick was to have the first, another Leeds architect, William Hill, the second, and Lockwood and Mawson the third. The building contract for £12,033 was let to Samuel Addy, the builder of the Town Hall tower, and this included the cost of the unusual roof which was to be constructed by Butler and Co. of Kirkstall Forge. Including the land, the total cost was to be about £25,000.

Brodrick's growing enthusiasm for Parisian architecture of an earlier generation as a source of his designs is perhaps at its most obvious in the

9 Linstrum, *WYAA*, p. 334, and plate 272.

10 Linstrum, *WYAA*, p. 347.

11 Linstrum, *WYAA*, p. 334, and plate 274.

12 *The Builder*, 18 (1860), 284.

13 *The Builder*, 18 (1860), 355.

14 *The Builder*, 18 (1860), 370.

62. The Corn Exchange, Leeds (1860): the ground-floor plan of Brodrick's competition design (redrawn from *The Builder*, 19 (1861), 651). 1. Entrance to the Market; 2. Entrance to the first-floor offices; 3. Entrance to the Sack Market; 4. Factors' Market; 5. Office; 6. Factors' Room; 7. News Room; 8. Farmers' Room; 9. Sacks.

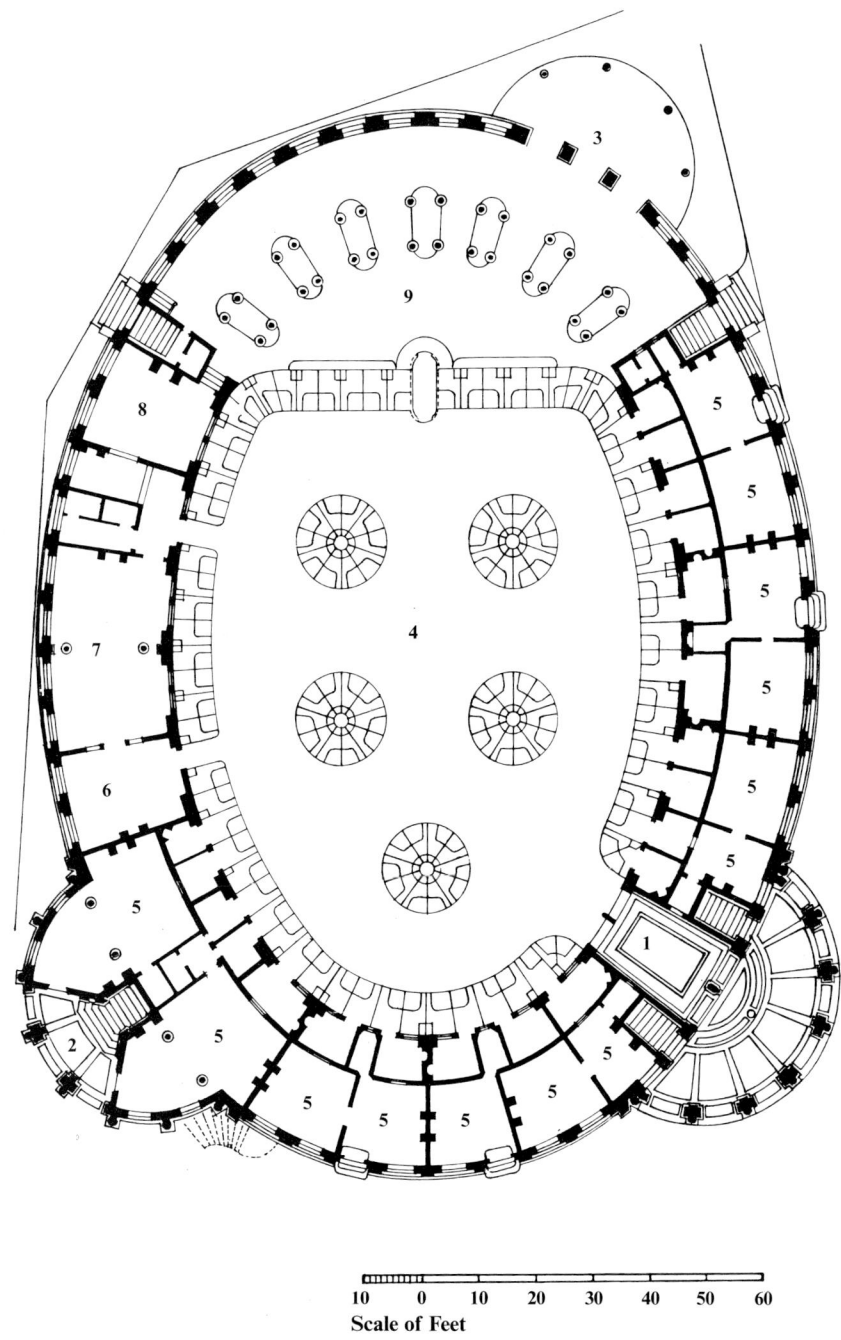

10 0 10 20 30 40 50 60

Scale of Feet

15 See M. K. Deming, *La Halle au Blé de Paris 1762–1813* (Brussels, 1984).

Corn Exchange. The Halle au Blé, the Paris corn exchange, was one of the most famous buildings in the capital. It had been erected in the 1760s by Nicolas Le Camus de Mézières as a large circular structure of two storeys, which was covered in the 1780s by a laminated timber dome one hundred and twenty-nine feet in diameter. The result, boldly geometrical in form, was much admired and likened to the Pantheon in Rome. After the dome was burned down in 1803, it was replaced by François-Joseph Bélanger with a glazed cast-iron construction.[15] The building quickly became one of the sights of Paris. The Abbé Laugier, one of the leading

63. The Halle au Blé, Paris: a structure of the 1760s which F.-J. Bélanger covered with a glazed cast-iron dome in 1803.

architectural writers of the eighteenth century, wrote in 1765 how the hall, surrounded by houses and roads whose construction would contrast with its rotundity, 'will be in Paris one of our most agreeable landmarks'.[16] Twenty years later the agriculturist, Arthur Young, wrote that it was the finest thing he had yet seen in Paris, 'so well-planned, and so admirably executed, that I know of no public building that exceeds it in either France or England'.[17] It was illustrated in several books, including Louis Bruyère's *Études relatives à l'art de construction*, published in 1823; interestingly on the same page is a reference to the choice at le Mans of a circular shape in preference to a rectangular for an exchange, partly because of the irregularity of the site. In almost identical words *The Builder* in September 1861 told its readers how in the Leeds building 'a form has been adopted unusual in this country, — the form of the Roman theatre — as best adapting itself to the site'.[18]

Obviously, the Halle au Blé, which had already been a source for John Bunstone Bunning's London Coal Exchange (1846–49), was the inspiration of the design for the Leeds building with which Brodrick won the competition, although the latter is elliptical in plan rather than circular, which might be interpreted as being Baroque rather than Neoclassical. In fact, the whole design seems to be a study in the use of the curve, in plan, in section, in the repeated arches of the windows and doors, and in its elliptical and semicircular roof ribs; but there is little affinity with the Baroque in its details. It might seem strange that Brodrick went back to an eighteenth-century model; but where was there a more distinguished precedent? Nevertheless, the Leeds building is not a copy of the Parisian original. Views of the latter, which was extensively remodelled in 1885 by Henri Blondel and renamed the Bourse du Commerce, shows the ground floor stacked with mountains of sacks of corn,[19] whereas in Brodrick's design, and according to the committee's instructions, all the storage is in the huge cellar which is so commodious that at first it was used as the headquarters of the fire brigade. The

16 Abbé M. A. Laugier, *Observations sur l'architecture* (Paris, 1765; reprint, Farnborough, 1966), p. 196.

17 A. Young, *Travels in France during the Years 1787, 1788 and 1789*, ed. C. Maxwell (Cambridge, 1929), pp. 81–82.

18 *The Builder*, 19 (1861), 651.

19 A. Braham, *The Architecture of the French Enlightenment* (London, 1980), plate 304.

64. The interior of the Halle au Blé, Paris.

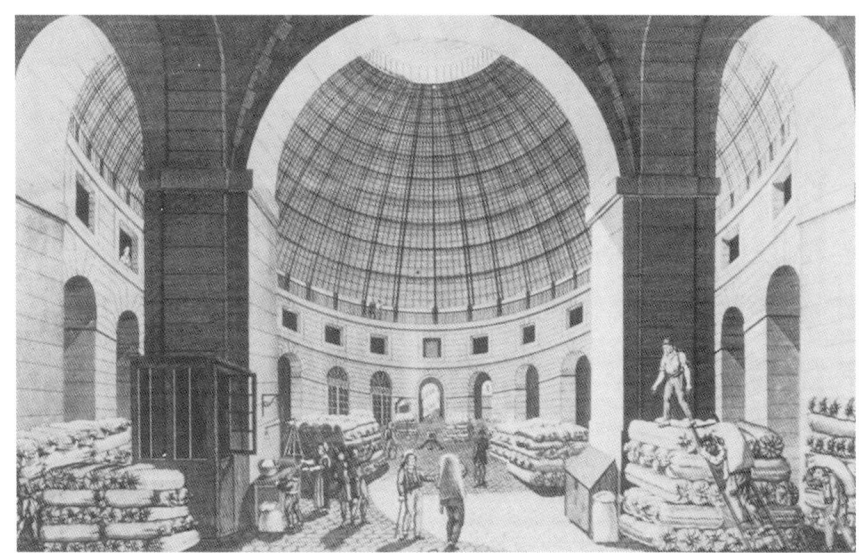

65. The Corn Exchange, Leeds (1860–62): the view from the west.

66. C. Brodrick: a watercolour perspective of the interior of the Corn Exchange, Leeds.

separation of activities allowed Brodrick to design a dignified interior in which the merchants conducted their business on rows of (still-surviving) tables which could be moved so as to liberate the large, clear floor area for other purposes.

In Paris the emphasis, both inside and outside, was on the lower of the two storeys of openings; these were semicircular-headed, while the upper row consisted of small rectangular windows. In Leeds, the two storeys are given equal emphasis with two tiers of semicircular-headed openings; the external ones are windows lighting the outer ring of offices, and the internal are glazed screens and doorways. A balcony with a richly moulded cast-iron balustrade gives access to the offices. Following the Parisian precedent, Brodrick made a great feature of the huge dome which is constructed of wrought iron and timber, all of which is exposed. A visitor

65

commented that 'No roof that it has been our fortune to see has ever impressed us more than this one, as a work of original genius and thorough practical utility'.[20] The fair-faced brickwork of the interior, which has decorative surrounds of diamond-pointed bricks around the repeated arches, is also left exposed.

The unity of design and precision of craftsmanship of the interior is matched on the exterior, which is constructed of local sandstone. The repeated arched windows on the two-storeyed elevation are set in precisely patterned rusticated walling of diamond-pointed ashlar. The Parisian building was plainly rusticated with buttress-like flat panels between the bays, but Brodrick's design is much richer and more monumental in character. He might have taken the idea for this remarkable treatment from one of the Renaissance buildings he had seen in Italy on his travels; Palazzo dei Diamanti in Ferrara or Palazzo Santacroce in Rome or the Gesù Nuovo in Naples could have been in his mind or in his sketchbook, but overall rustication without diamond pointing could also have been seen, not only in Florentine fifteenth-century buildings, but on nineteenth-century designs such as Schinkel's Palais Redern in Berlin. Brodrick's building is crowned with a frieze of garlands and ox skulls which binds the whole together, as does an unusually detailed string-course composed of what are probably representations of mill stones, while the parapet is crowned by three richly carved scrolled sculptures, unmistakably Parisian in flavour; two of them are placed above the semi-circular porticoes of the Tuscan order which swell out from the main mass in counterpointed curves and give a sense of movement to the whole domed mass of this extraordinary building, which has a unity of design, a relationship between decoration, form, and function, a precision of detailing, superior to any of his other buildings. While there is a precedent for its form in the Halle au Blé, and for some of the detailing in the Paris Bourse or the Bibliothèque Sainte Geneviève, the Leeds building, with its idiosyncratic, bold masonry detailing, is an inspired design. Brodrick's understanding of the quality and character of the local stone has been described in discussing the Town Hall, but it is even more

20 Originally the central oculus was the only natural lighting, but this was augmented later when a panel of glazing was inserted on the north side.

68–71. The Corn Exchange, Leeds: examples of the admirably detailed and executed masonry.

remarkable in the Corn Exchange, as in the Mannerist details such as the reversed console brackets which contrast with the bold horizontal tooling of the rusticated blocks in the basement. Once again, he made use of the stylized rosette which he seems to have adopted as his signature. It appears on every roundel between each pair of windows on the upper floor in an endless procession.

The Corn Exchange was completed in 1862, a year when Brodrick evidently felt the necessity to make a journey to Italy. He was in Genoa in April, Rome in May and June, Pompeii in September, and Capri in October. It was a time when he had been involved in two unpleasant contests, one in Leeds and one in Hull. Making watercolours in the Italian sunshine must have been a welcome diversion.

The Mechanics' Institute movement began around 1825, and twenty years later it could be said that Yorkshire possessed more 'and those, generally speaking, of a more active nature, than any other district of equal area or population in Great Britain'.[21] At first they were housed in modest, often converted, buildings, but as their status and popularity increased, so did their architectural images. In 1857 Lockwood and Mawson's Halifax Mechanics' Hall set a new standard with its *palazzo* style and its central location.[22] Leeds, where the Institute had been founded in 1825 in a house in Park Row, was not slow to follow, and almost at the same time as the competition for the Corn Exchange one was announced for an Institute on a site in Cookridge Street, a short distance from the Town Hall. Brodrick was awarded the first prize, but in December 1860 *The Builder* criticized the decision. The writer, presumably George Godwin, began suavely by praising Leeds for the improvement in its architecture, citing the Town Hall and the new warehouses in Wellington Street, which

21 See Linstrum, *WYAA*, pp. 252–55.

22 Linstrum, *WYAA*, plate 199.

67

72 and 73. C. Brodrick: The Leeds Institute (1860–65). His competition entry, showing alternative designs for the roof above the central arch.

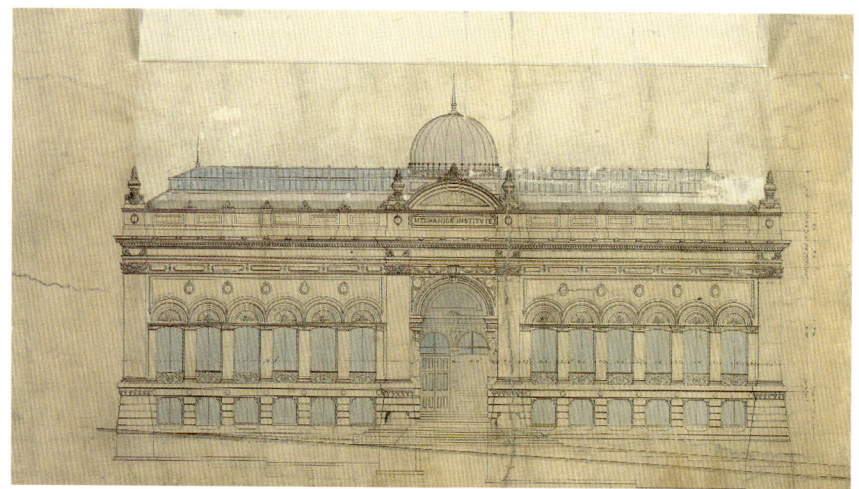

act as a standard by which all new buildings are tested . . . The standard has been raised and the public taste elevated . . . So that we were glad to hear the oft-repeated praises of the plans for the art schools, picture gallery and mechanics' institution; and believed that, in proposing to erect a building which should be a credit to the town, the committee was doing the best thing possible, and making a powerful claim on the generosity of subscribers and friends of the institution.[23]

However, out of the seventeen submissions, three had been selected.

The authors of these . . . were Mr. Brodrick, Messrs. Perkin and Backhouse, and Mr. Shaw; all, oddly enough, Leeds architects. It is, moreover, no secret as to who are the authors of the majority of the designs; and, whilst examining the plans for this criticism, we invariably heard the spectators speak of the designs of Mr. So-and-So's, and not by the motto attached to them.[24]

The Builder disagreed with the committee's choice, singling out two unplaced designs as being superior. Brodrick's design was severely criticized for not complying with the principal conditions, and the committee was criticized for its behaviour, implying that its decision had been swayed by Brodrick's reputation. The writer went on to say: 'It is due to those who have spent much valuable time in this competition that good faith should be observed towards them'. This was followed by a letter

23 *The Builder*, 18 (1860), 831.

24 *The Builder*, 18 (1860), 831.

from William Henry Crossland, once a pupil of George Gilbert Scott; his unplaced Gothic design had been singled out for praise by *The Builder*, and he asked if it was true that the designs had been sent to Scott for an opinion. If so, he would no longer feel himself an injured competitor, but he protested at the committee's 'underhand manner'.[25] The following week Henry Garling, Brodrick's friend and the author of an unplaced Italianate design which had been commended by the critic, contributed to the argument. He had been one of the three supporters, together with Sir Charles Barry and John Woody Papworth, of Brodrick's nomination in 1860 as a fellow of the RIBA.

Had the gentlemen of Leeds intended to have given the commission to their fellow-townsman, no one would have complained. Had they entrusted it to Mr. Brodrick, no one would have been more happy that they should have done so than myself. He is a personal and intimate friend, and among the rising men of the profession. None have won their position more fairly; none have so gallantly forced their way through the many difficulties that hedge round success in our laborious profession; and to better hands the commission could not have been trusted. But we have a right to complain that, with this foregone conclusion, they invite architects to lose money, and time more valuable than money, in a hopeless contest.[26]

The secretary of the Institute attempted to explain away the criticisms, but it was admitted that for some inexplicable reason Scott had not been sent the designs for an opinion, and Brodrick's had been chosen 'without any professional assistance whatever',[27] an admission quite properly criticized by *The Builder*.

However, the writer did find aspects of the design that could be praised. 'The internal arrangements . . . appear, except in some slight particulars, all that can be desired', and it was thought a 'grand and well-designed structure' except for the upper part which, 'for one-third of its entire height, is a dead wall, which, unbroken except by a cornice, gives a heavy leaden appearance'. The critic suggested that when it was blackened by the inevitable smoke the upper third would be 'like a huge leaden coffin, sepulchral, heavy, and excessively ugly'.[28] Undeterred, Brodrick exhibited his watercolour perspective (in which the stone was not black) at the Architectural Exhibition in London in April 1861, giving an opportunity to return to the attack to *The Builder*, which noted that, although it was monumental in aspect, displaying some of the ability shown in the Town Hall, the heavy part would be unbearable.

Despite the passage of time, building work had not started, and in April 1864 *The Builder* vouchsafed a mysterious turn of events.

Some time ago a design by Mr. Brodrick was recommended by the committee for adoption; but we understand that the tenders for carrying it out being in excess of the proposed expenditure, it had to be abandoned. The architects who had previously competed were invited again to submit their drawings and plans, and the choice has now fallen upon those sent by Mr. Crossland, architect, Leeds. The new building will be in the English Domestic Gothic Style.[29]

But it was not, despite what seems to have been *The Builder*'s attempt to have Brodrick's design put aside in favour of Crossland's, which was the

25 *The Builder*, 19 (1861), 14.

26 *The Builder*, 19 (1861), 29.

27 *The Builder*, 19 (1861), 43.

28 *The Builder*, 19 (1861), 244.

29 *The Builder*, 22 (1864), 281.

74. C. Brodrick: The Leeds Institute. The water-colour perspective view from the south-west.

Gothic one it had singled out for praise. When the Institute finally was built after the foundation stone had been laid in August 1865, it was to Brodrick's design.

The plan of the Institute centres on a large circular lecture theatre, 73 feet in diameter and two storeys in height, with a gallery supported on cast-iron columns and brackets; above, but now obscured because of the building's current use as the Civic Theatre, is an 'ornamental coved ceiling, a roof of somewhat novel construction, with windows immediately below it'.[30] Around the lecture theatre and fitting into a severe rectangle are classrooms and a library/reading room on the ground floor, and a picture gallery, with rooms for modelling, painting, and mechanical/architectural subjects on the first floor. Externally, the building appears larger than it is because of the way in which it is built up on a high battered podium, exaggeratedly rusticated and crowned by a course of bold anthemion-like motifs. On the main elevation the podium incorporates a monumental flight of steps, partly outside and partly within the high central archway. The latter has giant-order pilasters, above which is a sculptured tympanum similar to contemporary decoration on the New Louvre and the Opéra in Paris, and it is crowned by a pavilion roof which adds to the general Parisian character. The latter was offered as an alternative to a small, rather inadequate, dome.

30 *The Builder*, 25 (1867), 698.

**75. The Leeds Institute (1860): the ground-floor plan (redrawn from *The Builder*, 25 (1867), 696).
1. Entrance Vestibule; 2. Lecture Theatre; 3. Library; 4. Reading Room; 5. Classroom; 6. Teacher; 7. Lecturer; 8. Committee Room.**

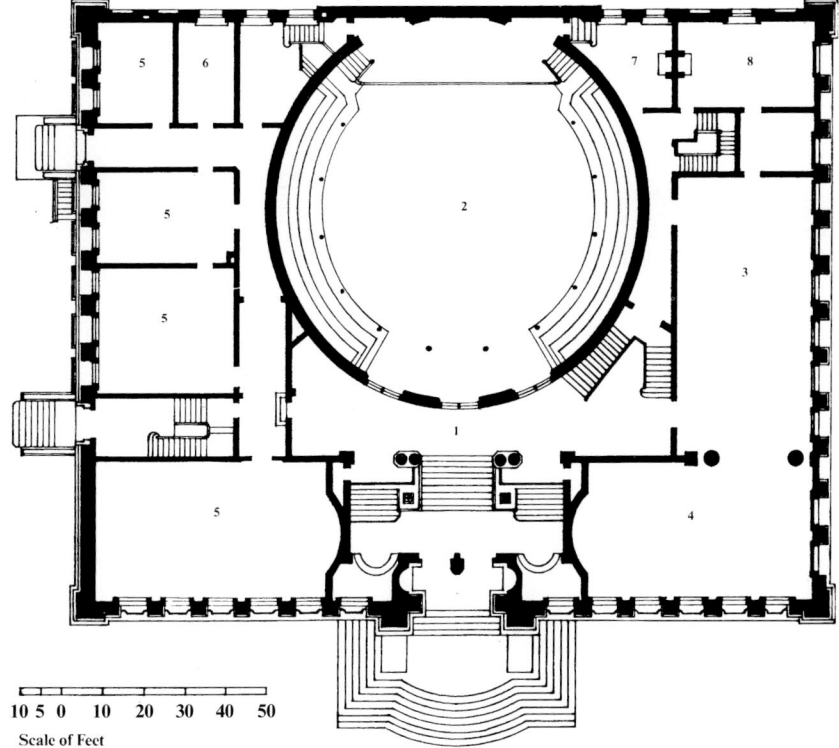

10 5 0   10   20   30   40   50
Scale of Feet

The two main façades of the Institute, which are at right angles to each other,[31] rely on a repeated element, that Durandesque formula to which Brodrick remained faithful; this one is a window set within an arch, with discs set in the interstices in the smooth ashlar. Maybe that was a recollection of the Bibliothèque Sainte Geneviève or of the interior of the Bourse, but it was not uncommon. Once again, too, we see the influence of Parisian architecture in the sculptured garlands and elaborate capitals which form part of the central archway, while the shells over the windows and the bold balconies seemingly derived from an Ionic capital are a part of the richness of Brodrick's idiosyncratic design methods. The Institute cannot match the perfection of the Corn Exchange. In some ways it is clumsy and it could have been better integrated; but it is a true Brodrick building with all his personal characteristics. In reality the Institute is an outstanding example of what was identified as well-meaning but excessive patronage, which produced such monumental structures that working men sometimes hesitated to cross the thresholds of the buildings erected for them.

The unfortunate circumstances surrounding the Institute seemed to forecast a sequel in Hull after the council promoted a competition for a new town hall on a restricted site fronting on to Lowgate. Entries were invited for not later than 31 May 1861, but there were complaints that some designs had been handed in and accepted as late as 4 June. 'An additional day at the end of a competition is no light matter, as those who have been compelled to send in half-finished drawings know',[32] wrote a disgruntled competitor; but all thirty-eight received were looked at by the

31 Only the south and west fronts are faced with stone; the north front was originally hidden from view and is faced with brick.

32 *The Builder*, 19 (1861), 415.

76. The Leeds Institute: the central pediment, which shows an increasingly Parisian influence. Compare with Figs. 77 and 78.

77 and 78. The Opéra, Paris (C. Garnier 1862–75): details of the sculptured pediments.

79. The Leeds Institute: the entrance arch.

33 *The Builder*, 19 (1861), 585.

34 R. G. Smith was the surveyor to the council; later he went into partnership with Frederick Stead Brodrick (1847–1927), Cuthbert's nephew.

35 *The Builder*, 19 (1861), 722.

36 J. J. Sheahan, *History of the Town and Port of Kingston-upon-Hull*, 2nd edn. (Hull, 1866), pp. 628–29.

committee without any professional advice, and it was announced that the first prize of £100 was to go to a local architect, R. G. Smith, and the second of £50 to Lockwood and Mawson. Where was Hull's famous architect son? 'Among the competitors were Mr. Brodrick, of Leeds, the architect for the Town-hall there, . . .', reported *The Builder* in August.[33] In September there was an accusation that 'the usual amount of blundering, or something worse, has been perpetrated', when it appeared that Smith's plan was not in accordance with the instructions, and that there had been only eight out of fourteen committee members present, of whom only five had voted for it. It was also said that the names of the competitors were known and the committee was voting for men rather than for the merits of the plan.[34] As for Smith, it transpired that he held the appointment of surveyor to the council. William Tite was invited to advise on the entries, but in November a frustrated competitor wrote to ask 'what the Hull people are doing about their proposed new town-hall . . . Surely six months is ample time even for the most antagonistic set of "common councilmen" to come to some understanding'.[35] Another month passed, and then Tite announced that 'Con Amore' was the winner. It was Brodrick, and Lockwood and Mawson remained in second place, while Smith was allowed to supervise the construction.

Unlike most of the great Victorian town halls, the smaller one at Hull did not contain a public hall for music and meetings. It was largely administrative, with committee rooms, offices for the town clerk, treasurer, and engineer, and a police court. At the rear it was built up to the existing sessions court. The only opportunity Brodrick had to attempt any architectural effects in the planning and decoration was in the staircase hall and the mayor's reception room. Evidently he made the most of these spaces:

The principal entrance leads through a short loggia or vestibule to the grand hall and staircase, where the *coup d'oeil* is such as is seldom seen in a building in any provincial town . . . Immediately opposite the entrance is the grand staircase, which is composed of red Mansfield stone steps. Caen stone perforated balustrades. and Sicilian marble hand rails about a foot in width. This noble staircase is surmounted by an elegant arcade, formed by clustered pillars of Mansfield stone, decorated to represent rouge royal, the bases Egyptian green and Aberdeen granite. The walls of the hall are painted a subdued red, the cornice is picked in tints of red, green, and buff, the ceilings are panelled in grey with light buff styles, and decorative corners and side centres in each . . . The skirting and shafts of the columns and pilasters are painted to represent Egyptian green marble, the caps are white, and the bases rouge royal. The pillars are coloured to represent marble.[36]

And so the staircase ascended in splendid polychromy, with more marbling, until the upper part was reached. There could be found Maw's encaustic tiles on the floor, while on the walls and ceiling was a riot of reds, buffs, greens, pinks, an orange fret border on a red ground, paterae of grey on a blue ground, allegories of Naval Architecture, Science, Agriculture, and Commerce, all surrounded with gilded arabesques. The mayor's reception room was equally lavishly decorated, including thirteen pilasters with 'painted arabesque ornaments of the light and chaste style of Louis XVI'. The breathless description ends with a declaration that

80. Hull Town Hall: a cork model, provenance unknown.

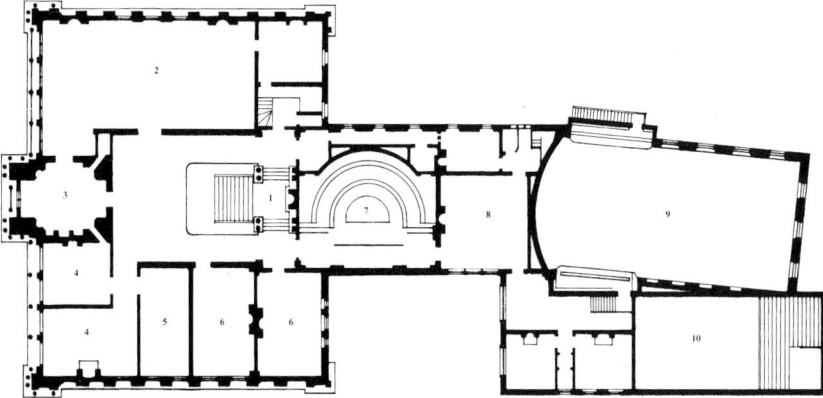

81. Hull Town Hall (1861): the first-floor plan (redrawn from *The Builder*, 22 (1864), 454). 1. Principal Staircase; 2. Mayor's Reception Room; 3. Mayor's Private Room; 4. Town Clerk; 5. Records Room; 6. Committee Room; 7. Council Chamber; 8. Grand Jury Room; 9. Upper part of Sessions Court; 10. Upper part of Police Court.

37 J. J. Sheahan, op. cit. (note 36), p. 631. The decorations were executed by J. L. Coulton of London (*The Builder*, 24 (1866), 92).

'the decorations of the principal apartments have been carried out in a style far surpassing anything yet seen in Hull'.[37]

Externally, the Town Hall was described by the convenient term Italianate, but it was more specifically Venetian in character, even though the general form of the façade to Lowgate recalled Théodore Ballu's contemporary Parisian church of La Trinité. It was dominated by a central

tower which rose from the face of the building, and this was flanked by Durandesque repetitive tiers of semicircular-headed Venetian *palazzo* windows separated by red Mansfield columns which contrasted with the Bradford stone plinth, the Portland stone cornices, and the Steetley stone masonry. At the angles of the building, and in the central bay, Brodrick seems to have been recalling the porticoes from the west front of the basilica of St. Mark. The *cinquecento* richness of the façade continued upwards:

The frieze of the main cornice is enriched with figures of naked boys holding festoons of flowers, and the parapet has an ornamental balustrade, with vases over each pedestal. At the angles of the building are four turrets, which rise to a height of about twenty-five feet above the cornice, and are surmounted by gilt finials . . . The tower . . . is 135 feet in height. It is enriched with beaded mouldings, forming panels . . . The upper part . . . which is circular, rests on eight Mansfield columns, with Corinthian caps, having red granite panels in the spandrils of the arches, and an ornamental balustrading on the upper stage, with vases on each shaft. The tower is surmounted by a large stone dome, highly ornamented, from which rises a cast iron spear-shaped finial, double gilt . . . The entire front is also enriched with polished granite panels, vase-shaped ornaments, &c.[38]

One wonders what can be left for inclusion in the final '&c.' in this colourful description of a design that marks a change from Brodrick's noble columnar compositions. It cost £28,000 and was the only town hall he built apart from his Leeds masterpiece. It survived until 1911 when it was decided to replace it with a new guildhall to a design by Sir Edwin Cooper.[39]

Brodrick's final design for a Hull building broke with the run of success, albeit not entirely straightforward, in Leeds and Hull. In 1866 a competition was announced for new Dock Offices on a triangular site overlooking what was then Queen's Dock and Prince's Dock. There were twenty-seven contestants, but little is known about the competition

---

38 Sheahan, op. cit. (note 36), p. 628.

39 A local poetaster wrote of the building:

> Talk of Athens, pride of Greece,
> Talk of Venice, talk of Nice,
> The Town Hall, Hull, in Lowgate stands,
> Competing with those classic lands
>   In architectural beauty.
> That noble pile of stone and brick
> Was designed by Cuthbert Brodrick,
> A Hull-born man of rising fame,
> A credit to his town and name;
>   Who has nobly done his duty.

When the Town Hall was demolished, the stone cupola was erected in Pearson Park, Hull, where it seems to have acquired an Indian character (see p. 109).

83. C. Brodrick: a watercolour perspective of the unsuccessful entry in the competition for Hull Dock Offices (1866).

84. C. Brodrick: a watercolour perspective of the unsuccessful entry in a limited private competition for a monument at Castle Howard to the 7th earl of Carlisle (1868).

entries since the company's records were destroyed during the Second World War. However, Brodrick's watercolour perspective has survived, showing a fairly conventional Italianate design for a rectangular building which apparently disregarded the shape of the site. It must have been a disappointing entry from the local man who had acquired a national reputation, but undoubtedly the submission of Christopher George Wray was superior. He was a London architect who held an appointment as civil architect to the government of Bengal for a time, during which he built St. James's church, Calcutta (1864), in association with Walter Granville, in an Early English style. In 1869 he designed the Oriental Hotel Company's hotel at Cairo. In Hull Wray recognized the potential of the site, which he used fully, placing a domed drum at each corner. Wray's façades are of two superimposed orders, Ionic and Corinthian, and there is a wealth of sculptured decoration. It is curious that Brodrick failed to make anything of the skyline. His design was placed second, and the £50 he received can have been poor compensation for a failure in his home town.[40] Nor was he any more successful in his native county in 1868 when he submitted a design in a competition limited to four for a monument at Castle Howard to the 7th earl of Carlisle, who had died four years earlier. He made a fine watercolour of a rather heavy Ionic structure with an upper storey supported by angelic caryatids; but a large classical column raised on a monumental podium,[41] the work of Frederick Pepys Cockerell, was preferred and erected in 1869–70. The county of the White Rose seemed to be turning against its son; had he fared any better in that of the Red Rose?

40 J. H. Rumsby, *The Hull Dock Offices 1787–1976* (Hull, 1976).

41 RIBA, *Catalogue*, B, p. 108; *The Builder*, 25 (1867), 623.

Trans-Pennine Disappointments

There was no lack of opportunities for an architect searching for public-building commissions in the middle of the century, especially in the increasingly prosperous industrial North, and Brodrick was looking across the Pennines as soon as he had established his office in Leeds and work had started on the site of the Town Hall. In 1853 there was a competition for a town hall at Preston, for which he made a design, although oddly enough his name does not appear in the list of competitors in *The Builder*. Did he not submit? It seems unlikely, after going to the trouble of making an elaborately rendered elevation.[1] The plan was unusual, as an exchange had to be incorporated; this was placed down one side of a long narrow building, with a colonnaded façade. There was a profusion

85. C. Brodrick: the entrance front of his unsuccessful competition design for Preston Town Hall (1853).

1 RIBA, *Catalogue*, B, p. 110.

78

of columns and pilasters, and the design was firmly in the Leeds mould. In effect, the entrance front was virtually one of the Leeds pavilions widened by two extra bays of semicircular-headed windows between giant-order Corinthian columns, over which was a heavy sculptured parapet; rising above all was a domed Corinthian *tempietto*, within which was a small dome to light the entrance vestibule. William Hill, the young Leeds architect who was to play a part later in Brodrick's story, was the winner, although he had been in practice for only two years; but he gained nothing. The Preston town council asked him to reduce his design so as to halve the cost from £30,000 to £16,000, and then, after further changes of mind, they abandoned the whole scheme and omitted to pay Hill the small sum due to him.[2] Later, in 1862, the council gave the commission to George Gilbert Scott for what was, surprisingly, his only Gothic town hall.[3]

Brodrick's next attempt to secure a commission in Lancashire was in 1859, when a competition was announced for new assize courts in Manchester, a booming town where *The Builder* drawn attention to the 'vigorous existence' of art, and the 'striking example [it displayed] of prevailing good taste'.[4] When Francis Goodwin, who designed the Ionic Central Market in Leeds (1824–27), built the first Town Hall in Manchester in 1822–25, the population was 133,788, and by 1859 it had more than doubled to over 300,000. The Free Trade Hall (Edward Walters 1853), an Italianate building contemporary with Leeds Town Hall, had equally set a high standard for the town's public architecture; but it was also the high-water mark of the *palazzo* style to which Manchester's banks and warehouses had been faithful in the 40s and 50s. It might have been assumed that the winning design for the Assize Courts would follow suit, but there were other styles on offer. The response to the announcement of the competition was said to be 'remarkable because of the amount of labour expended on the drawings, and because of the astonishing number of styles that were represented. One candidate submitted six alternative varieties from the same plan'.[5]

There were 940 drawings from 109 entrants on exhibition in Charles Barry's Royal Manchester Institution (1824, now the City Art Gallery); they filled the upper floors and galleries, covering an area of 8,410 square feet. Despite the large number of entries, they were dealt with expeditiously, so that *The Builder* commented: 'How on earth things could have been managed so adroitly is beyond my comprehension'.[6] Alfred Waterhouse, who was younger than Brodrick had been when he won the Leeds competition, was declared the winner; the second premium went to Thomas Allom, who had been Lockwood's partner for a short time, and the third to an obscure John Robinson, who was nevertheless a perpetual entrant who competed in twenty-five contests over thirty years and was premiated in sixteen. Waterhouse had already travelled on the Continent, and he had made a study of the great town halls of Bruges, Ypres, Ghent, Oudenaarde, Louvain, Malines, Antwerp, and Courtrai; these undoubtedly confirmed him in the belief that they offered a form and style appropriate for a public building in mid-nineteenth-century England, although, as Charles Eastlake commented, a compromise was necessary:

2 See C. Cunningham, *Victorian and Edwardian Town Halls* (London, 1981), pp. 82–83.

3 Illustrated in Cunningham, op. cit. (note 2), plate 40.

4 See C. Stewart, *The Stones of Manchester* (London, 1956), pp. 36ff.; J. H. G. Archer (ed.), *Art and Architecture in Victorian Manchester* (Manchester, 1985), pp. 1ff.

5 Stewart, op. cit. (note 4), p. 73.

6 *The Builder*, 17 (1859), 275.

Gothic architecture under its old conditions, and where the ordinary requirements of life are concerned, is impossible. Gothic architecture under modern conditions — improved methods of lighting and ventilating, sanitary conditions, the use of new materials, and habits of ease and luxury — may be, and indeed is, very possible.[7]

In the Assize Courts Waterhouse was breaking new ground, although various versions of secular Gothic had been presented in the 1857 competition for government offices in Whitehall, and Scott had also drawn on the town halls of the Low Countries for his unsuccessful bid in the competition for Hamburg Rathaus in 1854. How did Brodrick fare in the Manchester contest? *The Builder* drew attention to thirteen designs which were versions of Classical and columnar architecture, and to six Gothic entries. Surprisingly, Brodrick's was one of the latter group,

in all [of which] Gothic has the Continental impress; and the general grouping, and the details of pointed-arched windows and prominent tower, seem too nearly reproductive of the models — the Doge's Palace at Venice and the Town-halls of Belgium and the Netherlands. Exceptions, however, may be allowed to this generalisation. Mr. Brodrick's design has a larger amount of original thought than the others named.[8]

A photograph of a now lost perspective drawing shows what is believed to be a view of the exterior. It has a symmetrical façade of seven repetitive Gothic bays (presumably serving two storeys and continuing around the other façades in endless succession) on each side of a tall tower crowned with tiers of gablets and niches and a spire. There is a profusion of heavy traceried turrets or large pinnacles at the corners of the tower, of the main building, and of what is presumed to be the large central court which rises above the parapet level of the outer walls. The town

7 C. L. Eastlake, *A History of the Gothic Revival* (London, 1871; edn. ed. by J. M. Crook, Leicester, 1970), p. 315.

8 *The Builder*, 17 (1859), 339.

87. C. Brodrick: the design for the central court of Manchester Assize Courts.

halls of the Low Countries are obvious precedents, but in the relationship of the tower and the turreted skyline there is a curious resemblance to Leeds Town Hall. A perspective of the central court has survived,[9] and this shows an elaborately panelled roof of deep coves over what appear to be ashlar-faced walls. Below five tall windows, thirteenth-century in style, is a range of canopied seats on either side of a judge's throne, and there are galleries down the sides. The whole design did show an attempt to move away from Leeds Town Hall, but it was no match for Waterhouse's brilliant interiors.

The Gothic style seemed to be in the ascendant in the 60s. When John Ruskin gave his famous address in Bradford in April 1864 to a packed audience of Yorkshire men and women awaiting the oracle's recommendation of the style in which to build a new exchange, they were advised to consider Waterhouse's Manchester Assize Courts as an appropriate model. There they would see a 'hall of exquisite proportions, beautifully lighted, the roof full of playful fancy, and the corridors and staircases

9 RIBA, *Catalogue*, B, p. 110.

81

thoroughly attractive and charming'.[10] Ten architects had been invited to submit designs for the Bradford building. There were three from the town itself (Lockwood and Mawson, Milnes and France, Paull and Ayliffe), one from Liverpool (W. and G. Audsley), and Brodrick from Leeds, Bradford's traditional rival town. There were also five from outside Yorkshire: William Burges, Norman Shaw, Philip Webb, George Edmund Street, and Waterhouse, the apple of Ruskin's eye. Whether Brodrick intended to submit a Gothic design, a Classical, or even a Second Empire, is not known. Waterhouse and Street withdrew from the competition, and Webb and Brodrick failed to meet the timetabled deadline. The Italianate was Bradford's favoured style for the warehouses and mills which the mayor described as 'palaces of industry almost equal to the palaces of the Caesars' at the opening of Lockwood and Mawson's Saltaire Mill in 1853. Brodrick's Franco-Italian manner would have conformed; but Lockwood and Mawson adroitly changed allegiance from their accustomed Italianate style to embrace Ruskinian principles, or at any rate an external expression of them, and their entry of a building of 'Venetian Gothic . . . character, freely treated, and admitting of great picturesqueness of effect, and beauty of detail, without entailing heavy cost' was selected.[11] No doubt the last consideration helped.

Another opportunity to break into the Lancastrian architectural world came at the end of 1862 when a competition was announced for a new exchange in Liverpool, 'a place which, of all cities and towns in the United Kingdom is surpassed only by the metropolis in magnitude, wealth and importance, and which, in the quick yet solid growth of its commercial greatness, surpasses even the metropolis itself'. That was how *The Illustrated London News* hailed the city in 1854, when St. George's Hall was completed.[12] It is a building which, of course, in several ways had been a model for Leeds Town Hall, both to the promoters and to Brodrick, and its well-known genesis as the result of a reworking of two competition entries, both won by Harvey Lonsdale Elmes (1814–47), to bring together assize courts and two public halls in one building is a classic in the history of Victorian architectural competitions. After Elmes's early death the building was completed by Charles Robert Cockerell (1788–1863), who rightly praised his predecessor's achievement as 'the most magnificent work of modern times'; posterity has not disagreed.

The first of the later buildings on St. George's plateau, the William Brown Library and Museum (1857–60 Thomas Allom), was modelled on the Hall's Corinthian dignity (as were the later buildings in the civic group), and it might have been expected that in a design for the Liverpool Exchange Brodrick would have been in his element; but instead he chose to adopt as complete a Second Empire style as anything he designed.[13] Perhaps this decision reflected the Franco-Italian Municipal Buildings in Dale Street (1860–66 John Weightman and E. R. Robson), the most recent Liverpool public building which had added pavilion roofs to the town's skyline. Perhaps, too, Brodrick had finally begun to realize that his earlier columnar style was out of date and the Parisian mode was in. He needed another large commission as he had opened a second office, at 14 Buckingham Street, Strand, and London expenses had to be met.

10 Ruskin's lecture was reprinted under the title of 'Traffic' in *The Crown of Wild Olive* (1866), but it did not include the advice about using Waterhouse's Assize Courts as a model.

11 J. James, *Continuation and Additions to the History of Bradford and its Parish* (Bradford, 1866), p. 136.

12 Quoted in L. Knowles, *St. George's Hall, Liverpool* (Liverpool, 1988), p. 4.

13 RIBA, *Catalogue*, B, p. 109.

88. C. Brodrick: his unsuccessful entry in French Second Empire style for the Exchange, Liverpool (1862).

The new Exchange was to replace an older building (1803–09), the work of James Wyatt and/or John Foster senior. There were almost fifty entries. Brodrick planned his design around three sides of a large courtyard, but for some reason that is not now apparent, as plans have not survived, one wing is twice as wide as the other, so that the building is not symmetrical. The two-storeyed elevations are Durandesque in their repetitiveness, but unlike Durand, there is a richness of treatment, almost Baroque, in the sculptured façades, which leaves no stone untouched. The corners of the building are emphasized as slightly projecting pavilions and treated with greater elaboration before they rise above the balustrade level to become attics with Venetian windows and pavilion roofs. The middle section of the central wing is built up and crowned by a large square dome. There are many echoes here of the New Louvre and a reminder that Brodrick's francophilia was about to express itself at Scarborough. However, once again he was an unsuccessful competitor; Thomas Henry Wyatt from London was awarded the first premium for an equally Parisian design, while the second and third went respectively to a local firm, Cunningham and Audsley, and to a Newcastle man, W. Parnell.[14] Wyatt's design was built, but it was replaced in 1937. After this failure Brodrick had recourse to his favourite remedy — the Mediterranean. In March and April, as his surviving watercolours record, he was visiting the Sicilian sites at Agrigentum, Segesta, and Taormina, and in October he was in Venice; but more trans-Pennine disappointments were to come.

In 1863 a motion to build a town hall was approved by the town council of Bolton, another prospering Lancashire cotton town. A deputation visited 'various boroughs to inspect and derive lessons from similar erections; and the structure which appeared to have produced the most favourable impression upon the minds of the members of the committee

14 *The Builder*, 21 (1863), 420.

was the Leeds Town Hall',[15] although the cost was viewed with some alarm. £80,000 was being talked about as the likely cost of the Bolton building, but such a sum was 'deemed outrageous, if not absolutely ruinous'. However, one alderman 'presumed they would not dream of having a tower'. After the visit to Leeds, Brodrick was asked if he would be willing to provide a design, but in collaboration with a local architect; he was offered a half share of the fee, and presumably of the credit too.[16] He rejected the idea, but when the competition was advertised he entered a design.

Two hundred architects showed an interest, and thirty-nine entries were received. The brief included a public hall, court rooms, a council chamber, a suite of reception rooms for the mayor, municipal offices, and a free library and museum. It is notable that 'highly colored perspectives and elevations are not desired [although] perspective views may be sent'. There was a also a specific instruction that 'Architects should not adopt the Gothic style in their designs'.[17] Professor Thomas Leverton Donaldson, then president of the RIBA, was asked to make the assessment, selecting six out of the submissions. He reported that 'the designs generally conform to these directions in regard to the scale and mode of finishing the drawings, and as to the style of architecture [although] . . . six alone are treated with sufficient skill and taste worthy of the occasion'. He ventured to impress upon the committee

the necessity of having a lofty clock tower as an *essential part* of the design. Were this omitted the Town Hall would shrink into insignificance, and not be seen from the surrounding heights. Whereas, a huge turret or spire, properly ornamented, would successfully vie with numerous gigantic shafts which rise upon all sides of the town, and hold its own . . . as an important feature . . . If not executed now, it must be at some future period, and will then, as at Leeds, cost much more and bear the discredit of an afterthought.[18]

Donaldson recommended that the first prize should go to 'a design of remarkable skill and taste', although inexplicably, considering his urging, it did not include a tower. It had been submitted by William Hill, 'Experientia Docet', of Leeds. He had a respectable practice and had built a number of public buildings, despite his bad experience at Preston; but Bolton provided him with his great opportunity at Brodrick's expense. The latter, 'Nil Magnum Nisi Bonum', was placed third and, to add to his mortification, Hill 'knew enough of the antecedents of the competition to imitate as closely as was honourable the general character' of the Leeds building.[19] One of Hill's assistants remembered that his employer knew that Bolton's deputation had 'expressed their admiration for the design of Leeds Town Hall [and] decided to follow the lines of that building as closely as possible'.[20]

There is only a thin dividing line between inspiration and plagiarism. H. S. Goodhart-Rendel thought Hill's design was 'as original as it has any need to be, and, although smaller than its prototype, is no less satisfactory'.[21] But it is doubtful if Brodrick took such a view of the situation. Apparently the elevations of his entry were preferred to those of Hill, and he was asked if he would act as joint architect; but he was wise enough to refuse the offer, which must have appeared insulting. Hill

15 'Opening of the Bolton Town Hall', Bolton, 1873, p. 11 (reprinted from *The Bolton Weekly Journal & District News*, 7 June 1873 (Bolton Metropolitan Libraries, Arts and Archives)).

16 T. B. Wilson, *Two Leeds Architects* (Leeds, 1937), p. 31.

17 'Particulars of information and instruction to Architects competing for the intended Town Hall' (Bolton Metropolitan Libraries, Arts and Archives).

18 'Town Hall Designs. Report of Professor Donaldson' (Bolton Metropolitan Libraries, Arts and Archives: ABZ/41/2/1).

19 H. S. Goodhart-Rendel, 'Victorian Public Buildings', in P. Ferriday (ed.), *Victorian Architecture* (London, 1963), p. 94.

20 Wilson, op. cit. (note 16), p. 32. It has been said that Hill's behaviour was even more ungentlemanly as he had been a pupil in Brodrick's office; but Hill's obituary in *The Builder*, 47 (1889), 34, quite clearly placed the beginning of his career in the Leeds office of Perkin and Backhouse.

21 Goodhart-Rendel, op. cit. (note 19), pp. 94–95. Hill returned to Leeds Town Hall as a source of his design for Portsmouth Town Hall (1887–90).

modified his design, adding a domed tower which only increased his indebtedness to Brodrick's Leeds building, and he agreed to work with a local architect, George Woodhouse, whose design had been among the final six.

What might Bolton have had if Brodrick's design had been accepted? There are no signed or inscribed drawings, but Donaldson's assessment indicates two unusual features. One is the form of the main hall:

The Hall in its plan, that of a cross, is distinctly different from all the others, and the form is not so favourable as that of a simple parallelogram; the result is a deficiency of architectural effect, and a heaviness in the semi-circular vaulting — the decorations of which are too massive and plain and devoid of grace.[22]

The height of the hall was to be 83 feet 6 inches to the top of the vaulting, which means that it would almost certainly have been visible from the outside above the general roof level. Externally, the elevations were described as 'very grand, graceful, and imposing, bearing the impress of a noble municipal building'. Only in the comments on the design of the tower is there any indication of the architectural character and of Brodrick's megalomaniac tendencies.

The lofty tower, which forms the centre of the east front, is very effective, and recalls this characteristic feature of the municipal halls of the continent. It would be a stupendous object, whether seen from the square below or from afar in the country round about. The upper part or spire is composed of a multiplicity of small parts, too much resembling the Dutch or Flemish furniture or cabinet work, and would admit of greater simplicity of treatment. Still, *as a whole*, it is very fine, and the clock — a commanding feature — would rise above all the surrounding buildings of the town.

By now, soaring towers had become an obsession with Brodrick, and Donaldson's comments suggest that a competition with Bolton's mill chimneys would have been dramatic. Brodrick himself, in a letter to the town clerk, offered a clue to the character of his proposal:

I presume my design will be of no further use to the committee, therefore I shall feel obliged if they will allow me to exhibit it in the forthcoming exhibition here (London). I feel anxious to hear what opinions are expressed by the critics on the elevation, as it is an attempt to combine the Gothic outline with the classic details.[23]

Putting together the cruciform plan and great height of the hall and the Gothic/Classical tower, there is one design in the RIBA Drawings Collection which seems to incorporate both elements. This has been labelled 'Manchester Town Hall' in a later hand, but it is much more likely to be of Brodrick's entry for Bolton. The cross form of the central hall can be plainly seen, and the upper spired part of the tower conforms both to Brodrick's description and Donaldson's criticism.[24] The elevations are a Classical version of a Gothic town hall from the Low Countries, or of Brodrick's entry for the Manchester Assize Courts. Instead of the traceried windows there is a repetitive pattern of Sansovinesque windows and colonnettes; instead of the horizontal striping on the tower there is Venetian decoration as on the design for Hull Town Hall; and instead of the tier of Gothic aedicules encircling the round spire there are arcaded galleries around the four sides of a square

22 'Town Hall Designs. Report of Professor Donaldson', p. 2 (Bolton Metropolitan Libraries, Arts and Archives: ABZ/41/2/1).

23 *The Bolton Chronicle*, 25 March 1865, p. 7.

24 RIBA Drawings Collection. This drawing was originally listed in RIBA, *Catalogue*, B, p. 110, as part of a group of sketches for Manchester Town Hall. It has now been recatalogued as Brodrick's entry for the Bolton competition (C5/42).

89. C. Brodrick: an untitled design believed to be his entry for the competition for Bolton Town Hall (1863).

spire. Second Empire elements appear in the mansarded roofs and ornamented domes of the end pavilions. It would have been, as Donaldson wrote, 'a noble municipal building', although the tower does seem overloaded with ornament, and 'greater simplicity of treatment' would have been welcome. However, Bolton had no reason to be dissatisfied with Hill's more modest version of Leeds Town Hall, although it cost £167,000.

Did the town clerk return the drawings to Brodrick? If so, were they exhibited in London? And were there any comments about what Brodrick claimed as stylistic innovations? And was he right? In his description of Halifax Town Hall, Henry-Russell Hitchcock draws attention to

The assured quality . . . of its tremendous spire, more than worthy of Wren in the ingenuity with which the silhouette of a Gothic steeple was built up out of Renaissance elements.[25]

And Halifax Town Hall had been completed by 1863. The rest is silence; but the conclusion of Brodrick's letter to the town clerk reveals his feelings about the outcome of the competition:

If the committee wish to hear a pretty correct opinion on the other two designs [i.e. William Hill's and the one by Thomas Turner which was placed second], they should also send them to the exhibition.

The Yorkshireman was finding the thorns on the red rose.

Manchester, which had acquired the status of a city in 1851, offered two valuable architectural opportunities in 1866. The first was a new exchange, and the second was a new town hall, a latecomer in this respect among the major industrial towns and cities. The 'parliament house of the lords of cotton' was the centre of commercial life, and Thomas Harrison's Greek Doric building of 1806–08 had been enlarged in 1847–48 to become 'the largest Exchange room in Europe'.[26] However, less than twenty years later it was resolved to rebuild it on a larger scale and to advertise for designs, although 'Messrs. Mills and Murgatroyd

25 H.-R. Hitchcock, *Architecture: nineteenth and twentieth centuries* (Harmondsworth, 1958), p. 160. Halifax Town Hall was the last major work of Sir Charles Barry; it was completed after his death by his son, E. M. Barry, who made alterations to his father's design for the spire, which he also refaced with stone in 1869. Brodrick's proposed spire for Bolton was, as Donaldson implied, over-elaborate, but similar to Halifax in concept.

26 See *The Builder*, 29 (1871), 13, for a history of the Exchange.

90. C. Brodrick: three stylistically different elevations for his unsuccessful entry for the Exchange, Manchester (1866).

have been long the architects of the Exchange committee, and many thought in the first instance that they should have received the commission without competition'.[27]

Perhaps the outcome had already been decided, but fifty-three competitors sent in entries, of which 'all the selected designs may be described broadly as Italian'.[28] Despite the Gothic style of Waterhouse's Assize Courts, Manchester's predominant architectural style was still that of a version of the Italian Renaissance. The first and the second premiums were given to the sitting architects, Alexander William Mills and James Murgatroyd of Manchester, and the third to another local man, John Lowe. Brodrick made alternative stylistic designs in considering his submission, but finally he decided on an extrovert solution. Entered under the unlikely, maybe cynical, nom-de-plume, 'Lancashire', it was described as

27 *The Builder*, 24 (1866), 795.

28 *The Builder*, 24 (1866), 795.

Venetian, very richly treated, and well adapted for a building surrounded by streets, a fact which most of the competing architects seem to ignore. The interior is novel and good; but we do not like the arrangement of the capitals of the piers from which springs the groining.[29]

It is, in fact, a very accomplished design in a manner which seems, at last, to have thrown off the magnificent albatross of Leeds Town Hall, although it is still based on a repetition of elements which form a continuous arcuated envelope, three storeys high, which would have appeared to be a glazed screen from inside the building. The façades were to be lavishly ornamented, especially on the deep frieze of the entablature in which small circular windows were to be incorporated in an arrangement that seems to presage Louis Sullivan's Wainwright Building (1890–91) in St. Louis and the Guaranty Building (1894–95) in Buffalo; but the closest analogy to this design for the Exchange is the type of *grand magasin* being erected on the new Parisian boulevards, while details such as the monumental architectural frame in which a clock was to be set would not have been out of place on the New Louvre. There were also domes, grander versions of the contemporary ones on the Oriental Baths in Leeds. At each corner of the building was to be a dome with pedimented *oeil-de-boeuf* windows, while the roof was to be an elaborate building-up of glazed half-domes surrounding the drum of a huge flattened dome crowned by a glazed hemisphere. The internal effect would have been dramatic, as a now lost drawing illustrates. Brodrick's growing preoccupation with vast spaces and elaborate ornamentation seemed to be leading him into a world of Baroque fancy expressed in terms of the Venetian Renaissance, Islam, and the Second Empire. Despite the grey fuzziness of a photograph of his lost perspective, sufficient detail is visible to suggest the polychromatic splendour he intended on the massive piers and the pendentives and spandrels of the vaults and domes.

The eclectic monumentality of the design for the Exchange was evidently calculated to please the High Victorian world of commerce, but it

29 *The Builder*, 24 (1866), 807.

92. C. Brodrick: external perspective view of the unsuccessful entry for the Exchange, Manchester.

failed. However, according to *The Builder*, the event offered some serious thoughts about architectural competitions.

Although there are better designs than those premiated, at least some eight or ten rooms are superior; still Messrs. Mills & Murgatroyd have fairly gained their position, from the simple fact that they knew better than any other architect the requirements of the committee. If the latter had seen nine-tenths of the designs when the first sketches were made, they could at once have said how unsuitable they were, and saved the architects the great cost in thought, labour, and money, which the drawings must have entailed upon them. And what does this prove? Only what we have before frequently advocated, that (supposing competition desirable at all) they, the committee, should have invited architects to have sent sketches, and by these have made their selection for the future competition. It would, also, have saved an immense amount of labour if they had defined the style, for doubtless the majority of the committee had made up their minds to have what is usually termed a Classic design. Let us hope that the City Council of Manchester will not commit the same errors in the intended competition for the new town-hall, on which building they will probably spend £200,000.[30]

Manchester was surprisingly late in following the example of Liverpool and commissioning a new public building which would symbolize its prosperity. Francis Goodwin's Grecian Town Hall of 1822–25 was hardly good enough, and in March 1867 architects were invited to submit designs in competition for a new one on a site fronting on to Albert Square and the newly erected monument to the late Prince Consort, the work of Thomas Worthington and Matthew Noble. Some

30 *The Builder*, 24 (1866), 808.

93. C. Brodrick: internal perspective view of the unsuccessful entry for the Exchange, Manchester, taken from an old slide.

lessons had been learned from previous competitions and the subsequent wranglings, and this time there was to be a two-stage contest. An assurance was given that out of the first group of entries 'not fewer than six or more than twelve' would then be invited to submit in a second contest 'to be conducted on a much larger scale than that laid down for the first trial. In this final struggle the prize would be the erection of the building, with the usual professional remuneration; and each of the unsuccessful architects was to receive £300 as payment for his labour'.[31] The city council also announced that professional assistance would be sought to enable them to judge the entries. The first stage attracted 137 designs from 123 architects, and George Godwin, the editor of *The Builder*, assessed these. From them he selected entries by Edward Salomons, Speakman and Charlesworth, Thomas Worthington, and Alfred Waterhouse, all from Manchester, John Oldrid Scott, Thomas Henry Wyatt, William Lee, all from London, and Brodrick. As *The Builder* commented, the honours were equally divided amongst local and London architects — Brodrick was from Leeds *and* London.

A revised set of instructions was issued to each of the eight chosen men, and on 14 February the drawings arrived. *The Builder*, noting the date, ventured 'to say no enamoured swain or blushing maid received on that eventful morning a more valuable offering than did the worthy mayor of Manchester'.[32] The *Building News* reported: 'We hear that the drawings are most elaborately got up, and highly finished, and many of them are of great size'.[33] Rumours were soon circulating. Within days a correspondent wrote to the *Building News* that

Two of the designs have been imported from Paris, and drawn and finished by Frenchmen. As a political economist, don't you think they should be rattened? Scott's lot is high on the market, odds freely taken for place. Only one design will be Italian, or perhaps two, but the fiat has gone forth that Gothic is to win, in fact the Mayor says so.[34]

Professor Thomas Leverton Donaldson and George Edmund Street were appointed the assessors and requested to report. 'This they did after two

31 *The Builder*, 25 (1867), 223.

32 *The Builder*, 26 (1868), 259.

33 *Building News*, 15 (1868), 115.

34 *Building News*, 15 (1868), 120.

94. C. Brodrick: a design for Manchester Town Hall

35 *Building News*, 15 (1868), 237.

36 *The Builder*, 26 (1868), 259–62; see Archer (ed.), op. cit. (note 4), pp. 128–61, for a full account of the Town Hall competition and designs.

37 RIBA, *Catalogue*, в, p. 110.

38 RIBA, *Catalogue*, в, p. 110.

days' examination, which would allow them about five minutes per drawing.'[35] They were asked to judge according to four criteria; these were architectural excellence, plan and construction, economy and likelihood of being executed for the stipulated sum (£250,000), natural light and ventilation. Their first recommendation is one of the classic outcomes of the Victorian competition system. Waterhouse was placed first in all these criteria, except for the first, architectural excellence, in which he came fourth; but, after further explanations in a second report, he was declared the outright winner even if he had scored badly in something so apparently important as architectural excellence.[36] But this was beside the point for Brodrick, who was firmly out of the running in this last important competition for which he entered. What had he offered?

He had considered various styles for adoption, a Flemish Gothic or a domed Italian Renaissance,[37] but his final choice, with the motto 'Fides', was an idiosyncratic Gothic which he seems to have developed from the tiers of aedicules with which he had clothed the admired design for Lille Cathedral a decade earlier.[38] But despite the different stylistic dress, the composition of the main façade was once again a repetition of Brodrick's favourite design with corner pavilions and a megalomaniac tower.

95–96. C. Brodrick: two sketches of stylistic ideas for the Manchester Town Hall competition (1867).

The latter was to be built over a huge circular hall which was completely filled with a great staircase ascending to the first floor. Above it rose tier upon tier of arcades reaching up to a dome about 120 feet above the ground-floor entrance level. The main reception rooms were conceived in a similar vein of monumental fantasy, that characteristic which had been gaining an upper hand in Brodrick's unsuccessful competition designs. Was it a desperate last throw?

The architectural press had a field day. 'Of Mr. Brodrick's design we are very loth to speak', wrote the *Building News*, 'and the more so because he shows himself so very much moved by criticism'.[39] *The Builder* conceded 'the plan has merits'; but what they were was not specified.

39 *Building News*, 15 (1868), 256.

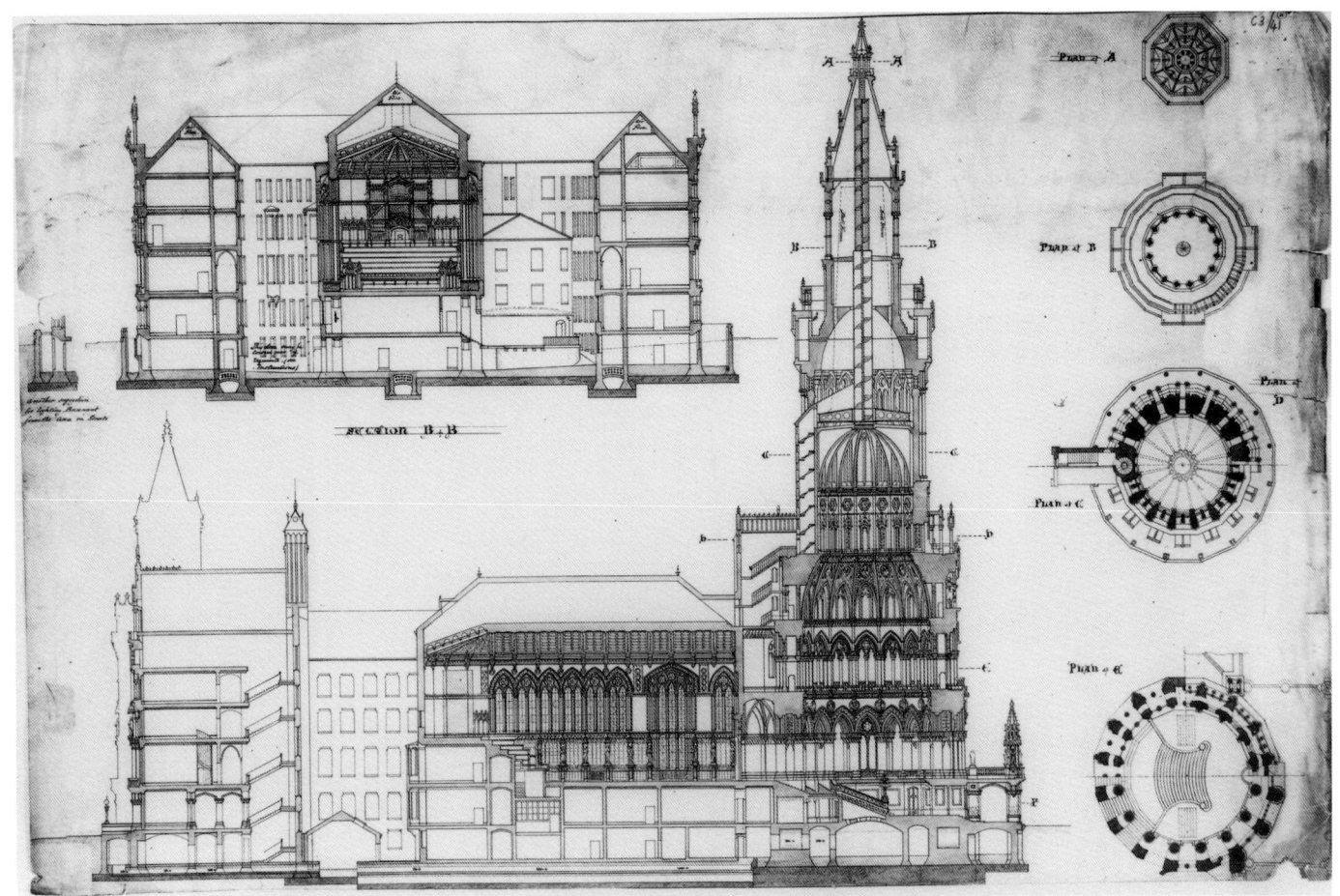

97. C. Brodrick: a section through the unsuccessful design for Manchester Town Hall.

On the ground floor, 'the base of the clock-tower, which is of great diameter, is devoted to a large entrance-hall, which swallows up the front part of his plan'.[40] The *Building News* ridiculed 'the apse of a church turned into the entrance for a town-hall, and [the] enormous circular entrance which swallows up all the best room and does nothing else, and there is — a tower?'.[41] *The Builder* was rather kinder in noting simply that 'all the towers are circular and very large [and] the group formed by the large towers is fine, [but only] when considered merely in outline'.[42] The *Building News* recalled how *Punch* had stigmatized Brodrick's

perpetual columns as candles, and forthwith he forsakes his wonted chandlery and betakes himself to confectionery, in which art he sends us 'the last sweet thing'. There are some of the much-wrought stones of Venice . . . but we really can't go on. Mr. Brodrick gains his £300, and we think but little else.[43]

The critic in *The Builder*, presumably George Godwin, offered sarcastic praise that 'part of the colouring of the exterior view is very spirited, especially the foreground'; but his final sneer was that Brodrick, 'best known by the "Leeds Town Hall", has collected the largest possible number of small shafts, and, with the assistance of pointed arches, has raised a palace for the — fairies'.[44]

So ended the fruitless expeditions across the Pennines and the last major competition for which Brodrick entered.

40 *The Builder*, 26 (1868), 260.

41 *Building News*, 15 (1868), 256.

42 *The Builder*, 26 (1868), 260.

43 *Building News*, 15 (1868), 256.

44 *The Builder*, 26 (1868), 260.

93

98. C. Brodrick: the elevation to Albert Square in his competition entry for Manchester Town Hall.

Antipodean Reflections

'Considering the means that have been taken to invite extensive competition, the expectations of many persons with regard to both the number and the character of the plans have been disappointed.'[1] That was the reaction of *The Sydney Morning Herald* in 1861 to the entries received for a design for a new houses of parliament and government buildings for the colony of New South Wales. The site selected was on Macquarie Street, then the fashionable part of Sydney; it was at the junction between the green Domain, in which Edward Blore's castellated Government House had been built in 1837–45, and the (Royal) Botanic Gardens, which date from 1816. Farther down Macquarie Street to the south is Parliament House, which had begun life as a part of a general hospital dating from 1811; in 1829 the northern wing had been relinquished and converted for use as the first home of the New South Wales parliament. Subsequently this had been extended to the north and the south to create Legislative Chambers in 1843 and in 1855. Why then did the government think in 1859 of erecting a new building so soon after the last addition?

It seems very likely that the stimulus was given because of the laying of a foundation stone in 1856 of a parliament house in Melbourne, the capital of the newly created colony of Victoria. Already there was a healthy rivalry between Sydney and Melbourne. Opinions had been offered about the type of building that was required for Victoria. One speaker wanted 'a plain and substantial building without cupolas, domes, pillars, and all sorts of ornamentation', and another inveighed against 'ostentation'; but in 1853 there was a competition for a building in the Classical style. It was decided that none of the entries was suitable, and in 1854 a plan submitted by the colonial engineer, Colonel Charles Pasley, was recommended for acceptance. In 1855 this design was handed to John George Knight and Peter Kerr, who made alterations to it.[2] The latter (1820–1912), who arrived in Australia in 1853, had worked for Sir Charles Barry, but maybe more significantly he had also worked for George Fowler Jones, a York architect.[3] Probably the Yorkshire connection accounts for the similarities of general character and elevational treatment between the Melbourne building and Leeds Town Hall. The intended tower of the Parliament House, which was to rise out of the colonnaded structure, has never been built; but it appears, as shown in the view published in *The Builder* in 1860,[4] to have derived from Brodrick's first design for a tower, which had been engraved and published in 1853.

The government of New South Wales appointed commissioners and advertised for designs for their new Houses of Parliament, taking two whole pages in the *Building News*.[5] A premium of £600 was offered for the best, and £300 for the second-best. As they were expecting to receive entries from architects who, for the most part, could have no knowledge

1 *Building News*, 7 (1861), 618, in which the comments of *The Sydney Morning Herald* are quoted.

2 M. Casey *et al.* (compilers and eds.), *Early Melbourne Architecture* (Melbourne, 1953), pp. 20–22; R. Davidson (ed.), *Historic Public Buildings of Australia* (Melbourne, 1971), pp. 152–63; Frances O'Neill, 'History of Parliament House', unpublished draft (1996).

3 *Australian Dictionary of Biography*, 16 vols. (Melbourne, 1966–), v (1974), pp. 22–23.

4 *The Builder*, 18 (1860), 577.

5 *Building News*, 6 (1860), 313–14.

99. Parliament House, Melbourne, Victoria, Australia (P. Kerr and J. G. Knight 1855–92). The tower shown in this illustration in *The Builder* in 1860 was not built.

of the chosen site, they offered 'photographic sketches' which exhibited 'the view from a spot near the centre of the proposed site, and also a view from the harbour, which will enable the architect to form an idea of the effect which the building will produce when seen from various parts of the surrounding country, or from the deck of a ship entering the port'. This latter was an important consideration, and one requirement was 'a perspective sketch of the whole as supposed to be seen from the Harbour, or from some spot in the direction of the Harbour'. The drawings and estimates were to be delivered to a London address before 1 January 1861, and an interval of three months was allowed for their transmission by mail steamer to the colony.

Twenty designs were received, of which eleven came from the home country and the other nine from Australia. It was said that

The principal reason offered for the fewness of the competitors was, that English and European architects were not disposed to compete where the successful competitor would not have the carrying out of the work. The supposition that a large number of English architects would send in plans, operated to deter colonial architects from competing, thinking no doubt, that they would stand little chance of success. Some of these are now, we understand, regretting that they did not tender, believing that they could have produced designs, if not of greater architectural merit, at all events better adapted to the situation and to the purpose than many of those exhibited.[6]

The Sydney Morning Herald published an account of the designs received. Twelve were Classical or Italianate in style, seven Gothic, and one Second Empire; but the principal worry seems to have been financial rather than aesthetic. 'Cost, it is thought, will stand in the way of selecting the design most approved of', was the ominous concluding sentence in the *Herald's* account as reprinted in *The Builder*.[7]

Six months later, after 'an inquiry, intrusted to the Colonial architect [Alexander Dawson, which] involved labour and care, and occupied several months in its performance', recommendations were made; but again there was the worry that 'each of them, with one exception, [was] found

6 *Building News*, 7 (1861), 618.

7 *The Builder*, 19 (1861), 508.

to cost over half a million of money to carry out'.[8] Evidently there was considerable apprehension about the expense of constructing a very large public building at the time when the small colonial town was only just beginning to evolve into a great Victorian city. The colonial architect's opinion was that the first prize should be awarded to William Henry Lynn, an Irish architect who was to win the Chester Town Hall competition in 1864; his design was Gothic, bearing 'a general resemblance to the Doge's Palace at Venice'. It was premiated even though the author had violated the condition that the elevations should be 'without colour or shading of any kind'; he had submitted an obviously eye-catching 'very artistically coloured perspective view'.[9] The second-prize winners, Stewart and Laver of London and Ottawa, had submitted Grecian and Gothic alternatives, but the former was favoured as it was the cheaper. Even so, the *Herald* had heard that

to erect any of the proposed buildings would involve an outlay of above £200,000, One of the designs — and that by no means the most elaborate — is estimated by its author to cost in execution £500,000, at English prices, and the cost of carrying out one of the more handsome designs has been computed at a million and a quarter.[10]

Could that exorbitant figure have been the magnificent design submitted under the motto of 'Res non Verba'? It had not been placed in the short-list of six, despite its evident quality as

a very striking Classical design. The intention of the artist has evidently been to produce a stately temple, and the elevation is certainly massive and commanding. There is a general resemblance in the design to the new Town Hall at Leeds. Handsome Corinthian columns surround the building, with a pediment and spacious peristyle at the east and at the west elevations, in the centre between which rises an enormous tower, of tasteful design, but apparently out of proportion with the edifice. The columns form quite a forest round the building, being in the peristyles five deep. The tower stands in the centre of a spacious court, and is connected with the floor of the building by a gallery. Midway between the tower and the pediment at either end, are corresponding domes, beneath which are circular halls, that towards the eastern side of the building being the Parliament Hall, and that to the western side the Official Hall. The former communicates with the Council Chamber on the right, and the Assembly on the left. The peristyles are ascended by broad flights of steps. The columns round the building form spacious colonnades.[11]

The combination of a multiplicity of columns and a huge tower renders an identification of 'Res non Verba' unnecessary. Brodrick's competition drawings have not been found, but some sketches survive in the RIBA collection.[12] They are drawn on the back of parts of an Ordnance Survey sheet of Sydney which includes the site. The concept is possibly Brodrick's most dramatic, and it confirms his ability to build up and control a complicated massing of elements. Together with his unsuccessful design for the Manchester Exchange, it is a castle in the air that would have greatly enhanced his reputation if he had been given the opportunity to develop and build it.

The elevations, like those of Leeds Town Hall and the designs for the War Office and the National Gallery, were to be completely surrounded by closely spaced bays separated by columns or pilasters, Ionic in the

8 *The Builder*, 20 (1862), 65–66.

9 *The Builder*, 20 (1862), 66, 86–87.

10 *Building News*, 7 (1861), 618.

11 *Building News*, 7 (1861), 618.

12 These unidentified drawings were not included in the published RIBA Drawings Collection catalogue; they are now on the card index as C5/33 (1–2).

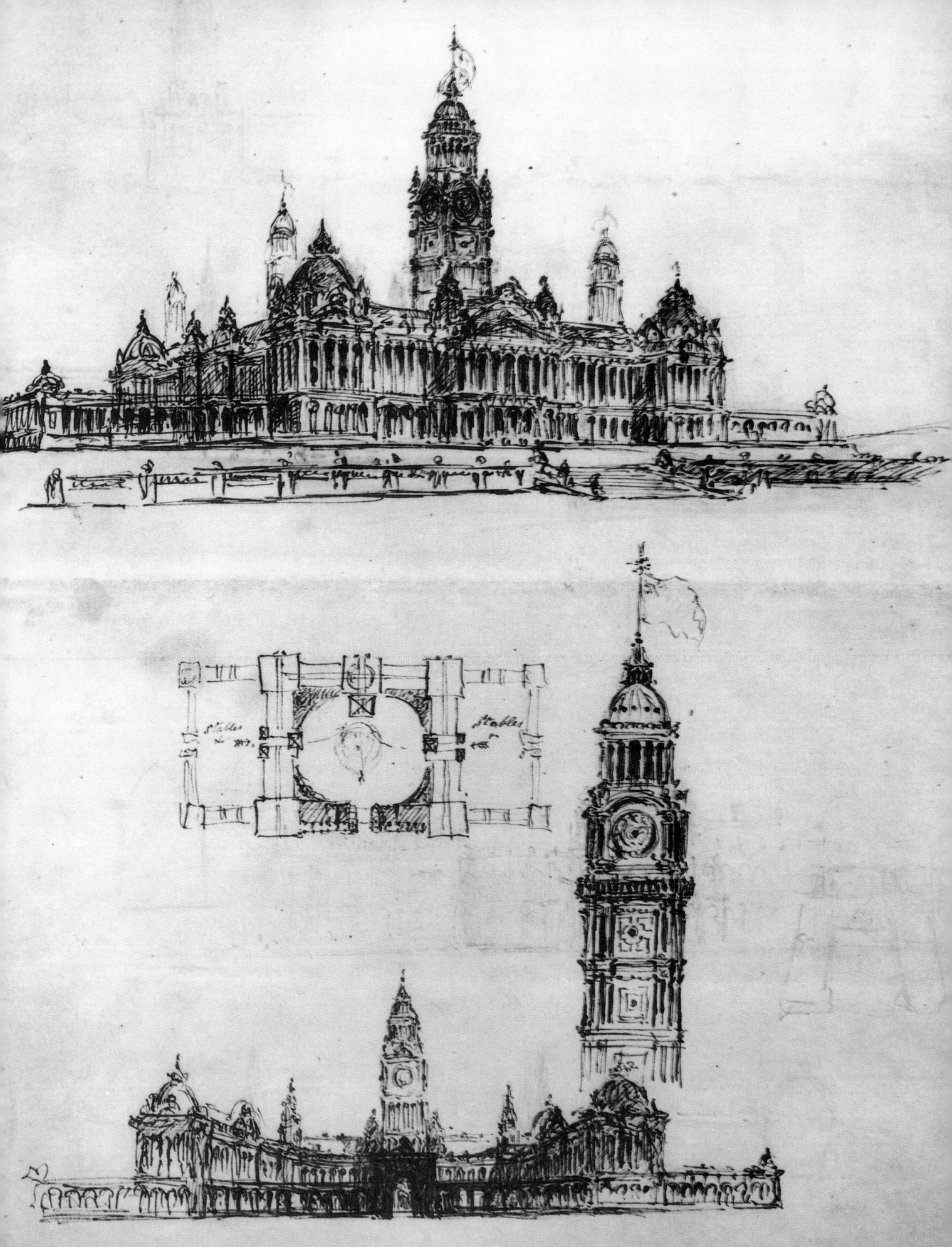

sketch rather than his usual Corinthian, but Brodrick was no longer following the severe Neoclassical models. One sketch shows that he was proposing to break and bring forward the entablature over every column, decorating it with garlands and rosettes or roundels. The parapet is fluted and panelled, and each division is crowned with an ornament. The three wings are grouped around a large rectangular *cour d'honneur*, on the fourth side of which Brodrick was proposing an open colonnaded screen with a Roman arch as the central entrance — a typically French arrangement. At each corner is a domed pavilion with ornamented dormers, and there are subsidiary domes and tall round-topped spires. The Baroque combination of domes, spires, pediments, porticoes, and columns would have been theatrically effective, but the richly varied skyline would have been dwarfed by the enormous tower rising out of the courtyard level in a manner reminiscent of the *campanile* of San Marco in Venice, or — an obvious source nearer home — Barry's recently completed clock tower containing the great bell, 'Big Ben', on the Palace of Westminster. The sketches suggest various treatments, one not unlike Leeds Town Hall at the summit, but all intended as a multi-storeyed colonnaded structure, crowned by a large domed *tempietto* surmounting a clock. The apparent height of this vertical feature, Brodrick's most ambitious projected tower, suggests that it would have been visible from the harbour, acting as a pharos or lighthouse that would have become as much an icon as the later Sydney Harbour Bridge or Opera House. The internal splendours of this extravagant design for what would have been a parliament building

102. Parliament House, Adelaide, South Australia (E. W. Wright and L. Taylor 1883–89).

second only to that of the mother of them all at Westminster have to be left to the imagination. The project never came to fruition. Lynn's pre-miated design[13] was exhibited at the 1867 Exposition in Paris, where it was awarded a gold medal. Probably Brodrick saw it there, where his own watercolour perspective of Leeds Town Hall was also hanging.

The New South Wales competition was his only known (and hitherto forgotten) contact with the Antipodes; but there was another, perhaps more distant, memory of Leeds Town Hall in the 1880s when there was a competition for a South Australian parliament house in Adelaide. A design by Edmund W. Wright and Lloyd Taylor was selected.[14] Although the first phase was completed in 1889, the building was only finished fifty years later and, as in Melbourne, the projected tower has not been constructed: but the colonnaded building with its decastyle portico illustrates the longevity of the Brodrick tradition.

13 RIBA, *Catalogue*, L–N, p. 52. Lynn's design included two towers, following the model of Barry's Palace of Westminster.

14 E. J. R. Morgan and S. H. Gilbert, *Early Adelaide Architecture* (Melbourne, 1969), pp. 10–11; R. Davidson (ed.), op. cit. (note 2), pp. 138–45.

Restorations and Innovations

Ecclesiastical architecture is not the first association that comes to mind in Brodrick's work, but he did hold an appointment as diocesan surveyor, and churches do figure in the list of his achievements, as they did in almost any nineteenth-century practice.

It is very likely that he was working on the restoration of the huge medieval parish church of Holy Trinity, Hull, during the time he was in Lockwood's office;[1] but certainly on his own account he restored in 1852–53 All Saints, Hessle, a church that had undergone many changes since its Norman foundation.[2] It is not clear what 'restoration' meant to Brodrick at the time in the middle of the century when *The Ecclesiologist* was pronouncing authoritatively on the treatment of medieval buildings. 'To restore is to recover the original appearance which has been lost by decay, accident or ill-judged alteration'[3] was its definition in 1842, and that was most likely what Brodrick did; but there was much later work at Hessle in 1868–71, and again in 1896. At the same time, in 1853, he was rebuilding the nave, north aisle, porch, and top of the tower of All Saints, Lund.[4]

Then, five years later in 1858–59, he had the unusual task of rebuilding the fifteenth-century church of St. Nicholas at Withernsea. This building had been left as a ruin since its roof was blown off in 1609; but as part of the generally unsuccessful attempt to establish the town as a genteel holiday resort (in which Brodrick was closely involved as the

103. St. Nicholas, Withernsea: the south elevation of the ruined church as rehabilitated in 1858–59.

1 This restoration took place between 1841 and 1845 (N. Pevsner and D. Neave, *The Buildings of England: York and the East Riding* (2nd edn., London, 1995), p. 505).

2 Pevsner and Neave, op. cit. (note 1), p. 267.

3 *The Ecclesiologist*, 1 (1842), 70.

4 Pevsner and Neave, op. cit. (note 1), p. 607.

104. C. Brodrick: an interior view of the unsuccessful competition entry for the church of St. Martin-on-the-Hill, Scarborough (1861).

designer of the Queen's Hotel and of an abortive residential layout) he was commissioned to rehabilitate the ruin.

Apparently a large part of the structure was still intact, including the chancel walls, the nave arcades, the north aisle, the clerestorey, and the west tower; but the south aisle seems to have been destroyed, and the whole shell lacked both roof and window tracery. So far as one can tell from the evidence today, Brodrick undertook a very creditable, conservative restoration. He retained what was left of the old structure, rebuilding the missing aisle walls, the south porch, and the tower parapet. Following the original building materials, he used both ashlar and cobbles, and he

5 Pevsner and Neave, op. cit. (note 1), p. 761. *The Hull News*, 4 June 1859: 'We are assured that, with the exception of the internal fitting, the original building has been faithfully reproduced, sufficient remains having been found in different parts of the ruins to leave no doubt upon the matter'.

6 Pevsner and Neave, op. cit. (note 1), p. 297. Brodrick oversaw the recording, repairing, and repainting of the painted ceilings, including that of the chancel, which depicts forty English kings. The work was done by William Padgett jr.

7 RIBA, *Catalogue*, B, p. 110.

8 RIBA, *Catalogue*, B, p. 110.

9 York, Borthwick Institute, Faculty 1863/2. The east window appears to have been a characteristic design incorporating circles, as in the contemporary Headingley Hill Congregational Church. See D. Neave, *Lost Churches and Chapels of Hull* (Hull, 1991), p. 17.

10 Brodrick's design is in Beverley, County Hall, East Riding of Yorkshire Council Archives and Record Service: SGP/31.

11 Beverley, County Hall, East Riding of Yorkshire Council Archives and Record Service: SGP 28.

12 Pevsner and Neave, op. cit. (note 1), pp. 646, 724.

13 West Yorkshire Archive Service, Leeds District Archives, Headingley Hill Congregational Church, item 3: undated newspaper cutting (1864) pasted in Headingley Hill Congregational Church, Church Building Committee Minute Book 1864–66.

14 T. B. Wilson, *Two Leeds Architects* (Leeds, 1937), p. 33.

15 Wilson, op. cit. (note 14), p. 25.

appears to have modelled new angel corbels on those that remained.[5] He probably worked on other churches too; in 1860–62 he was doing some unspecified work on St. Mary's, Beverley, following E. W. Pugin, who had been there in the 50s,[6] but this was probably relatively minor.

In the social life of Scarborough, Sunday morning was set apart for the ritual of church-going and the subsequent church parade along the Esplanade. A new church was required for the fashionable South Cliff, and Brodrick was one of the competitors who submitted designs for St. Martin-on-the-Hill in 1861. The only drawing that survives shows a rather bleak interior with some characteristics of George Edmund Street who, at the time of the competition, had embarked on a series of churches in the East Riding.[7] Evidently Brodrick intended to use coloured brickwork, and his proposed roof construction is interesting, but it cannot be regretted that George Frederick Bodley's design for the church, which became a treasure-house of early Pre-Raphaelite art and decoration, was selected. It was consecrated in 1863.

Still in Scarborough, Brodrick entered a design for a new baptismal font and cover for the old parish church of St. Mary in 1860;[8] and four years later he was dealing with a different sort of church, the brick-built Late Georgian St. John's, Hull (1790–92), where he extended the chancel and remodelled the whole building.[9] As a diocesan architect, his duties would have included responsibility for schools and vicarages. In Hull there was Christ Church Schools of 1847,[10] built of white brick with stone dressings in a mixed Gothic style, and in Driffield there was an institutional Gothic National School of 1853.[11] Two vicarages are known to have been his work, both of 1857, at Paull and at Thorpe Bassett.[12] They are brick-built, Late Georgian in style, and of only minor interest. Brodrick needed to work on a large scale.

The one ecclesiastical commission of any real significance that came Brodrick's way was in Leeds, where 'for some years past there had been a growing inclination on the part of their more opulent townsmen to leave the centre of the town for a residence in some of the more pleasing suburbs, and Headingley has been as much selected as any'.[13] This suburb on the north and elevated side of Leeds, which had been developed with stone-built villas in spacious gardens from the 1830s, was a part of the town that Brodrick would have known well. He lived in lodgings in Far Headingley, although precisely where is not known,[14] and the handful of houses which form a minor but interesting part of his work are in the Hyde Park/Headingley area.

In 1859 he designed a terrace of three brick houses with stone dressings, Moorland Terrace in Reservoir Street.[15] The client was Alderman Joseph Ogden March. In the same year he made a design for a villa, 7 Alma Road, for John Henry Smalpage; this illustrates how Brodrick was able to scale down the characteristics of his large public buildings, using bold architectural forms and meticulous detailing of the masonry. The idiosyncratic Grecian doorway contains two of his favourite rosettes, and the roof structure ingeniously incorporates a proto-pediment with large coupled eaves brackets. The neighbouring villa, no. 9, is different in detail but similar in character, and is very likely a Brodrick design. The

16 West Yorkshire Archive Service, Leeds District Archives: Headingley Hill Congregational Church, Church Building Committee Minute Book, meeting of 22 January 1864.

17 West Yorkshire Archive Service, Leeds District Archives: Headingley Hill Congregational Church, Church Building Committee Minute Book, meeting of 20 February 1864. The other suggested names were Thomas Ambler, Paull and Ayliffe, Lockwood and Mawson, James Fraser.

18 West Yorkshire Archive Service, Leeds District Archives: Headingley Hill Congregational Church, Church Building Committee Minute Book, meeting of 27 February 1864.

19 See note 13.

105. 7 Alma Road, Leeds; Brodrick's public style modified for a villa in Headingley (1859).

frame to the semicircular-headed doorway, set in an unusual rusticated surround, is ornamented with large bosses, and there is a similar detail on Bardon Grange, Weetwood, which is the work of John Simpson, a pupil of Brodrick. Again, Ashfield in Grove Road has large eaves brackets and a semicircular stone bay window very similar to those on 7 Alma Road. All these, and probably others in the Headingley area, were the sort of desirable residence that appealed to the 'more opulent townsmen' who set up the Headingley Hill Church Building Committee on 22 January 1864, which agreed on a site for a Congregational place of worship in Headingley Lane at the corner of Cumberland Road.

The committee's intention was to build 'an Elegant Structure' capable of holding six hundred people.[16] A month later they met to discuss the appointment of an architect and selected four from a list of eight; these were Joseph James of London, Pritchett and Son of Darlington, and William Hill and Brodrick from Leeds.[17] They were invited to submit designs, but Brodrick declined on account of numerous engagements (maybe a euphemism for a disillusion with local competitions), and Thomas Ambler was chosen as a fourth contestant.[18] The cost was to be no more than £3,500 (later raised to £4,500) and the style was to be 'Gothic with a Spire or Spirelet'. At the stone-laying ceremony the speaker said of this stylistic preference that there were those who regarded the adoption of the Gothic style of architecture as a retrograde movement;

but he believed that in raising a house to God (who has built this great and beautiful world, had made the forests and woven their branches into Gothic arches, and given them nowhere an idea of straightness and squareness, but everywhere the suggestion of beauty), they should build it in his own fashion.[19]

106. C. Brodrick: the south elevation of Headingley Hill Church, Leeds (1864).

107. Headingley Hill Church: the view from the east.

Three of the four chosen architects sent in designs, of which 'Hope' seems to have been the best. It turned out to have been Hill's, but apparently it was not good enough for the committee, and they decided to begin again *de novo* and invite Brodrick to be their architect.[20] His plans, elevations, and specification were submitted and accepted on 25 June and the foundation stone was laid on 22 October 1864. An appeal for funds was launched, in which the design was described as being 'marked by appropriateness to Congregational worship, by architectural honesty, and by sobriety of ornament'.

That the building possesses more elegance than in past years has been thought necessary to such structures, and more than is even now required in certain districts, will not, it is hoped, be objected to by those who remember the character of the neighbourhood and the growing demand for correct taste in all public buildings.[21]

The church is elevated above a basement, well above the level of Headingley Lane, a situation that adds to the impact of the building in the suburban landscape. As one might expect from Brodrick, the Gothic style is neither conventional, nor one of any particular phase. In form the church is rectangular, with six gabled bays on each long side. Each bay has a tall two-light window fitted within a pointed head that is almost more circular than pointed so as to enclose a circular element. Between each pair of bays is a buttress topped by a crouching-animal gargoyle. The south elevation to Headingley Lane has a double pointed-arched doorway under a gable enriched with carved rosettes and other ornaments, while the capitals of the red-sandstone colonnettes are of an unusual order, a sort of Gothic Corinthian. Above is a rose window made up of ten small roundels revolving around a large decafoil circle. Indeed,

20 West Yorkshire Archive Service, Leeds District Archives: Headingley Hill Congregational Church, Church Building Committee Minute Book, meeting of 18 May 1864.

21 West Yorkshire Archive Service, Leeds District Archives: Headingley Hill Congregational Church, Church Building Committee Minute Book, undated appeal leaflet (1864).

108. C. Brodrick: an unsuccessful design for the Wesleyan Theological College, Headingley Hill, Leeds (1866), in an unusual style.

109. 49–51 Cookridge Street, Leeds (1864). A rare example of a commercial design by Brodrick, but one which incorporates a typically idiosyncratic version of a Gothic style.

110. Yokefleet Hall, near Goole; attributed to Brodrick (1868).

22 RIBA, *Catalogue*, B, p. 109.

23 Reference must be made here to Blenheim Baptist Church, Leeds, which T. B. Wilson attributed to Brodrick (1864), with a west front and tower added by Walter A. Hobson in 1892. This attribution was followed by Pevsner in the first edition of *The Buildings of England: Yorkshire, the West Riding* (London, 1959), but altered to William Hill in the second edition (1967). That, in turn, was followed by the present author in his *West Yorkshire Architects and Architecture* (London, 1978). Unpublished research by John Goodchild has found that six architects (not including Brodrick) were invited to submit designs in 1862. Five did so and Lockwood and Mawson, Hill, and W. J. Paull were shortlisted. Paull (by then Paull and Ayliffe) was finally appointed. It is correct that Hobson added the west front in 1892.

circles are to be found in all the windows, including the large one at the north end; and there are Brodrick's favourite rosettes, as well as a variation on their formalized petalled form above the east porch. The committee's request for a 'Spire or Spirelet' was more than met by the tall slim tower to one side of the church, which terminates in a louvred bell chamber, on top of which is an obelisk-like ashlar structure, which is discussed in the next chapter. The building was opened on 29 August 1866, the year in which Brodrick made an unsuccessful bid for another building in the Headingley Hill district. This was for the Wesleyan Theological College, for which he unaccountably designed a castellated elevation with turreted chimney-stacks and battlemented parapets, but it was, nevertheless, still his favourite five-part composition of a central building with symmetrical wings and pavilions, despite its unusual and inappropriate dress.[22] The Wesleyans preferred a design by Wilson and Willcox of Bath.[23]

The Gothic style featured little in Brodrick's work, and when it did in his later years it was an unconventional interpretation, as in the

106

Headingley Hill Church. In 1864, the year in which he received the commission, it was almost as if he had been reminded of the style's existence when he designed shops and offices, 49–51 Cookridge Street, Leeds. The façades incorporate pointed-arched windows and foliate corbels, but otherwise one might hesitate to call them Gothic, even though there is a sort of Venetian character in the grouped windows at first- and second-floor levels. Once again Brodrick put his characteristic rosettes in the blank arches, and in each gable he inserted a framed triangle enclosing a square and three circles which is almost cabbalistic in character. There are similar features in the brick-built Yokefleet Hall near Goole, which is attributed to Brodrick and to a late date of 1868. The groups of pointed-arched windows and the multiplicity of circles on the façades seem to confirm the attribution.

The Exotic East

Egypt, Arabia, Greece, India, have all contributed to enrich our national resources. . . . and where treated with artist-like feeling, most happily . . . where graceful and effective arrangement of parts and characteristic conventionalities of detail are harmonised . . . with the forms necessary to our various applications of architecture, the art gains by such eclecticism, and I will instance the treatment of the square columns and their intervals at St. George's Hall, and the form of the cupola in the new town-hall at Leeds; the first as pointing to Egypt, and the latter to Northern India, as suggestive respectively of their arrangement and outline.

That attribution, at first sight surprising, of a Northern Indian influence on the design of the Town Hall tower was offered in a paper read on 3 November 1858 by H. P. Horner, then president of the Liverpool Architectural and Archaeological Society.[1] Can there be any truth in it? And if so, how could Brodrick have known about such structures, other than through English versions such as the Royal Pavilion, Brighton, or Sezincote in Gloucestershire?

The collection of beautiful aquatints made from the paintings of Thomas and William Daniell and published between 1795 and 1810 was certainly available, but in limited numbers only.[2] Among them is the plate entitled 'Hindoo Temples at Bindrabund on the River Jumna', which had earlier been the source of Humphry Repton's aviary for the Royal Pavilion in 1806. If Brodrick had seen it, one could suggest a possible connection, but perhaps more likely could be one of James Fergusson's remarkable pioneering publications about Indian architecture.

It is true that his *History of Indian and Eastern Architecture*, with its valuable illustrations, was twenty years away; and even his *The Illustrated Handbook of Architecture*, in which there is a section on India, was not published until 1855, by which time Brodrick had designed his domed version of the tower. In the *Handbook* there is an engraving of the Ghateshvara Temple at Barroli (Badoli), which has a square portico and an elegantly curved superstructure, giving it an outline not unlike that of the Town Hall tower.[3] But how could Brodrick have known about it in 1854?

He could, in fact, have known an even earlier publication by Fergusson, *Picturesque Illustrations of Ancient Architecture of Hindostan*, dated 1847. In this handsome folio volume, there are three relevant plates, of the Great Temple of Bobaneswar (Bhubaneshwar), the Temple of Jugganath (Jagannatha) at Puri, and the group of temples at Barroli (Badoli).[4] Fergusson's text stresses that

The principal part of all Hindu temples . . . is the vimana or great tower . . . Externally the vimana consists of a base perpendicular to a height varying from half its width to a whole diameter; and this is surmounted by the sikra (sechata), a sort of spire always of a curvilinear outline, though square or nearly so in section. In the older temples the diminution in diameter at the top is very slight, and the term tower is more applicable than spire.[5]

1 *The Builder*, 16 (1858), 811–13.

2 M. Archer, *Early Views of India* (London, 1980), plate 32.

3 J. Fergusson, *The Illustrated Handbook of Architecture*, 2 vols. (London, 1855), I, p. 111.

4 J. Fergusson, *Picturesque Illustrations of Ancient Architecture of Hindostan* (London, 1847–48), plates 1, 2, and 7.

5 Fergusson, op. cit. (note 4), p. 16.

111. An illustration, 'Temples at Barroli', from J. Fergusson's *Picturesque Illustrations of Ancient Architecture of Hindostan* (1847–48). Could such structures have been a source of the design of the domed tower of Leeds Town Hall?

The description could almost be of the Town Hall tower, and possibly some credence can be given to the idea of an Indian influence because of another of Brodrick's designs. The tower of Headingley Hill Congregational Church, Leeds, of 1864–66 terminates in a stone obelisk-like spire of which the four angles are given a slight inward curve towards the top. It is a singular spire for a Congregational church, but one might detect a similarity to some Hindu structures which, like the Leeds spire, often have bands of decoration with rosettes that are reminiscent of Brodrick's favourites.[6] One other aspect of this unlikely suggestion of an Eastern interest is in Hull. When the 1861 Town Hall was demolished in 1911, the domed cupola of the tower was re-erected in Pearson Park, and its appearance is curiously similar to the type of small mausoleum or garden pavilion such as one finds in Northern India. For a moment one can imagine one is in the Lodi Gardens in New Delhi, and not in Pearson Park. Perhaps Fergusson's words in another context are appropriate at this point:

I have occasionally asserted broadly what I have not attempted to prove, and what it is possible I could not prove satisfactorily were I to make the attempt, as sufficient evidence, either for or against it, may not yet have been collated to settle the matter definitively either one way or the other.[7]

6 In writing of the 'Hindoo Temples at Bindrabund' (see note 2), Daniell was impressed by the 'beautiful and singular Pagodas . . . certain carved ribs go equidistant with small figures prettily filled with rosettes'.

7 Fergusson, op. cit. (note 4), p. iii.

112. C. Brodrick: an unexecuted design for a Customs House commissioned for Bombay (1866).

But if all this seems uncorroborated fantasy, an Indian design made in 1866 does have real substance, even if it remained on paper.

With the sudden loss of cotton supplies from the United States during the American Civil War (1861–65), Bombay boomed as a source of supply from India, and this set in train a massive public-building programme which gave the town one of the finest groups of monumental Victorian architecture in the empire. This included the General Post Office (James Trubshawe 1869–72), the Public Works Office (Henry St. Clair Wilkins 1869–72), the University (George Gilbert Scott 1869–78), the High Court (James Augustus Fuller 1871–79), the Secretariat (Wilkins 1874), and the stunning Victoria Terminus (Frederick William Stevens 1878–87).[8] To this impressive list should have been added 'the Customs House (Cuthbert Brodrick 1866)', but it is still housed today in an old building, some parts of which probably date back to the Portuguese colony in the seventeenth century, after when it was taken over by the East India Company.

It was presumably as a replacement for this building that Brodrick designed a large structure in 1866. There is no record of a competition, so who commissioned the design? Presumably the government of India; but why Brodrick? And why was not it or any other design for the Customs House built in the 60s and 70s when the other new public buildings were constructed? There is an extraordinary lack of information — only an elevation in the RIBA Drawings Collection,[9] and a plan and elevation with a brief note in *The Builder,* which described the style of the building as being 'a mixture of Hindoo and Mohammedan'[10], an early example of political correctness.

Brodrick had done his research, probably using the Daniells' plates and Fergusson's *The Illustrated Handbook of Architecture.* In his interesting design there are more 'Mohammedan' than 'Hindoo' elements, such as the 'iwan' or high central arched entrance leading in to an open courtyard, the 'chattri' or domed kiosks above roof level, the 'jarokha' or hooded balconies. The design consists of a central building, three storeys high, deriving in form from characteristic gateways opening on to tombs or gardens. To each side is a long wing divided into five bays, each with

8 See G. Michell and P. Davies, *The Penguin Guide to the Monuments of India*, 2 vols. (Harmondsworth, 1990), II (by P. Davies), pp. 443–44.

9 RIBA, *Catalogue*, B, p. 108.

10 *The Builder*, 24 (1866), 724–25.

113. C. Brodrick: the Oriental Baths, Cookridge Street, Leeds (1866).

triple cusped openings, which reflect the courtyard screens of Jami Masjids or Friday Mosques such as those at Delhi and Fatehpur Sikri. These terminate in gateway pavilions and long wings at right angles to the main building. As in all Anglo-Indian buildings, open arcades are a feature of the design for ventilation. Perhaps this very creditable Anglo-Indian essay, which predates all those in Bombay listed above, illustrates some of the similarities between Islamic and European (especially Venetian) architecture. On the other hand, one can almost see behind this façade, on which Brodrick would undoubtedly have used with pleasure the coloured marbles that are traditional facing materials, the ghost of the large central arch and heavy attic of the Leeds Mechanics' Institute, as well as his favourite corner pavilions which terminate the wings.

Presumably, it was the estimated cost of £270,000, twice the final cost of Leeds Town Hall, which prevented the realization of this ambitious design; but then it was twice the size on plan, 970 feet long and 300 deep, and so long in plan and elevation that Brodrick had to have drawing boards specially made thirteen feet long so as to produce the necessary drawings.[11] These boards survived until the 1930s in the Hull office of Brodrick's direct successors. He was paid £3,000 for the abortive work he had done.[12]

It was a misfortune that this Indian commission was not realized, but in the same year, 1866, Brodrick did build an oriental design, and on a

11 T. B. Wilson, *Two Leeds Architects* (Leeds, 1937), p. 29.

12 Wilson, op. cit. (note 11), p. 29.

111

site in Cookridge Street, Leeds, opposite the Institute and next to the pair of shops and offices, 49–51, which he had designed in 1864. These latter are in an individual Gothic style, which must have contrasted strangely with their neighbour. Looking at the colourfully presented perspective in the RIBA Drawings Collection,[13] one might assume that the Oriental Baths were designed for a site in Roundhay Park (although the extensive estate had not yet become the property of the Leeds citizens). In the background and at the sides are feathery trees, and in front of the building appears to be an open site on which two riders on horseback are talking to a lady in her carriage while family groups stroll around as if the scene were in the Champs Elysées. The reality of Cookridge Street was never like Paris. The building which occupies most of the beautifully rendered watercolour is single-storey with a central section, wings, and pavilions — the standard Brodrick composition that goes back to Great Thornton Street Chapel, Hull. The façade is faced with horizontal coloured stripes, 'bands of red, blue, and black brick with freestone dressings'[14] around the cusped oriental/Gothic windows. There are Brodrick's rosettes below the windows, and on a frieze, above which is a crested parapet. On top of all this there is a central group of three small domes in front of a large flat one, out of which rises a tall striped minaret. There are small domes, too, on the end pavilions.

This extraordinary building was commissioned by the Oriental and General Bath Company of Leeds for £13,000. One might be forgiven for wondering if this design was ever built, especially as the public baths within living memory on the Cookridge Street site had an undistinguished Gothic frontage from 1882 until the building was demolished in 1969.[15] However, newspaper advertisements for Turkish, warm, and vapour baths, which include an illustration of a domed, striped building,[16] confirm that this unusual sight was to be seen in sober Leeds for almost twenty years, even though some of the richer details on the perspective were probably modified.

Presumably it was Brodrick's immersion in the novel style of the Customs House that directed his ideas towards other non-European examples, although the design of the Baths seems more in a late-eighteenth-century playful Picturesque tradition, while the Bombay building would have been a more serious Indo-Saracenic experiment. The associational quality of an oriental style with Turkish baths had already led to other attempts to capture the glamour and mystery of the East. In 1862 George Somers Clarke had provided the fashionable men about town with the 'Hammam' in Jermyn Street, which was described as 'the one perfect Turkish Bath in London'.[17] Perhaps Brodrick was a patron; but nearer home there was a building on the Foreshore at Scarborough, at the junction with Bland's Cliff, which had been built in 1859 to a design by J. J. Fairbank 'in the Saracenic style of architecture [with] a lofty Mooresque water tower and dome, besides a minaretted chimney shaft. The sea front has a series of Moorish arches, in red and white bricks, and stone pilasters and dressings, inlaid with encaustic tiles'. There was a tidal swimming-bath, medicated, and plunge baths, hot, cold, shower, and slipper baths, all, with the greatest delicacy, 'being lighted entirely from the

13 RIBA, *Catalogue*, B, p. 109.

14 Wilson, op. cit. (note 11), pp. 29–30.

15 The Gothic façade included the figure of a swimmer about to dive out of a canopied Gothic niche; see D. Linstrum, *Historic Architecture of Leeds* (Newcastle-upon-Tyne, 1969), p. 75.

16 See S. Burt and K. Grady, *The Illustrated History of Leeds* (Derby, 1994), p. 150.

17 *Building News*, 8 (1862), 12.

top'.[18] Maybe this local building suggested Brodrick's Leeds fantasy, or perhaps he knew the *moschee* which Ludwig Persius (1803–45) had designed at Potsdam in 1841 'in the style of a Turkish mosque with a minaret as chimney', a dome, and horizontally striped treatment of the façades with elaborate cresting.[19] Persius' interiors were Moorish; were Brodrick's? There is no record.

As a pendant to these colourful episodes in Brodrick's practice, mention should be made of an influence in the opposite direction, from west to east. Between 1872 and 1874, Maharaja Jayaji Rao of Gwalior built for himself a new city palace, the Jai Vilas. The architect was Lieutenant-Colonel Sir Michael Filose. At the centre of the building, approached up a crystal staircase, is the Durbar Hall. On the floor is the largest carpet in Asia; the furniture and ornaments are made from solid crystal, and from the ceiling hang two of the world's largest chandeliers, each weighing over three tons and holding two hundred and forty-eight candles. One visitor described it as 'like a pantomime palace with its vast chandeliers, its glass fountains, glass banisters, glass furniture and lustre fringes'.[20] But a closer look beyond the dazzle of glass and flickering flames reveals that the 'finest and most beautifully proportioned room in India' could owe something to Brodrick's Leeds Town Hall. There are the bays divided by coupled Corinthian columns, the lunette windows, the arched ribs of the vaulted ceiling, all very reminiscent of the Victoria Hall. Brodrick would have been in his element working for the Indian princes.

18 *The Builder*, 17 (1859), 374.

19 See G. Streidt and K. Frahm, *Potsdam: palaces and gardens of the Hohenzollerns* (Cologne, 1996), pp. 220–23.

20 The Maharaja of Baroda, *The Palaces of India* (London, 1980), pp. 108–13.

Living Like Lords

As a Hull-born man and the son of a shipping owner, Brodrick would certainly have known Scarborough well from his childhood. In 1837, the year he was articled to Lockwood, the town was described as

beautifully and romantically situated in the recess of a fine bay, on the coast of the North Sea, and [it] consists of several spacious streets of handsome well-built houses, rising in successive tiers from the shore, in the form of an amphitheatre . . . On the Cliffs are many new and handsome houses for private residence, and numerous lodging houses have been erected for the accommodation of visitors.[1]

As a port, Scarborough could not compare in importance with Hull, of which it was a member port, but there was a not inconsiderable trade with Portugal, Holland, and the Baltic countries. The principal imports were wine, brandy, gin, timber, hemp, flax, and iron, and there was a coastal trade in corn, butter, bacon, and salt-fish with Newcastle, Sunderland, and other places on the coast, and with the port of London for groceries. But Scarborough had been developing as a spa town since 1626. Gradually its fame spread, and during the eighteenth century it was increasingly visited by members of the nobility and gentry. It became a favourite town of travel diarists and, by the time Thomas Rowlandson's illustrations in *Poetical Sketches of Scarborough* (1812) had been published, sea bathing had been added to the health-giving activities; for the less hardy indoor baths had been provided.

St. Nicholas Cliff was considered the best part of the town where the most commodious lodgings were to be found, but early-nineteenth-century developments gave a change of social and architectural emphasis. The key to this was the Cliff Bridge which was started in 1826 to link St. Nicholas Cliff to the South Cliff, spanning the Valley between at a height of seventy feet. In importance it may be likened to the North Bridge in Edinburgh, which allowed the old town to expand into the formal spaciousness of the Classical new town, and it was vital to Scarborough's expansion to the south as well as to the development of the Spa, which was immediately granted on a long lease to the Cliff Bridge Company. The Bridge became a part of an early-nineteenth-century Picturesque landscape. Close to it, at the end of the Valley, Richard Hey Sharp of York built a museum in the form of a Classical rotunda. The Crescent, part of a development dating from the early 1830s, was built above the Valley in a sober Neoclassical design,[2] and in front of it a grand layout was envisaged of a series of seven linked villas set in the landscaped Valley,[3] at the sea end of which was to be a long colonnaded building with a portico. In the end, only three villas were built, and to a different, larger, design.

The development of the South Cliff began in the 1840s with the building of the terrace with the porticoed Crown Hotel as its centrepiece, and

1 S. Lewis, *A Topographical Dictionary of England...*, 4 vols. (London, 1831, 1837 reprint), IV, *s.n.* Scarborough.

2 H. Colvin, *A Biographical Dictionary of British Architects 1600–1840* (New Haven and London, 1995), p. 860.

3 Shown in an engraving dated 1832, reproduced in *Country Life,* 168 (18 April 1974), 942, fig. 5. The three villas are now the Natural History Museum, the Art Gallery, and offices of Scarborough Borough Council.

by 1852 there were thirty houses on the Cliff. Terraces and squares were added, and down below the Spa had been improved in 1837 when Henry Wyatt built a 'convenient and handsome building' in the castellated style. The town was slowly and sedately growing larger and more elegant when, in 1845, the railway came, and then the visitors began to arrive in even greater numbers from Newcastle and the north-east, but even more from Leeds and the West Riding. The development of the North Cliff, mainly as lodging-houses, dates from this time; but the more fashionable South Cliff also grew at a much quicker rate from the 1850s. Wyatt's building on the Spa proved too small, and in 1856 Sir Joseph Paxton was invited by the Cliff Bridge Company to advise them. He made a design in a Second Empire style for a large new saloon, built of stone and surrounded by cast-iron colonnades. This was destroyed in a fire, and replaced in 1877–80 by the present one designed in a similar style by Verity and Hunt.

In the early 1860s the newest hotels were the Crown and the Prince of Wales on the South Cliff above the gardens laid out according to Paxton's design with flower-beds, shrubberies, winding walks, and terraces. There was a custom in these hotels that the visitors should 'install a president, and subscribe, and give balls to those at another, to which they will invite any stranger they please'. But the fifty-bedroomed Crown and the sixty-bedroomed Prince of Wales with their little evening entertainments were soon to be overshadowed by a gigantic rival at the other end of the Cliff Bridge. The development of the railway brought with it an increased demand for accommodation. The Crown and the Prince of Wales had set a standard for better-class hotels, and the new ones attached to the stations at Hull (1849) and York (1852–53) were pioneers in catering for railway travellers in Yorkshire; but when the Scarborough Cliff Hotel Company was formed in 1862 its directors were thinking on a different scale. Their ambition was to build a great new hotel, metropolitan in character, not close to the station but on the most prominent site in the town overlooking the entire bay. It was to be modelled on the American hotels, with impressive public rooms and hundreds of bedrooms, which had been built in the 1850s in summer resorts.

Already some of the English railway companies had adopted a similar pattern for their London termini; and, as Prosper Mérimée wrote to Viollet-le-Duc from London in 1863, these huge buildings were 'dans le goût du Louvre'.[4] The first was at Paddington where the Great Western Hotel was built in 1851–53 (Philip Charles Hardwick), and then came the Grosvenor Hotel at Victoria (1859–60 James Knowles). These two were quickly followed by others in London, including the Charing Cross (1864 E. M. Barry) and the Langham (1864 John Giles), and the new company in Scarborough intended to emulate what had been done in London, despite the shortness of the spa town's holiday season. Doubtless they were also aware of similar developments in Paris, where the Grand Hôtel du Louvre had been built to cater for visitors to the 1855 Exposition universelle with such a profusion of bedrooms (seven hundred) and public rooms that it was described as 'a little town'. It was the result of a collaboration between Jacques-Ignace Hittorff and three other architects,

4 C. Mignot, *L'Architecture au XIXe siècle* (Fribourg, 1983), p. 158: 'le nouveau Louvre de Lefuel a été la référence culturelle du boum hôtelier des années 1850–80'.

115

114. Wells House, Ilkley (1854): the ground-floor plan (partly reconstructed and redrawn from an altered plan of the 1950s). 1. Drawing Room; 2. Dining Room; 3. Coffee Room(?); 4. Billiards Room(?). The other rooms have not been identified; nor is it certain if the rooms in the central part of the building are part of the original plan or a later remodelling.

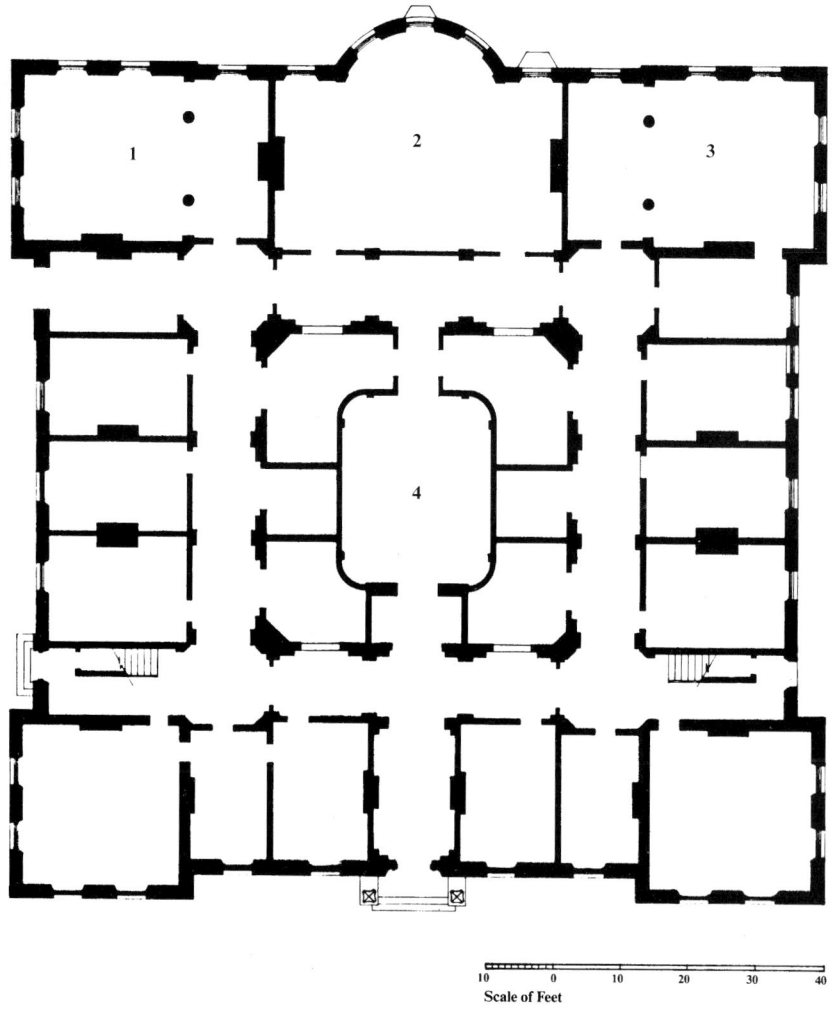

Scale of Feet

one of whom, Alfred Armand, was alone responsible for another Parisian Grand Hôtel close to the new Opéra.[5] It was completed in 1862, and it can be assumed that Brodrick, who had been appointed architect for the Scarborough hotel, was familiar with these Parisian innovations. It does not appear there was a competition for the building, which was to be called the Cliff Hotel, and his appointment was probably due to Dr. John Deakin Heaton, who had been such a force behind the realization of Leeds Town Hall and was actively and financially involved in the Scarborough enterprise.

Brodrick had already had some experience of designing hotels, although not on the scale of what was proposed. In February 1854 he received a commission to build Wells House, a hydropathic establishment on a moorland site overlooking the then small township of Ilkley, a place 'much frequented in the summer, for the benefit of a cold bath, which is supplied from a spring issuing out of a neighbouring hill'.[6] The health-giving qualities of its waters had been more comfortably reorganized in 1843–44 when the Ben Rhydding Hydropathic Establishment had been built in a Scottish baronial style. Nine years later a joint-stock company,

5 P. Boissel, *Le Grand Hôtel Inter-Continental, Paris 1862–1992* (Paris, 1992), pp. 5ff.

6 Lewis, op. cit. (note 1), II, *s.n.* Ilkley.

the Wells House Hydropathic Company and their architect, built in a very different style. Coming as it did at the same time as Brodrick was immersed in the problems of building Leeds Town Hall, it is hardly surprising that Wells House, which cost more than £30,000, shares something of its monumental character, and even its form to some extent. It is also the most Barry-esque Italianate of all Brodrick's buildings, and like the former's country-house palaces, such as Trentham and Cliveden, it would have been a more appropriate design for an urban site.

The plan resembles, to some extent, Barry's Reform Club (1837) in Pall Mall. The rooms are arranged around a central rectangle, but a local guide book rightly says that whereas

Italian buildings of this description have usually an open court in the centre, . . . here the space is occupied by offices, billiard-rooms, etc. . . . The corridors are broad and well-lighted, and form a valuable promenade when the weather is too inclement for outdoor exercise, and at all times for the most delicate of patients, being artificially heated.[7]

This wide corridor, again reminiscent of that surrounding the cortile in the Reform Club, gives access to the large rooms around the perimeter. All this accommodation is fitted within a solid, almost square building with projecting corner towers topped with belvedere attics and little cupolas. The lower storey is faced with the 'astrakhan'-type vermiculation used on parts of the Louvre, and the entrance doorway is reminiscent of that to the north-east wing of Castle Howard. In the centre of the front overlooking the then unobstructed spectacular view of Wharfedale from a wide terrace, there is a large shallow bow window which helps to create the effect of a miniature Blenheim Palace. On the east side of the building steps led down to marble-lined baths under a flat roof which was designed as a terrace for recreation. The masonry is beautifully detailed and executed, as the Town Hall clerk of works noted on 15 September 1856: 'Went to Ilkley . . . & saw the new Establishment Designed by Mr. Brodrick and was very much satisfied with the Building as a whole, and think the workmanship very creditable to all concerned with it'.[8]

7 J. Shuttleworth, *Shuttleworth's Guide Book to Ilkley and Vicinity* (Ilkley, 1863), p. 21.

8 West Yorkshire Archive Service, Leeds District Archives, LC/TO, Bin 42, C: extracts from the journal of the clerk of works.

116 and 117. Wells House, Ilkley: details of the stonework.

118. C. Brodrick: Wells House, Ilkley. A perspective view of the corridor leading to the Drawing Room.

9 J. Mayhall, *The Annals of Yorkshire, . . .*, 2nd edn., 3 vols. (London, 1878), I, p. 679. It was opened on 28 May 1856. In the previous year Brodrick had exhibited the design at the Royal Academy.

10 See Linstrum, *WYAA*, p. 105, note 4. The site layout included other attractions: 'A colonade

The accommodation in Wells House was spacious, with

a noble dining-room, calculated to dine comfortably from 80 to 100 guests, a large public drawing-room, a private drawing-room for ladies only, a coffee-room for general visitors, or those not wishing to join the company at the table d'hote, a billiard-room, thirteen private sitting-rooms, and six bath-rooms, &c., &c.[9]

The rooms were plain and dignified with little decorative plasterwork and austere fireplaces; but a watercolour by Brodrick of one of the wide corridors gives a good idea of how the decorations must have enhanced the spaces. Borrowed light enters through huge lunettes which probably contained coloured glass, one to each bay as in the Victoria Hall in Leeds; there are Greek ornaments over the doors, and the numerous pilasters are marbled. In the spandrels of the arches which cross the corridor between each bay, Brodrick placed his favourite stylized rosette. A design for an unidentified 'Board Room' probably dates from this time, and might have been intended for either Wells House or Leeds Town Hall. Wells House is the only building by Brodrick which is known to have been surrounded by a designed landscape. It was (to some extent probably is still) the work of Joshua Major (1787–1856), an important Yorkshire landscape gardener who lived at Knostrop, near Leeds, and was the author of several books on the subject.[10]

In the same year, 1854, as Brodrick was working on Wells House *and* Leeds Town Hall, he had a commission to design a layout and buildings for what it was hoped would prove a popular seaside resort. In 1854 the railway connected Hull to Withernsea, and Brodrick is credited with the modest station buildings along the line. His brief was to lay out a twenty-one-acre site as a residential development for the new resort, partly with semi-detached villas but mainly with streets of long

119. C. Brodrick: a design for an unidentified board room which seems to be contemporary with Wells House.

120. The Queen's Hotel, Withernsea (1854–55). An early lithograph of a now much-altered building.

[sic] was erected at a convenient distance from the house, 70 feet in length, in which is placed an American bowling alley. Here in wet weather the visitors resort, and amuse themselves with a variety of interesting games . . . In another part of the grounds is a building for Turkish baths'.

11 Beverley, County Hall, East Riding of Yorkshire Council Archives and Record Service, DDCC(2), plan 53: 'Plan of an Estate situated at Owthorn in Holderness' (1854).

brick-built terraces of two-bay lodging houses.[11] They were to be in a plain Late Georgian tradition with occasional pediments to relieve their length. This ambitious scheme was not executed, although the streets were laid out and developed later in a piecemeal fashion. But the other part of his brief, a forty-bedroom hotel, the Queen's, was built in 1854–55 in a form not unlike Wells House, but plainer, without the belvedere attics, and faced with grey bricks and minimal stone dressings. It is three

119

121. The Queen's Hotel, Leeds (1862): the ground-floor plan of the unsuccessful entry (redrawn from an old photograph of the original drawing). 1. Vestibule; 2. Hall; 3. Coffee Room; 4. Commercial Room; 5. Bar Parlour; 6. Bar; 7. First-class Refreshment Room; 8. Second-class Refreshment Room; 9. Smoking Room; 10. Sitting Room; 11. Dining Room; 12. Billiards Room.

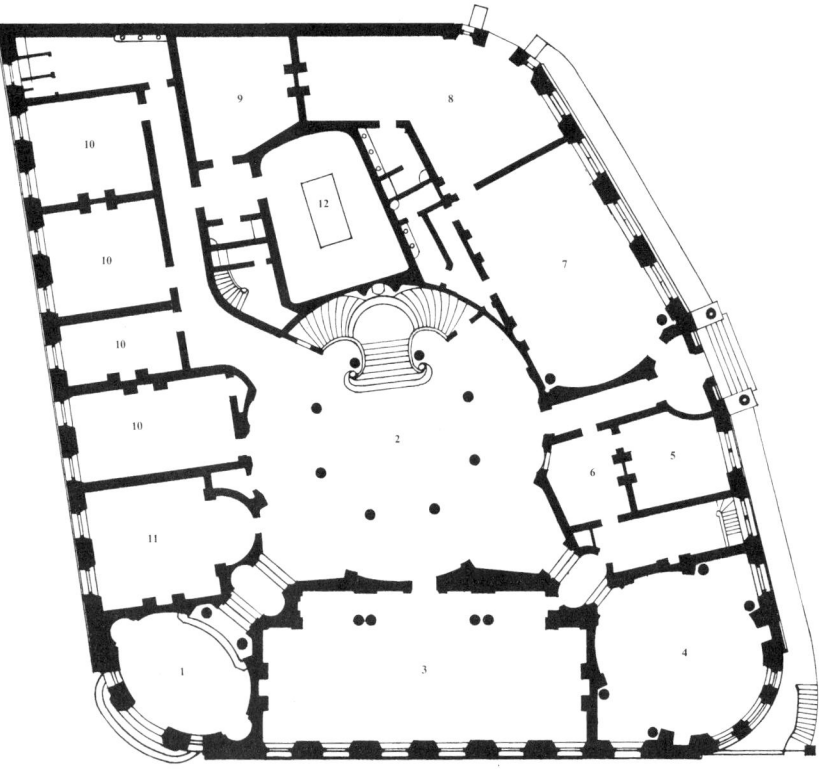

storeys high, eleven bays long, with slight projections at the two ends of the front façade which once overlooked the sea. The ground-floor windows are semicircular-headed, and there is a slightly ornamented frieze in the entablature, but otherwise it is an austere, sober design, more institutional in character than its advertisement as 'a most desirable Residence for Visitors, unsurpassed by any other Hotel on the coast' would suggest. It had a 'Ladies' Drawing Room, elegant Coffee Room, Billiard and Smoke Room, Baths', and its sanitary arrangements were said to be 'perfect'. So far as one can see from the much altered interior, there was little decoration; only two rooms seem to have had decorative plastered ceilings. There were pleasure grounds (possibly laid out by Major), which adjoined the land surrounding the church, which Brodrick rebuilt, and there was a music pavilion; but Withernsea failed to attract the expected visitors and the hotel proved 'too large and too costly'. In 1892 it became part of Hull Royal Infirmary.

Brodrick's third design for an hotel, of which he made alternative versions, would have been by far the most interesting of the three.[12] It is quite different in character, and although it was not built, it foreshadows his Scarborough hotel. In 1862 the Midland Railway Company held a competition for a building adjacent to the Wellington Station, Leeds. The site was restricted, but Brodrick made the most of the available space by using diagonal axes in the planning. In the more imaginative (and doubtless more expensive) design, the principal entrance was to be at the rounded corner of the building, through an elliptical vestibule, between columns, and up a short flight of wide steps into a central circular hall. A

12 The plans exist only in prints made from old slides.

120

122. C. Brodrick: the Queen's Hotel, Leeds. A perspective view of the Parisian-inspired, unsuccessful design.

balancing diagonal from the other corner would have passed through an elliptical Commercial Room, and between the two ellipses there was to be a long rectangular Coffee Room facing on to the street. True to Brodrick's taste for columns, there were to be eighteen within these four rooms, and a Baroque staircase with curving flights was to be fitted into the circular hall that would undoubtedly have been crowned with a glazed dome. There were also sitting rooms, a dining room, a billiards room, and public refreshment rooms for travellers.

This design raises an interesting question: did Brodrick know the plan of the Parisian hôtel de Montmorency, which had been designed by Claude-Nicolas Ledoux in 1769–71?[13] It has been pointed out that Ledoux's plan, which had been published, was based on a diagonal, so that the house seemed larger than it really was, and that in its ingenious planning, in which no two rooms were alike, he had made the most of a confined site. Exactly the same could be said of Brodrick's plan, except that he introduced two diagonals in an even more ingenious solution. Was it a coincidence? Or was this another case, like the Royal Institution, Hull, and the Corn Exchange, Leeds, of his looking to an historical precedent in Parisian architecture for inspiration? But externally the hotel

13 See Daniel Ramée (ed.), *Architecture de C. N. Ledoux,* 2 vols. (Paris, 1847; reprinted edn., London, 1983), plate 159; A. Vidler, *Claude-Nicolas Ledoux* (Massachusetts, 1990), pp. 36–39.

121

123. The Grand Hotel, Scarborough (1862–67), with the linking Cliff Bridge to the South Cliff and the Spa.

124. The Grand Hotel, Scarborough, from the Foreshore.

14 RIBA, *Catalogue*, B, p. 109.

15 See, e.g., an illustration in H.-R. Hitchcock, *Architecture: nineteenth and twentieth centuries* (Harmondsworth, 1958), plate 75A, of an apartment block *c.* 1860, 11 rue de Milan, Paris.

would have been up-to-date Second Empire, quite different from those at Ilkley and Withernsea.

The design shows a rusticated ground floor, and three storeys of windows set within dressed surrounds. Above the bracketed cornice is a row of pedimented dormer windows, and the corner entrance is treated with tiers of tripartite windows surmounted by an ornate, large dormer with scrolls, caryatids, and a broken segmental pediment.[14] The design could be for an apartment building in one of the new Parisian boulevards;[15] but apparently it did not suit the Midland Railway Company. Perhaps it was the costly decoration, including eighteen columns with pilaster responds, that lost Brodrick the commission and favoured William Perkin's less disciplined but stylistically not dissimilar design for the hotel, which was given the name of the Queen's and survived until 1935. However, there is

125. The Grand Hotel, Scarborough, from St. Nicholas Cliff.

126. C. Brodrick: an early design for the Grand Hotel before the final form of the domes and French Second Empire richness above the cornice. The intention at the time seems to have been to build a terrace of lodging houses at the Foreshore level where the Grand Restaurant (now demolished) was built in 1871 after Brodrick had given up practice.

a clear link between Brodrick's two 1862 hotel designs — the rejected one in Leeds and the executed one in Scarborough.

The site of the Scarborough hotel is on the seaward side of St. Nicholas Cliff, adjoining the north end of the Cliff Bridge. Perched, as it is, high above the level of the shore below, this meant expensive substructural work and resulted in a building which is nineteen bays in width, eight storeys high (including attics for servants in the domes) on the south-west side, and a total of eleven facing the sea. The three lower floors, which consisted of bedrooms and sitting rooms, are set forward of the main building so as to provide originally for a flat roof which was designed as a wide, planted terrace; at each end was a curved, ramped access and a domed 'guérite' or sentry-box. This level still exists, but a glazed superstructure was built over it in 1949 as a dining-room. The lowest level of the whole massive structure was apparently intended to be

127. The Grand Hotel, Scarborough, from the Cliff Bridge.

developed as a terrace of houses with access from the Foreshore; but instead it became the Grand Restaurant, which was built in 1871, but was demolished after being gutted by fire in 1942.

A design, known only from an old photograph of a perspective drawing, shows an earlier version of the hotel. It is not greatly different in general form from what was built, but there were some important changes. Brodrick's later thoughts about the design above the huge bracketed cornice are what give the building its extrovert, flamboyant character. Instead of the conventional mansard pavilion roofs, such as he had used on the Leeds Institute, he substituted domes with *oeil-de-boeuf* windows, and spiky finials. The present balustraded tops are a later addition. In front of each dome he placed an elaborate dormer window with a pediment and flanking caryatids, undoubtedly inspired by the similar features on Visconti and Lefuel's New Louvre. A row of smaller ornamental dormer windows around the entire roof, like those he had proposed for his unsuccessful design for the Midland Railway Company's hotel in Leeds, adds to the richness of the dominating skyline. There are some similarities to the Grosvenor Hotel in London; but the breathtaking siting and mass of Brodrick's building adds a Sublime quality. It seems not so much to be built on the hill, but to have become part of the hill itself, growing up out of it.

Henry-Russell Hitchcock succinctly identified the hotel as 'the climax of English Second Empire' and 'internationally the most notable example of its type'.[16] It is the decorative elements above the cornice level that are largely responsible for the Parisian character, but it is very probable that they were added after the completion of the building had become uncertain. It was first started by a company with twelve thousand £10 shares, but after the contractor had failed to complete his contract its future was in doubt.[17] In July 1865 Dr. Heaton wrote to his wife

I understand it is decided to 'wind up the Hotel'; a great pity that so good an undertaking should come to so bad an end . . . The building is now up to the cornice, and looking handsome; but it is standing still without any roof.[18]

16 Hitchcock, op. cit. (note 15), p. 162.

17 Mayhall, op. cit. (note 9), III, p. 122.

18 Unpublished letter from Heaton to his wife, 26 July 1865. The letters and diaries of Dr. Heaton are in the possession of Brian and Dorothy Payne.

128. The Grand Hotel, Scarborough: one of the crowning domes on the St. Nicholas Cliff frontage.

In August he wrote that the company 'came to a sudden collapse . . . in which process nearly all the money hitherto expended was absorbed'.[19] The unfinished building was sold to another company for £43,000, having then cost, with the site, upwards of £90,000, and Brodrick estimated that about £60,000 would be required to finish and furnish the hotel.[20] In November Heaton 'agreed to take shares in a new Company to buy the estate and complete the building'.[21] It is very likely that this was when Brodrick revised the design for the upper part above the cornice. Maybe he had been inspired by more visits to Paris; he was in Italy in 1862 and 1863,[22] and it is believed that 'not infrequently he made visits to Paris',[23] which would account for the increased use of Second Empire elements and decoration in his designs of the 60s. A sketch in the RIBA Drawings Collection, unfortunately undated, shows the final design of the hotel and is probably a preparatory setting-up drawing for the magnificent watercolour of the building in all its splendour which was exhibited at the Royal Academy in 1867, the year of its opening.[24]

Near the end of 1866 *The Builder* could report that the hotel was nearing completion.[25] On 7 June 1867 Dr. Heaton

went to Scarbro' . . . on this occasion, for the first time we were lodged and boarded in the Hotel. A serious crack was found in a massive brick column in the basement, which supported a wall rising to the top of the building; this was ordered to be strengthened with iron rods and plates. It was determined to give a public dinner on the opening of the Hotel, to be followed by a grand ball the next night.[26]

The grand opening took place on 24 July 1867 with a great banquet, the tables 'glittering with the splendid and massive plate of Elkington and Co., and with crystals, floral decorations, and banners profusely displayed'.[27] The following evening there was a ball which was inaugurated with a newly composed waltz by M. Lutz, 'Grand Hotel'. On these two occasions the public, or at least the two hundred privileged guests, could inspect the interior of the rechristened Grand Hotel. For once the name was appropriate.

They would have entered through a monumental tripartite porch, very Baroque in form, which incorporates a sculptured fantasy of shells, fishes, and other marine imagery, reminiscent of rich Parisian ornamentation, but also of some of the detailing in Trinity House Chapel, Hull. A small lobby then opens out into the central hall which, because of the trapezoidal site, is itself wedge-shaped and surrounded by giant arches two storeys high. The capitals of the piers are inventive and include shells and ammonites such as could be found on the local beaches. Above is a glazed dome, now underceiled, which would have emphasized the colour of the encaustic tiled floor and the dadoes. The other wall surfaces appear to have been marbled or else faced with decorative tiling, and there were painted figures in the spandrels of the arches. At the narrow end of the hall a staircase ascends, the first long flight branching out at a half-landing where an open archway discloses further spaces beyond. Above this arch another space is framed by detached columns and is cut across by a balcony. From the half-landing shorter flights on each side go up to the first-floor level, where the boldly patterned bronzed balustrade originally

19 Extract from Dr. Heaton's unpublished diary, August 1865.

20 *The Builder*, 23 (1865), 719.

21 Extract from Dr. Heaton's unpublished diary, November 1865.

22 This is known from Brodrick's dated drawings and watercolours of Italian views in the RIBA Drawings Collection; see RIBA, *Catalogue*, B, p. 111.

23 T. B. Wilson, *Two Leeds Architects* (Leeds, 1937), p. 33.

24 RIBA, *Catalogue*, B, p. 111.

25 *The Builder*, 24 (1866), 813.

26 Extract from Dr. Heaton's unpublished diary, 7 June 1867.

27 *The Scarborough Gazette*, 25 July 1867.

129–131. The Grand Hotel, Scarborough: carved stonework on the dormer windows and doorway, inspired by the New Louvre, Paris.

132. C. Brodrick: an outline perspective view of the Grand Hotel, Scarborough, intended as a preparatory setting-out drawing for the large watercolour (Fig. 133).

continued around the open arcades.[28] This Baroque concept could have been suggested by the staircase in the Painted Hall at Chatsworth, but it is more likely to derive from the Paris Opéra, which was under construction from 1862. Charles Garnier's design had been approved in the previous year and it had been well publicized. Brodrick could have seen the model that was exhibited in the Palais de l'Industrie in 1863. Like Garnier, Brodrick 'transformed a simple element of circulation into a major architectural statement . . . its cage an auditorium, and its staircase a stage'.[29]

As Mark Girouard wrote, 'in a big Victorian hotel a grand staircase was an essential'. It was part of the make-believe, if temporary, life that could be led in such an hotel as the Grand.

The clientele could live like lords — even more lavishly, if less selectly, than in a club — moreover their wives, who were not allowed into the club, could live like ladies. They could stand on the top of the great staircase and walk down it to the music of a string band and feel like Lady Manvers walking down the great stairs at Thoresby to open a ball.[30]

At the narrow end of the central hall, beyond the main flight of the staircase, was the Coffee Room, a quatrefoil on plan, of which the southern apse formed the bay commanding 'a range of view hardly equalled by any establishment on the East Coast'. The principal Drawing Room was

28 The balustrades at first-floor level were destroyed during the Second World War when the hotel was requisitioned by the Royal Air Force; see B. Perrett, *A Sense of Style* (Ormskirk, 1991), no page references.

29 C. C. Mead, *Charles Garnier's Paris Opera: architectural empathy and the renaissance of French classicism* (Cambridge (Mass.), 1991), p. 120.

30 M. Girouard, *The Spirit of the Age* (London, 1975), p. 168 (in chapter entitled 'All that money could buy').

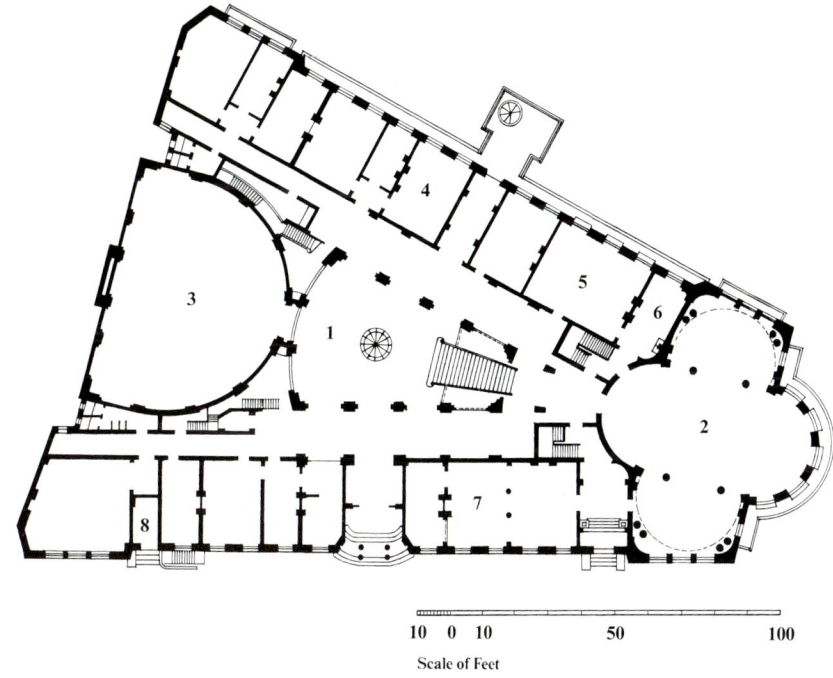

133. C. Brodrick: the presentation perspective of the Grand Hotel which was exhibited at the Royal Academy in 1867.

134. The Grand Hotel, Scarborough (1862): the ground-floor plan (redrawn from an old diagrammatic plan lacking the uses of the rooms). 1. Central Hall; 2. Coffee Room (Drawing Room above); 3. Ballroom/Dining Room; 4. Breakfast Room; 5. Dining Room; 6. Servery; 7. Club(?); 8. Telegraph Room.

10 0 10   50   100

Scale of Feet

31 *The Scarborough Gazette*, 25 July 1867.

above, following it in plan form and offering a more exalted panoramic view across to the South Cliff, to the Spa below, and of the next bays beyond. The 'apartment devoted to the daily *table d'hôte*' could seat three hundred diners and faced directly on to the sea. Apparently, 'by competent authorities [it was] pronounced one of the most magnificent dining-rooms in the United Kingdom',[31] although in fact it was too small.

135. Grand Hotel, Scarborough. A dormer window flanked by atlantes (male caryatids), inspired by the sculpture on the New Louvre.

At the wide end of the central hall was the Ballroom, which was lit by a dome. It was semicircular in plan and the walls were arcaded; the upper parts of the arches were open to the first-floor level to allow views of the dancing below, and to provide a background of music throughout the public spaces. There can be little doubt that in this room Brodrick had in mind the hemispherical salle des fêtes in the Grand Hôtel (or hôtel de la Paix) facing on to the new Paris Opéra. This luxurious establishment, the largest in Europe at the time, was designed by Alfred Armand and built over the surprisingly short period of fifteen months between April 1861 and June 1862. There were eight hundred rooms with bathrooms, lifts,

136. The Grand Hotel, Scarborough: the central hall in 1898. In common with the other interiors, much of its grandeur has been lost.

telephones, and hydropathic facilities, and the elegantly decorated small rooms of the café de la Paix occupied part of the perimeter on the ground floor. But the salle des fêtes, described as a 'monument unique au monde' and still in existence, was the most elaborately decorated interior with a double colonnade, caryatid figures, pendentives supporting a glazed dome, and glittering chandeliers. The Empress Eugénie, who attended the inauguration on 5 May 1862, exclaimed 'C'est absolument chez moi; je me suis crue a Compiègne ou à Fontainebleau'; and Offenbach conducted the music.[32] Scarborough could not rise to quite these heights, but Brodrick did his best, and after descending the great staircase the ladies could continue to feel like Lady Manvers, if not the empress herself, as they consulted their *carnets de bal*.

It was only to be expected that the manager, M. Augustus Fricour, should have been brought from the Hôtel Mirabeau in Paris, and that 'a Parisian *chef* of high repute' should have been put in charge of the cuisine. The *fourneau de cuisine* and broiling stoves were supplied by Messrs. Baudon et Fils of Paris. Equally predictably, the public rooms were furnished in French Second Empire style. *The Scarborough Gazette* drew attention particularly to the furnishing of the Drawing Room,

32 P. Boissel, op. cit. (note 5), p. 7.

129

137. The Grand Hotel, Scarborough: a detail of the coloured brickwork.

one of the most splendid rooms ever seen [which] is decorated in a most chaste manner, white, gris perle, and gold being the predominating colours. The seatings are in amber silk and brocade. White and gold . . . fauteuils and chairs, covered in gris perle reps, tufted with amber, break the monotony of amber that would otherwise prevail. The room is lit by four bronze statues, made by Messrs. Moray and Sons, purveyors to the Emperor, Paris and London, each bearing a cluster of twenty lights, with crystal pendants, which produce the most brilliant effect. The land and sea views from this room are so splendid that the novel experiment of dispensing with window hangings has been tried. It has often been remarked that when architects have done their best to produce rooms that are grand in prospect, lofty draperies are introduced, which are perfectly useless, and only serve to screen from the admirers of the sea one of the most splendid panoramas.[33]

The furniture for the hotel was mainly provided by William Smee and Sons, a London firm that 'ranked as one of the largest wholesalers of the mid-century' and issued its own catalogues, 'Designs for Furniture'. They had a reputation for products of good quality in the favourite styles, including French, and they exhibited in Paris at the 1855, 1867, and 1878 *expositions*.[34] The best pieces in their catalogues were labelled 'Superior', and no doubt these were the ones selected for the public rooms in the Grand Hotel. Apart from these impressive apartments, of which photographic records do not seem to have survived, there were also 'elegantly appropriate billiard and smoke rooms, bathrooms and lavatories supplied with hot, cold and sea water, quite a large number of private sitting and bedrooms en suite'. There were three hundred bedrooms, which appear to have found occupants. Dr. Heaton was able to write in 1868 that 'the Hotel is quite full, and many are being turned away; only the most expensive sitting-rooms don't let, which is a pity'.[35] For those guests who wished

to obviate the inconvenience generally complained of in large hotels, arising more from the size of the building than from any defect in the management, a complete system of Electric Bells, Steam Kitchen Lifts, Speaking and Despatch Tubes, Hydraulic Ascending Room, &c., &c., has been established, at a cost of several thousand pounds, which will place every public and private room of the Hotel in almost immediate connection with the Reception Room on the ground floor.[36]

The international character of the hotel was emphasized by the provision of a 'Telegraph Office, whence messages may be transmitted to all parts of the world'.

Externally, the bold and dominating form of the hotel on top of the cliff became the symbol of the moneyed West Riding on holiday. The luxury of the public rooms with their magnificent views would have compensated for what some visitors might have thought was external austerity despite the domes and dormers above the cornice, although Brodrick tempered the rows of identical windows by using orange moulded-brickwork surrounds, contrasting with the buff brick and the sandstone stringcourses. Evidently he had recently discovered the potential of moulded brickwork, since he also used it extensively in 1862 on the façade of a palatial group of warehouses in King Street, Leeds.[37] The red brickwork and the sandstone dressings were boldly detailed with characteristic ornament, and there was a frieze of garlands below a bracketed cornice. *The*

33 *The Scarborough Gazette*, 15 July 1867.

34 E. Joy, *Pictorial Dictionary of British 19th-Century Furniture* (Woodbridge, 1977), p. xxix. Smee's name is known as the supplier of furniture to the hotel because of an entry in Dr. Heaton's unpublished diary, May 1868; 'the large cabinet-maker who has furnished the Hotel . . . and who had invited us [Dr. and Mrs. Heaton] to spend a night at his home at Epping'. Smee's London factory was at 6 Finsbury Pavement.

35 Extract from an unpublished letter from Dr. Heaton, 12 September 1868.

36 A brochure in Scarborough Public Library, Local History Library: 'Grand Hotel, Scarboro', opened to the public, July 1867'.

37 Demolished in 1967, this was a fine building oddly reminiscent of Leo von Klenze's War Office in Munich (1824–26); see H.-R. Hitchcock, op. cit. (note 15), p. 26, fig. 4. Maybe Brodrick had been to Bavaria. Similar materials and details to the warehouse can still be seen on another in Leeds, at 1–2 York Place (Ernest Smith *c*. 1870).

138. C. Brodrick: the King Street warehouses, Leeds (1862). Now demolished.

139. A detail of a window in the King Street warehouses, Leeds.

38 *The Builder*, 20 (1862), 623.

Builder wrote of these warehouses that Brodrick had done good service by introducing 'the use of moulded brickwork':

Thus, with red, blue and black brick, moulded brick string-courses and mouldings, encaustic tiles and terracotta, we have a stock of materials which no climate will touch or destroy; and with them a field for design, both in form and colour, that will give our architects opportunities for exercising every artistic faculty they possess.[38]

There is a similar character in the brick-built pair of semi-detached houses, 37–39 North Bar Within, which Brodrick built in Beverley in 1861. The five-bay façade is strongly modelled, with arched windows on all three floors; those on the first floor have panelled stone heads within the arched openings, not unlike the detail on the ground-floor windows of the warehouses. The repetitive character of the elevations of these three buildings of such varied sizes — the hotel, the warehouses, and the pair of houses — was probably a legacy from Durand's writings, in which he also stressed that utility should take precedence of unnecessary extravagance and decoration; but Brodrick would not have entirely agreed with the latter dictum once he had experienced the heady pleasures of the Second Empire style. When he exhibited his magnificent perspective view of the hotel at the Royal Academy in 1867, the *Building News* wrote:

Mr. Brodrick treats us to the Palace of Aladdin of our youth, only considerably increased since then. That, if we recollect aright had only one dome; now we have four roc's eggs and more, each capped by its own particular incubator. Oh! that they would hatch a dividend; great would be their use, and we might then forgive their want of beauty. The rest of the building is of ordinary hotel character, but

140. 37–39 North Bar Within, Beverley (1861). An intrusion by Brodrick into a Georgian street.

39 *Building News*, 14 (1867), 334.

40 *Building News*, 4 (1858), 1289.

41 *The Scarborough Gazette*, 25 July 1867. The statistics are impressive. 'The building covers 3,996 square yards of ground; the total area of the several floors is 17,500 square yards. About 6,000,000 bricks were used, and 50,000 cubic feet of stone, excluding floors and staircases'.

42 A. Robertson, *Atkinson Grimshaw* (Oxford, 1988), p. 67. There is a similar painting of this subject, 'Scarborough Lights' (1877), in the Scarborough Art Gallery.

43 'circular façades of the "Grands" and the "Royals" of Scarborough and of Brooklyn; and their railways flank, cut through, and overhang this hotel whose plan was selected in the history of the most elegant and most colossal edifices of Italy, America, and Asia, and whose windows and terraces, at the moment full of expensive illumination, drinks and breezes, are open to the fancy of the travelers and the nobles who, — during the day allow all the tarantellas of the coast, — and even the ritornels of the illustrious valleys of art, to decorate most wonderfully the façades of Promontory Palace'. This version is on pp. 105–07 of the English translation by Louise Varèse, published under the title *Prose Poems from the Illuminations* (New York, 1946).

counterchanged; heretofore they have generally been red with white facings. This puts on a sort of bandsman's uniform of white faced with red.[39]

The sneering was unjustified

Just as Leeds Town Hall had taken on the character of a noble municipal palace resulting from West Riding industry and prosperity, so one can see that the Grand Hotel represents the ideal of an hotel in the 60s, as well as success and prosperity at play. The *Building News* had described the former as representing 'an age in which wealth has passed beyond simple comfort to the enjoyment of luxury. It speaks of abundance, and displays it'.[40] Exactly the same words could be used of the hotel, of which an awestruck writer commented after the opening:

The day of small things is apparently despised . . . The tastes and tendencies of the present age, in every place and department of life and society, are towards greatness, vastness of enterprise, magnificence of appearance, and often, of what may be described as sensational result.[41]

The hotel in its setting became a popular subject for painters, although few captured its grandeur better than Atkinson Grimshaw, especially in his 'Scarborough Bay' of 1871. As his biographer comments:

The brilliance of this night scene, with fisher-folk landing the catch, is watched over by the massive new hotel, symbol of the new wealth of the industrial age. The guests on holiday are unaware of the essential night-time activity for those who still earned their living in the old ways.[42]

The hotel has also found a place in literature. In 1886 the French Symbolist writer, Arthur Rimbaud, published his collection of prose poems under the title *Les Illuminations*. The hotel seems to have been in his mind when he wrote 'Promontoire', a poem that relies on the sound of the French words and almost defies translation. He writes of 'les façades circulaires des "Royal" ou des "Grand" de Scarbro' et de Brooklyn',

et leurs railways flanquent, creusent, surplombent les dispositions dans cet Hôtel, choisies dans l'histoire des plus élégantes et des plus colossales constructions de l'Italie, de l'Amérique, et de l'Asie, dont les fenêtres et les terrassses à present pleines d'éclairages, de boissons et de brises riches, sont ouvertes a l'esprit des voyageurs et des nobles, — qui permettent, aux heures du jour, a toutes les tarantelles des côtes, — et même aux ritournelles des vallées illustres de l'art, de décorer merveilleusement les façades du Palais-Promontoire.[43]

A later writer, Sir Osbert Sitwell, paid his tribute to the hotel in his novel *Before the Bombardment*. 'It uprose from the town', he wrote,

dominating the entire prospect, in the manner of Landseer's Monarch of the Glen, its four domes, instead of antlers, towering up into the glowering winter sky . . . It offers no comfort, spiritual, mental or bodily, but it is impossible to challenge its possession of a certain quality of stern, grandiose beauty . . . It stands there, its two vast façades capable of holding out against the four winds, a rock composed of yellow brick in an undeniably rare tint, decorated with surface patterns in other bricks of equally unusual red and purple, crowned with a high slate roof and four barrel-like domes. No building could crown an important site more satisfactorily. Even the porch, in shape akin to the fashionable bonnet of the period . . . possesses an indisputable atmosphere. When it was built no other social system was deemed possible, and so it was intended like the Great Pyramid to stand through all eternity, but an eternity that was to differ in no

141. John Atkinson Grimshaw (1836–93), the Leeds painter, made several romantic views of Scarborough, where he rented a house in the 1870s. 'Scarborough Bay' (1871) shows the dominating effect of the Grand Hotel in the wide panorama of the South Bay.

respect from the present . . . Upon this monstrous hub the entire system of the town's summer life revolves. Bath chairs, cabs, funiculars, tramways, shops, public gardens, promenades, crescents, terraces, the sands, the sea even, flutter round it as coloured ribbons whirl round an electric fan.[44]

The Scarborough building, which Sitwell described as 'obviously the work of an architect, as opposed to that of a commercial builder or latter-day luxury expert of the great hotel companies', was to be Brodrick's swan-song, although he did continue to enter competitions up to 1870 without being premiated. His Grand Hotel had been likened to the 'Palace of Aladdin', while his proposal for Manchester Town Hall had been sneered at as a palace for fairies. Something had gone wrong since his early successes, and the prospect of retirement from it all and a life of ease in his favourite city, Paris, must have been very tempting even although he was not yet fifty.

44 O. Sitwell, *Before the Bombardment* (London, 1926), pp. 112–14.

Parisian Epilogue

Brodrick had not entirely given up practice in 1870, as he submitted a competitive design in that year for a corn exchange in Mark Lane, London. Sixteen architects were invited, including W. H. Crossland, Banks and Barry, George Gilbert Scott junior, and thirteen submitted.[1] Almost as if making a final throw, Brodrick once again had recourse to Leeds Town Hall for inspiration. The fenestration of the three giant glazed arches of the frontage to Mark Lane is virtually a triplication of the large window between the Vestibule and the Victoria Hall, while the glazed vault over the entire space closely resembles that of the Victoria Hall itself transformed into an iron and glass structure.[2] The presentation drawings are, as usual, handsomely executed; but it is an extraordinary design. The submissions were examined by a committee which 'peremptorily refused admittance to any representative of the press',[3] but the winner was a fairly obscure Henry Stock. For Brodrick, it seems, that was that.

Apparently it was to be a total break. Dudley Harbron wrote that in his Hull–Leeds days Brodrick was 'a tall, dashing-looking man, clean shaven except for sideboards like those worn by Prince Albert. His hair was brushed back from his forehead, and he affected an artistic negligence in his dress. He was a striking-looking man'. But after he went to live in France he grew a beard and became less slim — a common result of French cuisine — and so the studio portrait of Brodrick wearing a top hat and looking every inch a Parisian presumably dates from the 70s when he was in his fifties. The self-portrait reproduced in Harbron's article appears to be later in date after the beard had grown bushier and more grizzled.

When did Brodrick decide to retire? In 1865 there had been a brief note in *The Builder* that about three hundred residences had already been built in a new and fashionable town outside Paris, le Vésinet;[4] did he see it and retain the information for further consideration? In 1867, even before the humiliating reception of his design for Manchester Town Hall, he was invited to accept nomination for the RIBA council, but he replied from his London address to decline the offer: 'I have no time to devote to the duties & think those only should be elected who can devote at least a certain amount of their time'.[5] Perhaps he had already thought about an early retirement. In 1870 he wrote from Paris, once again declining an offer that had apparently been repeated, although the letter of invitation had not been forwarded to him: 'I should not be able to act if elected'.[6] Despite these refusals, in 1874 he was elected,[7] but not surprisingly he never attended a meeting. In the following year, again from Paris, he wrote to resign from the institute, adding a postscript that 'I was not aware I had been elected to serve on the Committee last year until I found your letter which had been placed amongst the "Transactions" which I

1 *The Builder*, 28 (1870), 210.

2 RIBA, *Catalogue*, B, p. 109.

3 *The Builder*, 28 (1870), 569.

4 *The Builder*, 23 (1865), 800.

5 RIBA, Library, LC/4/10/26.

6 RIBA, Library, LC/7/5/13.

7 RIBA, Council Minutes, 16 March 1874, pp. 410, 413.

142 and 143. C. Brodrick: his final unsuccessful competition entry, for the Corn Exchange, Mark Lane, London (1870). It appears to show a revival of faith in Leeds Town Hall as a source of design.

saw for the first time last August'.[8] This final break with his profession was recorded in the council minutes for 3 January 1876.[9] Neither of the letters from Paris gives an address and the mystery that surrounded his departure from England was maintained.

The year, 1870, when Brodrick is believed to have taken up residence in Paris where he is said to have rented an apartment, was not an auspicious time. On 3 September Edmond de Goncourt wrote in his celebrated journal of Parisian life, men, and manners:

What a sight, that of Paris this evening, with the news of MacMahon's defeat and the capture of the Emperor spreading from group to group! Who can describe the consternation written on every face, the sound of aimless steps pacing the streets at random, the anxious conversations of shopkeepers and concierges on their doorsteps, the crowds collecting at street-corners and outside town-halls, the siege of the newspaper-kiosks, the triple line of readers gathering around every gas-lamp, and on chairs at the back of shops the dejected figures of women whom one senses to be alone and deprived of their men?[10]

On the next day a republic was declared and 'at the gate of the Tuileries, near the great pool, the gilt "N"s were hidden beneath old newspapers, and wreaths of immortelles hung in the place of the missing eagles'.[11] On 31 October the Commune was established, and then began the Prussian bombardment of Paris, first of the suburbs when the palace of Saint-Cloud was destroyed, and then on 6 January 1871 Goncourt wrote 'the shells have

8 RIBA, Library, LC/13/4/13.

9 RIBA, Council Minutes, 3 January 1876, p. 76.

10 R. Baldick (ed.), *Pages from the Goncourt Journal* (London, 1962), p. 169.

11 Baldick (ed.), op. cit. (note 10), p. 170.

144. J.-L.-E. Meissonier: 'The Palace of the Tuileries after the Commune' (1871).

begun falling' in the city itself. After that came the formal French capitulation to Prussia and the enthronement of King Wilhelm as emperor of Germany 'at Versailles, in the Hall of Mirrors, under the nose of the stone Louis XIV in the courtyard outside. That really marks the end of the greatness of France', lamented Goncourt.[12] But then came civil war, and in May the followers of the Commune began to set fire to the principal buildings as well as murdering the archbishop of Paris. Goncourt reported that

the Palais-Royal has been burnt down . . . The Tuileries need to be rebuilt along the garden and overlooking the Rue de Rivoli [it never was]. There is smoke everywhere, the air smells of burning and varnish, and on all sides one can hear the hissing of hose-pipes . . . The large-scale destruction begins at the Châtelet and carries on from there . . . On the other side of the embankment, the Palais de Justice has had the roof of its round tower decapitated. There is nothing left of the new buildings but the iron skeleton of the roof. The Prefecture of Police is a smouldering ruin, in whose bluish smoke the brand-new gold of the Sainte-Chapelle shines brightly.[13]

This was vandalism and terrorism on a grand scale. The large additions to the Palais de Justice had been completed according to the designs of Louis Duc in 1869 and awarded the Prix Napoléon III, having been judged the greatest artistic achievement of the Second Empire. As well as the Tuileries and the Palais Royal, a total of 238 private or public buildings were destroyed, including the Palais de la Légion d'Honneur in the hôtel de Salm, the cour des Comptes, and the library of the Louvre. But it was the sight of the ruined sixteenth-century Hôtel de Ville that moved Goncourt more than any other:

It is a splendid, a magnificent ruin. All pink and ash-green and the colour of white-hot steel, or turned to shining agate where the stone work has been burnt by paraffin, it looks like the ruin of an Italian palace, tinted by the sunshine of several centuries, or better still like the ruin of a magic palace, bathed in the theatrical glow of electric light. With its empty niches, its shattered or truncated statues, its broken clock, its tall window-frames and chimneys still standing in mid-air by some miracle of equilibrium, and its jagged silhouette outlined against the blue sky, it is a picturesque wonder which ought to be preserved if the country were not irrevocably condemned to the restorations of M. Viollet-le-Duc.[14]

It would have been a heartbreaking time for an architect who had conceived a great admiration for Parisian architecture; but how long did Brodrick stay when, as Goncourt reported on 19 April 1871, 'it was estimated that seven hundred thousand people had left Paris'? According to Dudley Harbron:

During the Commune [Brodrick] had to live in the basement. He saved his furniture and pictures by allowing a French officer and some of his men to share his flat, over which he hung out a large Union Jack.[15]

What other hardships did Brodrick have to put up with at this time? Was he still there when the shortage of food was partly answered by slaughtering the animals at the zoo? Goncourt wrote:

Out of curiosity I went into Roos's, the English butcher's shop on the Boulevard Haussmann, where I saw all sorts of weird remains. On the wall, hung in a place of honour, was the skinned trunk of young Pollux, the elephant at the Zoo; and in the midst of nameless meats and unusual horns, a boy was offering some camel's kidneys for sale . . . I fell back on a couple of larks which I carried off for my lunch tomorrow.[16]

12 Baldick (ed.), op. cit. (note 10), p. 183.

13 Baldick (ed.), op. cit. (note 10), pp. 192–93.

14 Baldick (ed.), op. cit. (note 10), p. 193.

15 D. Harbron, 'Cuthbert Brodrick: or Cabbages at Salona', *The Architectural Review,* 79 (1936), 35.

16 Baldick (ed.), op. cit. (note 10), p. 179.

It can hardly have been at this time that Brodrick, according to a persistent but unlikely story, was so short of money that he had to work as a waiter. Neither Harbron nor Wilson made mention of this, but neither did they suggest that Brodrick might not have been living alone in Paris. He is said to have moved from the flat, from which he was evicted by soldiers, and gone to Neuilly-sur-Seine,[17] a fashionable suburb to the north-west of the city which consisted largely of villas built on the grounds formerly surrounding a château burnt down during the 1848 Revolution. But in 1876 he moved yet again, this time further to the west and close to St. Germain-en-Laye. His choice of places in which to reside does not suggest he was short of money. The idea of creating a colony on the outskirts of Paris came in the first place from the duc de Morny, Napoleon III's elegant and influential half-brother, who was minister for the interior from 1863 until his death two years later. He was involved in many affairs, both of a business and a more personal nature; but in 1865 the emperor's enthusiasm for the large-scale rebuilding of Paris evidently caused de Morny to initiate his own ideas about planning. One result was the creation of Deauville as a fashionable watering place on the Normandy coast. The other was le Vésinet, in the *département* of Seine-et-Oise ten miles to the west of Paris.[18]

Morny suggested building a *ville-parc* on picturesque English lines to Alphonse Pallu, an industrialist and politician from Auvergne, who became so enthusiastic about it that he left his native province and settled in Paris to devote himself to developing the colony as an expression of original views on bourgeois life. It coincided with Haussmann's great reorganization of the capital and his creation of the bois de Boulogne, les Buttes-Chaumont, and the bois de Vincennes, with their winding paths, irregular lakes, and informally planted trees. In the case of le Vésinet, some of the last were indigenous since the 450-hectare site was a part of the ancient forest of Saint-Germain. But Haussmann had no connection with le Vésinet. Pallu consulted Paul de Lavenne, comte de Choulot, an amateur *compositeur des paysages*, who seems to have been the originator of the layout; he had assistance from M. Olive, a landscape architect, M. Petit, an engineer from the Ponts et Chaussées, and M. Dufrayer, a hydraulics engineer. One of Choulot's ideas was that there should be no walls between the different plots and gardens which are, in effect, part of the park, and he carefully controlled the planting of the trees in designated positions as well as protecting mature ones from being taken down.

The initial site work and the sale of building plots began in 1858, when an inducement to purchasers was the offer of a free ticket on the railway to and from Paris for three years. The plots varied considerably in size, as did the houses themselves, and among the early purchasers were wealthy industrialists who built large mansions as second homes which they occupied during the summer. But there were also artists; Gabriel Fauré lived there for a time, as did Georges Bizet, who wrote most of *La Jolie Fille de Perth* during his residence in the town. Another type of artist was Céleste Mogador, who sang every night in a *café-chantant* in Paris, returning to le Vésinet afterwards. Maurice de Vlaminck spent the early years of his life there, and later the flamboyant Count Robert de

17 T. B. Wilson, *Two Leeds Architects* (Leeds, 1937), p. 34.

18 See G. Poisson, *La Curieuse Histoire du Vésinet* (le Vésinet, 1986); G. Bauer, G. Baudez, J.-M. Roux, *Banlieus de charme ou l'art des quartiers-jardins* (Aix-en-Provence, 1980), pp. 38–57.

145. Le Vésinet: le lac Supérieur.

146. Le Vésinet: la rivière Anglaise.

19 See P. Jullian, *Robert de Montesquiou* (London, 1967), pp. 229–30. The Palais Rose is illustrated in Poisson, op. cit. (note 18), p. 165.

Montesquiou lived in the Palais Rose, a miniature Grand Trianon which had been built by a Parsee millionaire.[19]

By 1875 the population had reached 1,500 and le Vésinet became a municipality, of which Pallu became the first mayor; in 1877 a town hall was built, but not on a scale to which Brodrick was accustomed. By that time, too, the general character and layout had become established. The streets and roads varied considerably; some were formal, straight, and intersected at *ronds-points*, and some were winding; some were wide and some narrow, some tree-lined, others not. But there were trees everywhere. Water was a pervading feature, in the lac de Station and in the lac Supérieur, which was linked by the winding rivière Anglaise to the île des Ibis in the middle of a lake. The houses varied stylistically as well as in size, many of the earlier ones being narrow and tall with steep gables; but

138

in maturity the trees dominated the houses, framing them picturesquely or being reflected in the moving water.

Brodrick bought an existing house and garden at le Vésinet on 4 March 1876 from a M. E. F. Guibal. Initially the land was only 1,742 square metres in area, but later that year he enlarged his property by purchasing a further 2,285 square metres from the Société Pallu, at first the sole landowner.[20] This gave him around an acre of land. According to Wilson, Brodrick devoted a great deal of time to developing his garden, which it is said friends likened to a smaller Parc Monceau,[21] the eighteenth-century Parisian garden with its artificial ruins which Haussmann had extended and remodelled in the 1850s.[22] It was completed in 1861 and Brodrick must have admired this new *jardin anglais* which was, of course, much larger than his acre at le Vésinet.

The avenue du Belloy, in which his house was number 11, is a long, straight road, but he had a prime site, and from his veranda he had a fine view of the beautiful tree-fringed lac Supérieur. Like many of these houses, this one is three-storeyed, tall, and narrow, with 'à pans de bois' or half-timbering on the façade. A cast-iron veranda at the front opens into the dining room, behind which is a library, and to one side a drawing room. French windows open on to the garden from the latter rooms.

20 I am indebted to Mme. J. M. Paute, who did valuable research in the le Vésinet archives under the supervision of Professor André Parreaux.

21 Wilson, op. cit. (note 17), p. 35.

22 P. de Moncan, *Les Jardins du Baron Haussmann* (Paris, 1992), pp. 41–43.

The kitchen is set back to one side beyond the staircase. Above are the bedrooms, from some of which there is a fine view of the lake through trees and across an open green space, with an oblique view of the reinforced concrete *château d'eau* through which the water was introduced to le Vésinet's lakes and streams.

It may seem curious that an architect with such individual ideas did not design and build his own house, but there were probably good reasons why he wanted to move in without delay. For one thing, he was in his midfifties, and evidently there was someone else who had to be consulted. The census for 1876, the year in which he bought the house, shows that there were three in the household. There was a French servant, but there was also a Marguerite Cawling (more likely Cowling), who was described as English and 'sa femme'. This would bear out a family tale that he had not gone alone to France. According to the 1876 census, she had been born in England and was 48. The next census of 1881, five years later, gives her age as 59, and not 53 as one would expect. But what happened to her? And was she his wife? One asks because in the 1886 census Marguerite has become Margaret and aged 62, whereas Marguerite should have been 58. A woman does not usually add four years to her age. Even more confusing is a certificate of a marriage at the Marylebone Registry Office on 7 May 1885 between Cuthbert Brodrick, bachelor, aged 63, and Margaret Chatham, widow, aged 70; both were living in Berners Street, London. She had been born in York in 1814 as Margaret Barber; but she died at le Vésinet in 1888 and is buried in the cemetery. Her tombstone gives her age as 74; this seems to be one of the few fairly certain facts in a confused story of Marguerite and Margaret, of Cawling, Barber, and Chatham.

What did Brodrick do during the years he lived at le Vésinet, apart from cultivating his garden? Evidently he had nothing more to do with his profession after 1875, and he is said to have devoted his time to painting, exhibiting his works in the Salon until the late 80s,[23] but it has not

23 Harbron, op. cit. (note 15), 35.

been possible to verify this; and which Salon? There was the old-established one which, in 1881 and subsequent years, was given over to the artists who were members of the Société des artistes français; but that did not prevent internal dissension and a major split in 1889 which led to the founding of the Salon de la Société nationale des beaux-arts.[24] Maybe it is significant that Brodrick is said to have made his last drawing, of his residence at le Vésinet, in 1889. It is believed that one of his nieces went to look after him, but his name does not appear in the 1892 census, although Harbron and Wilson thought he had remained at le Vésinet until 1898. His last years were spent in Jersey, where he rented a house at Gorey, la Colline, in which he died on 2 March 1905 when 'his prowess in the 'sixties was dimly recalled by the newspapers'; but, as one of them commented, 'the generation which knew the famous architect had passed away'.[25]

24 J. Milner, *The Studios of Paris* (New Haven and London, 1998), pp. 55–56.

25 *The Yorkshire Post*, 4 March 1905. His nephews, John Henry Brodrick and William Stead Brodrick, were his executors and he left £7,490 9s. 1d. (Probate Record, 1905, A–B, 325), at least £350,000 at 1998 values.

Appendix A

Henry Francis Lockwood: list of works 1837–43 during Brodrick's time in his office

1837	Hull. Kingston College
	Hull. 44 Beverley Road
1838	Hull. British School, Dansom Lane
1839	Kirk Ella. Vicarage
	Beverley. Beverley and East Riding Public Rooms
	Hull. Trinity House Chapel
1840	Hull. Royal Infirmary, alterations and additions
	Welton. Eastdale
	Hull. Zoological Gardens
1841	Beverley. St. John's Anglican Chapel
	Driffield. Corn Exchange
	Hull. Great Thornton Street Chapel
	Hull. Holy Trinity Church, restoration and pulpit
1842	Hull. Albion Independent Congregational Chapel
	Burton Constable Hall, conservatory
1843	Liverpool. Workhouse, alterations
	Kirkdale. Industrial Schools
	Driffield. Police Station
	Market Weighton. Police Station
	Howden. Police Station
	Hull. Sculcoates Hospital

Appendix B

Cuthbert Brodrick: list of works executed or submitted in competitions

1846	Railway station in the East Riding (?)
	Hull. General Cemetery, lodges and chapel*
	Hull. Fish Market and Corn Exchange (C)
1847	Hull. Christ Church Schools
	Hessle. Layout for villa residences for Hull Charterhouse
1848	Hull. 4, 5, and 6 Silver Street for Hull Charterhouse
	Hull. Royal Flower Pot Hotel*
1850	Sigglesthorne Hall, enlargement
1852	Hessle. All Saints, restoration
	Hull. Royal Institution*
	Leeds. Town Hall
1853	Lund. All Saints, rebuilding
	Preston Town Hall (C)
	Driffield. National School
1854	Ilkley. Wells House Hydropathic Establishment
	Withernsea. Layout of terraces
	Withernsea. Queen's Hotel
	Withernsea. Railway Station, attributed*
1856	Driffield. 51 Market Place, bank
	Lille. Cathedral (C)
	London. Government offices (C)
1857	Paull. Vicarage (now Manor)
	Thorpe Bassett. Vicarage (now The Lowlands)
	Cherry Burton Hall, remodelling
1858	Withernsea. St. Nicholas, restoration
1859	Leeds. 7 Alma Road
	Leeds. Moorland Terrace*
	Manchester. Assize Courts (C)
1860	Scarborough. St. Mary, baptismal font and cover (C)
	Leeds. Corn Exchange
	Leeds. Mechanics' Institute
	Beverley. St. Mary, unspecified work
1861	Hull. Town Hall*
	Scarborough. St. Martin-on-the-Hill (C)
	Sydney. Houses of Parliament (C)
	Beverley. 37–39 North Bar Within

1862	Leeds. Queen's Hotel (C)
	Scarborough. Grand Hotel
	Leeds. King Street warehouses*
1863	Liverpool. Exchange Buildings (C)
	Bolton. Town Hall (C)
1864	Hull. St. John, remodelling*
	Leeds. 49–51 Cookridge Street
	Leeds. Headingley Hill Congregational Church
	London. Natural History Museum (C)
1866	Leeds. Oriental Baths*
	Hull. Dock Offices (C)
	Manchester. Exchange (C)
	Bombay. Custom House (unexecuted)
	London. National Gallery (C)
	Leeds. Wesleyan Theological College (C)
1867	Manchester. Town Hall (C)
1868	Castle Howard. Monument to 7th earl of Carlisle (C)
	Yokefleet Hall
1870	London. Corn Exchange, Mark Lane (C)
undated	Grimston Hall, design for staircase (probably unexecuted)

*	executed but subsequently demolished
(C)	unsuccessful competition entry

Appendix C

Leeds Town Hall: specification attached to Cuthbert Brodrick's competition entry (West Yorkshire Archive Service, Leeds District Archives, Acc. 4232)

<u>Leeds Town Hall</u>

<u>Description of Design marked "Honor alit Artes"</u>

The Buildings are placed at the North of the proposed site so as to give as large an area as possible in front of the principal façade.

The style of Architecture adopted is Roman and of the Corinthian Order.

The Building is two stories high with a Basement floor under part of it.

The Ground floor is principally devoted to the Law Courts and Music Hall with their respective rooms, the Music Hall being in the centre, and the Courts at each angle of the Building. On the first floor are the Town Clerks Offices, Borough Treasurers, Engineers, Surveyor and Inspectors Offices, with the Council Room, Mayors parlour, Committee Rooms &c.

The Police Offices are on the Basement Plan with the Gaol, Stables &c and other conveniences as required by the printed instructions.

On the East side of the Basement floor underneath the Refreshment Rooms are the Kitchens, Servants Hall, Cellars &c conveniently situated for the use of the public room, with a seperate staircase leading to them and to the first floor and Roof.

There is a seperate hot water apparatus for heating each of the Courts, Public Rooms and Council Room.

The Hall is 150 feet by 72 feet and 72 feet high with a semicircular arched roof reaching from wall to wall, it is divided into five large bays or compartments by means of coupled Corinthian Columns 30 feet high placed on a stylobate 12 feet high, in each bay there are two large windows spanning from side to side making with the one at the south end of the Room 11 windows to light the Hall. The North end of the Room is semicircular and occupied by the Orchestra. The other end of the Room is square with a gallery 25 feet deep running from side to side. At the back of the Gallery is the Council Room of semicircular form corresponding with the North End of the Hall which can upon any particular occasion be made to form part of the Hall by merely opening the folding doors. This will give additional space for at least 300 spectators sitting.

The length of the room will be nearly 200 feet when the Council Room is thrown open to it, in an ordinary shaped room of this length it would be almost impossible to hear any one speaking from the Orchestra, to remedy that defect as much as possible, it will be perceived that each end of the room is semicircular with coved ceilings, also the ceiling of the Room itself is semicircular, thus forming one of the best possible shaped room for acoustic properties.

The available space in the Hall for spectators is 8389 feet on the Ground floor, in the Orchestra 1363 feet, Gallery 1872 feet, and in the Council Room 2254 feet, altogether 13878 feet which at 4 feet for each person sitting will give 3470 and allowing 1½ feet for each person standing it will hold 9278 with the Council Room.

The Courts of Justice are as before stated at the four corners of the Building on the Ground floor, the two larger Courts are at the North, One for Criminals and the other for Civil business. they are 50 by 42 feet and 40 feet high with a Gallery in each, and are lighted from windows in the end and have the necessary rooms and offices mentioned in the furnished instructions adjoining.

The one for Criminal cases is immediately over the Prison to which as well as to the Police Offices there is an underground communication.

The two other Courts for the Justices are at the south, and are 40 by 30 feet and 35 feet high lighted from the sides, with a Gallery at one end. they have each a communication underground to the Police Station and Gaol as well as the necessary rooms adjoining.

The number of rooms and offices for the Town Clerk, Surveyor, Engineer, Town Treasurer, Police and Gaol &c are according to the instructions, for their sizes see the Drawings where each is shown.

The principal Entrance to the Building is in the south front. On entering you come into a large vestibule 90 feet long by 30 feet wide, on each side of the Doorways there are large staircases 8 feet wide which conducts you to the first floor, connecting the Vestibule with the Courts, is a Corridor 10 feet wide, which runs round the large Hall on each floor, serving as a means of access to all the apartments. [Faintly pencilled: 'How are the Corridors lit?']. Underneath the Staircase on the left hand side is another which conducts you to the Police Establishment and Gaol.

At the North end there are two other Staircases and Entrances of a smaller description which give immediate access to the Courts and offices the furthest from the principal Entrance, there is likewise a spacious Vestibule at that end of the Building formed by the Corridors and the circular end of the Hall.

The Police Establishment and Gaol although on the Basement floor are entirely above ground in consequence of their being placed on that part of the site which is lowest.

The Kitchen department is partly underground (that is the floor) in consequence of its being placed immediately under the Refreshment and Retiring Rooms.

146

It is proposed to face the whole of the Exterior of the Building with Park spring Stone according to the Drawings and to build the inner walls with either brick or stone for which seperate estimates are given, also an estimate is given for making the East side next to Calverley Street of a plainer character similar to that facing Oxford Place.

The Exterior of the large Hall is proposed to be covered with Galvanized Iron it being better adapted for a circular Roof, than slates.

The total cost of the Building as shown in the Drawing with Park Spring Stone and brick walls inside will be -.-.-.-.-.-.-.-.-.-.	£31632.7.0
If the inner walls are all stone -and-	£27900.7.0
If the East side is of a plain character	£26250.7.0

Appendix D

Leeds Town Hall: final costs (J. Mayhall, *The Annals of Yorkshire*, . . ., 2nd edn., 3 vols. (London, 1878), III, p. 14)

Purchase of land	9,084	16	9
Samuel Atack	8,637	7	0
Addy and Nichols	14,096	6	11
Architect's commission	3,685	0	0
Clerk of the works salary	1,027	14	10
Examining plans and prize money	728	15	6
Plasterer's work	2,658	14	4
Iron work	4,626	11	8
Plumber's work	1,692	18	11
Stone, bricks, lime, cement, &c	2,400	18	6
Joiner's and Mason's work	803	3	2
Wages paid to workmen on account of Atack's contract, &c	1,523	3	5
Chandeliers	2,491	14	0
Organ	5,837	4	6
Decorating large hall, vestibule, &c	1,595	10	0
Painting and papering	1,071	4	10
Models	747	10	1
Law charges and disbursements	706	10	0
Court fittings and furniture; including furniture, &c for her Majesty's visit	6,962	13	0
Paving vestibule	364	0	0
Bell	662	12	0
Printing, stationery and advertising	194	13	7
Miscellaneous expenses, including railway carriage	140	17	0
	111,739	0	0
Paid for additions and alterations since, on account of the Assizes, &c	10,261	0	0
	122,000	0	0

Appendix E

The Queen's Visit to Leeds, 6 and 7 September 1858 (J. Mayhall, *The Annals of Yorkshire, . . .*, 2nd edn., 3 vols. (London, 1878), I, pp. 717–28)

Queen Victoria's visit to Leeds for the purpose of inaugurating the Town Hall, forms one of the brightest events in local history. No sooner was it known that her Majesty would arrive in Leeds on Monday the 6th of Sept. and open the Town Hall on the following day, than a general anxiety was manifested to give her a right loyal welcome. The inhabitants seized the occasion to dress the town in the gayest costume. The preparations to receive her Majesty were on a gigantic scale, and of the utmost splendour; and notwithstanding the unfavourable state of the weather — a heavy sleety drizzle, falling in the afternoon of the 6th, accompanied by gusts of cold raw wind, — yet the streets were crowded to excess. The station was very tastefully and handsomely decorated. Sheds and rows of seats covered with scarlet cloth, and filled with ladies and gentlemen, gave an air of animation and pleasure to the scene. That part of the platform where the Queen was to alight was draped with scarlet cloth, and here were assembled the Earl of Derby, Earl Fitzwilliam, the Earl of Hardwicke, the Mayor and Mayoress, Viscount Goderich, Sir Harry Smith, Mr. William Fairbairn, the nephew of the Mayor, Mr. Denison M.P., the chairman of the company, the High Sheriff, and the whole of the Aldermen and Town Council of the borough. A quarter past six p.m. was the time her Majesty was expected to arrive; and accordingly, at that period, almost to the very second, the train glided into the station. The guard of honour of the 22nd saluted; the artillery began its regular salvos; and amid cheers and waving of handkerchiefs her Majesty alighted on the platform. The Earl of Derby and the Mayor were the first to welcome her to Leeds. The Mayoress gracefully bowed a profound welcome, and had the honour of presenting her Majesty with a magnificent bouquet of the most costly flowers. A few minutes were occupied in conversation, when the Queen, leaning on the arm of the Prince Consort, and followed by the Princesses Alice and Helena, passed out of the station, the Mayor going before them, the members of the corporation standing at each side and cheering. Once her Majesty's carriage was fairly seen outside the railway station, there arose such a cheer as has seldom been heard before. It was the cheer not only of the thousands to whom she was visible, but the cheers of all along the line of route: it was caught up and passed from street to street, over crowded housetops, and into places far removed from where the Queen would pass — one long sustained outburst of loyal enthusiasm. It was not alone a shout of welcome to her Majesty, but one of gratification at the knowledge that she was at last the guest of Leeds, and that for a time, if only for a few hours, the borough became the seat of empire of the greatest monarchy of the earth. Slowly from the railway the royal carriage descended into the streets — a little speck among the great mass of human beings who, shouting and cheering, pushing and throwing their hats and handkerchiefs into the air, as if they were demented, thronged up the streets, half wild with exultation and delight. From the station her Majesty proceeded to Woodsley House, the seat of Mr. Fairbairn, the Mayor of Leeds, everywhere meeting with the same ovation. The route taken was along Wellington Street, Queen Street, Park Street, Park Square, and past St. George's Church, up Clarendon Road to Woodsley House. Soon after her Majesty's arrival at the house, the royal commands were laid on Mr. Fairbairn to join the dinner party that evening. The other guests were the Earl of Derby, Lady Churchill, the Hon. Miss Stopford, Sir Charles Phipps, Major-General the Hon. G. Grey, and Lieutenant-Colonel the Hon. F. Ponsonby, with Miss Hildyard.

ILLUMINATION. — From all parts of the country round, the visitors had been flocking in on foot, in carts, by rail or road, or any avenue that led to Leeds. Every conveyance that could bear the strain of a beast of draught, and many that would not, and with which the experiment ought never to have been attempted, was pressed into the service. Not less than 150,000 or 200,000 people were crowded into the streets. Briggate, Boar Lane, Wellington Street, and Upperhead Row; and, in fact, all the places best illuminated were thronged. In Briggate and Upperhead Row the effect was beautiful; for neither money nor trouble had been spared upon the adornment of these thoroughfares. The first-named street was crossed in all directions with festoons of artificial flowers, so as to form across both road and paths a perfect arcade, from the wreaths of which depended coloured lamps. The transparencies and illuminations too, along the house-fronts were brilliant and varied, equalling those which once before were displayed in Leeds on the occasion of the fall of Sebastopol. It was past twelve o'clock before the last of the lamps went out.

Tuesday the 7th was looked forward to as the greatest day that Leeds had yet seen; but alas! the morning broke with heavy clouds, thick mist, and drizzling rain. From the earliest hours, however, thousands upon thousands came flocking into Leeds from all parts. Every street and alley of the town seemed thronged, and still thousands upon thousands kept coming in per rail from York, Bradford, Wakefield, Halifax, &c., until it seemed a question whether the last comers would find room enough even to get out of the trains. The arrangements made on the line of route from Woodsley House to the Town Hall were excellent. The streets were transformed for the day into a series of floral avenues, colonnades, and triumphal arches. Not only was the line throughout well kept by the constables of London and the district police, but by the friendly societies of Leeds, who were wisely pressed into the service, and lined the barriers inside along the whole route. Their members wore no insignia or badge, except a laurel leaf in the buttonhole, and white gloves, and on the royal procession passing they simply removed their hats, but took no part in the cheering. The greatest scene along the whole route of her Majesty's procession was at Woodhouse Moor, where the children of the Sunday Schools were mustered to the number of more than 32,000, of almost every age and every religious denomination. On the banks of the reservoir which bounds the western extremity of the plain of Woodhouse Moor were collected some 60,000 or 70,000 persons, who had made the best of the vantage ground which was here presented. Tier above tier they rose in dense masses, and it may be questioned whether such a multitude was ever before seen packed into so small a space. In the centre of the amphitheatre formed by these living walls stood the children, in two huge divisions, amounting to (inclusive of teachers) more than 16,000 each, divided into districts, parishes, and schools, and distinguished by their orange, crimson, or blue banners. The children were disposed upon two immense platforms or galleries, between which the royal cortège passed, each being about 170 yards in length; depth 27 and 45 ft. respectively. In the centre was a sort of elevated pulpit for the general director and his assistants, and above this was a tall rostrum, in which stood the musical conductor, Mr. Longbottom, the movements of whose baton were to sway and to modulate the fresh young voices of the crowd beneath him. From this centre, radiating equally on all sides, were posted signalmen, with huge boards, on which were printed in the largest of letters the various signals as "Prepare to cheer!" "Sing!" "Silence!" and "Dismiss!"

THE PROCESSION TO THE TOWN HALL. — Her Majesty left Woodsley House at half-past ten, and proceeded up Clarendon Road, along St. John's Hill, across Woodhouse Moor, down Woodhouse Lane, Upperhead Row, Briggate, Boar Lane, Wellington St., West St., Park Place, East Parade, to the Town Hall. The procession was a very long one, and consisted of the Mayor and corporation in their robes, and in carriages, &c.; a squadron of the 18th Hussars, and a squadron of the 2nd West York Light Infantry, &c. The royal procession however consisted only of three carriages. The first contained General Grey, her Majesty's Equerry; Sir Charles Phipps, K.C.B., Privy Purse; and Colonel Ponsonby, the Prince Consort's Equerry. The second contained the Earl of Derby, Minister in attendance; Miss Hildyard, the Princesses' Governess; Lady Churchill and the Hon. Miss Stopford, Maids of Honour to the Queen. The third contained the Queen, the Prince Consort, the Princess Alice, and the Princess Helena. Sir Harry Smith, K.C.B., rode on the left of her Majesty, and Earl Fitzwilliam (Lord Lieutenant of the West-Riding) on the right. At the time her Majesty started, the clouds broke up, and the sun shone fully as she came upon the moor amid the children. As the cortège came in sight of the children's platforms the signals "Prepare to cheer" rose up on every side, but they were needless; the difficulty was to keep the children quiet. 30,000 little trebles set agoing are not so easily stopped; and some time elapsed before the shouts ceased, and the thundering bass accompaniment of the populace outside went rumbling way in the distance. Then the conductor waved his hand, and slowly swelling upwards, like a vast organ of human voices, came "God save the Queen." With the first notes her Majesty held up her hand, and the carriage halted in the centre of the moor amid the children, while the great choir of singers went pealing forth their anthem with such a truth and sublimity as seemed to move even the most distant hearers. When this was over the procession continued its way, and the hymns of the children continued — the long soft notes of every psalm resounding far and near, and making themselves heard above the cheering, even when the procession was wending its way through the most crowded parts of Leeds. From this point her Majesty's reception was as grand in its enthusiasm as any thing could be. For nearly four miles it was one continued ovation. At the Town Hall the crowds were so great that the barriers seemed quite inadequate, and at last bent, cracked, and splintered before the immense pressure. The admirable arrangements of the police, however, averted all mishap. The crowd was pacified, the barriers shored up and bound with iron bands, and with such aids and exhortations to quietness the affair was managed.

THE INAUGURAL CEREMONIES. — At twenty minutes to twelve o'clock the royal cortege entered the great square in which the hall is situated, when the scene quite defies all attempts to pourtray it in words. The cheers literally seemed to rend the air. After acknowledging these salutes and those of the guard of honour, her Majesty and the Prince Consort gave their undivided attention to the noble building they had come to inaugurate. The Mayor and Mayoress received the royal party as they alighted, and the mayor conducted her Majesty and the Prince up the steps of the south facade. Repeatedly her Majesty stopped to examine and admire the edifice, till she entered the vestibule, where the architect, Mr. Brodrick, was in attendance, and had the honour of being presented. Here her Majesty had an opportunity of seeing the Mayor's princely gift to the town — her statue, by Noble, the sculptor. The hall was thronged with all the rank and fashion of the county, the varied dresses of the choirs above the northern end of the hall showing out like a rich parterre, a kind of background to the magnificent dresses and uniforms that thronged it in every part. As her Majesty entered, the whole mass of visitors rose and made the hall echo and vibrate again under the great welcome given to their Queen. Yet almost as suddenly as this began it ended, as the Queen, reaching the dais, stood with the Princess Alice on her right, the Prince Consort and Princess Helena on her left. The Bishop of Ripon, advancing, read aloud, with much solemnity, a prayer specially composed for the occasion. The national anthem followed. Mrs. Sunderland taking the second verse in solo, and then, advancing with the Mayor to the foot of the dais, the town clerk, Mr. Ikin, in a distinct tone of voice read the following address:—

TO THE QUEEN'S MOST EXCELLENT MAJESTY.

MAY IT PLEASE YOUR MAJESTY,

We, the Mayor, Aldermen, and Burgesses of the borough of Leeds, bid your Majesty welcome to this your faithful and loving town, and thank you from our hearts for having granted our prayer that you would make this happy and memorable day doubly happy and doubly memorable by your auspicious presence. We venture to hope that so excellent a judge of art as your Majesty; may find something to approve in the hall in which we are now for the first time assembled, and may be well pleased to see a stirring and thriving seat of English industry embellished by an edifice not inferior to those stately piles which still attest the ancient opulence of the great commercial cities of Italy and Flanders. For the mere purpose of municipal government a less spacious and costly building might have

152

sufficed. But in our architectural plans we have borne in mind the probability that at no very distant time civil and criminal justice may be dispensed to an extensive region in this town, the real capital of the West-Riding. We were also desirous to provide a place where large assemblies might meet in comfort to exercise their constitutional right of discussing public questions, to listen to instruction on literary and philosophical subjects, or to enjoy innocent amusements. Confident that nothing which concerns the happiness of your subjects, from the solemn administration of those laws which protect our lives and our property, down to the harmless recreations from which a laborious population returns with new vigour to its toils, can be uninteresting to your Majesty, we were encouraged to prefer our request that the opening of our hall might be graced by your presence; and we see with pride and pleasure the fulfilment of our hopes. We pray God to bless your Majesty; we pray God to prolong your reign; and we know that, in so praying, we are praying for our own happiness and for that of all your people. May a long line of descendants be, like you, repaid for the mild and constitutional exercise of regal power by the respect and love of a free and high-spirited nation. It is probable that in the days of those descendants experimental science will have made great progress; that inventions of which we have seen the promising infancy will have been brought by successive improvements near to perfection; and that the material wealth of our island may be such as would now seem fabulous. Yet we trust that even then our hall will be seen with interest as a memorial of a time when England already enjoyed order and freedom, profound tranquility, and steadily increasing prosperity, under a Sovereign exemplary in the discharge of every political and of every domestic duty; and that those who visit this building will contemplate it with double interest when they are told that it was inaugurated by the good Queen Victoria.

As this address was presented, her Majesty sent for the Earl of Derby, who was in the hall, to stand on the dais, and taking from his lordship her written reply, Her Majesty read aloud, amid breathless silence, as follows:—

Mr. Mayor and Gentlemen,
I accept with pleasure your loyal address; and I thank you sincerely for the cordial welcome with which I have been received. It is highly gratifying to me to witness the opening of this noble hall — a work well worthy of your active industry and enterprising spirit; and, while it will reflect a lasting honour on the town of Leeds, I feel assured that it will also secure to the thriving community whom you represent, the important social and municipal advantages for which it is designed.

The Mayor, the Town Clerk, with the mover and seconder of the address, Mr. Alderman Botterill, and Mr. Councillor Irwin, had then the honour of kissing hands; after which each member of the corporation was presented to her Majesty by name. The Town Clerk then read an address to the Prince Consort, which his royal highness gracefully acknowledged. Her Majesty then conferred for a few minutes with the Earl of Derby, and taking the sword of General Grey, signalled to the Mayor to kneel, and touching him lightly first on the right and then on the left shoulder, saying "Rise Sir Peter Fairbairn," the Mayor of Leeds rose up, amidst tremendous cheering. The Earl of Derby then came forward, and addressing the assembly, said, "I am commanded by her Majesty to declare that this hall is now opened" — an announcement which was responded to by loud cheers from all parts of the hall. The Hallelujah Chorus formed the fitting finale of the opening, which was sung by the entire choir in a very effective manner. Her Majesty, the Prince Consort, and the Royal Princesses then retired from the room amid the cordial farewell acclamations and manifestations of all assembled, and proceeded to a suite of private apartments in the building, where luncheon had been prepared for them. After the lapse of about half an hour the royal party again entered their carriages, and a few minutes after one o'clock they drove through the streets leading to the North-Eastern Station, which was gaily decorated for their reception. A few minutes later, about half past one o'clock, amid reiterated cheers from the spectators, her Majesty, accompanied by the Prince Consort, the Princesses Alice and Helena, the members of the household before mentioned, and the Earl of Derby, was on her way to Balmoral. Her Majesty was richly but simply attired, with that discriminating taste for which she is remarkable, as well in dress as in other matters. Her dress was a rich mauve silk with brocaded flounces. Her mantle was of white lace, ornamented very elaborately, apparently with needlework. Her bonnet also was of white lace, with a few simple flowers inside, and a short white veil also of lace. Her hair was plainly parted on each side of the face in what, we believe, is the "Victoria" fashion. The dress was of sufficient amplitude, but nothing to the mountains which some ladies indulge in. The Princesses were dressed exactly alike, — green and white silk dresses, with violet coloured mantles, and light bonnets trimmed with green. The Prince Consort wore an ordinary morning dress, with his blue ribbon of the Garter. In the afternoon, the Mayor, Sir Peter Fairbairn, gave a grand banquet at the Town Hall to a large number of guests, in honour of her Majesty's gracious visit.

DESCRIPTION OF THE TOWN HALL. — This magnificent building covers an area of 5600 square yards, and is bounded on the south by Park Lane, on the north by Great George's Street, on the west by Oxford Place, and on the east by Calverley Street. The site on which it is erected was purchased from John Blayds, Esq. for £9000. The form of the structure is a parallelogram, being 250 feet long by 200 feet in breadth. It stands on an elevated platform, and is surrounded by Corinthian columns and pilasters, supporting an entablature and balustrade, altogether about 67 feet in height. The large hall rises out of the centre of the building, to a height of 92 feet from the ground. The south or principal facade, which is approached by a handsome flight of 19 steps, 110 feet in length, has a deeply recessed portico of 12 columns, ten of them being in front, and two recessed. In the centre of this facade, and adjoining the south end of the large hall, rises the dome, or tower, which is 225 feet in height. The two sides and north end of the building are somewhat similar to the south front, excepting that the columns and pilasters which surround them are near to the walls, and the intercolumns, or spaces between them, have two tiers of circular-headed windows. The principal entrance is under the south portico, and consists of a large archway, 32 feet high by 21 feet wide. The lower part contains three splendid doors, composed of highly ornamented wrought and cast iron work, glazed. The tympanum of the arch has been filled in with an emblematic group of figures, and the panels have been elaborately carved, the work being executed by Mr. Thomas, of London, the celebrated sculptor of the Houses of Parliament. The group represents Leeds in its commercial and industrial character, fostering and encouraging the Arts and Sciences. The central figure, which is almost colossal, is that of a female, in free and elegant drapery, having in the outstretched right hand a wreath, and in the left the distaff. Immediately behind this figure is a judicial chair, ornamented with rays of light, and flanked by owls, emblematical of wisdom, as well as being supporters of the arms of Leeds. On the right there is a personification of Poetry and Music, with the lyre and pipe, a Faun's head, and wreath of flowers in the background; and also a figure of Industry looking with anxious care towards the principal figure, and holding in her hands samples of textile fabrics. She is represented as seated on a bale of goods, and resting her arm on an anvil, surrounded by various implements of trade. On the left there are also two figures, the one representing the Fine Arts, and the other Science. The former bears in her hands the emblems of painting, and leans upon a Corinthian capital, at the base of which is a bust of Minerva, the latter is represented in an attitude of repose, looking with a calm expression upon the figure of the Fine Arts, and holding in one hand the compass, in the other a globe, marked with the rudiments of geometry, and at her feet lie various portions of machinery. The panels forming the architrave to the arch, and spanning the group, are tastefully carved with various devices, selected from the arms of the town, with scroll ornaments, &c. The centre panel contains the scales of justice, surrounded with palm branches. The large panels on each side of the entrance doorways are filled in with bold and classic scrolls and foliage, in the centre of which is a child bearing the fleece, having beneath the fasces and other emblems of Power and Justice, and above the caduceus of Mercury, symbolic of Order, Peace, and Prosperity. The interior of the building is characterised by almost unequalled adaptation to the various municipal and judicial purposes it is intended to subserve, besides which it is in several important portions marked by ornamentation of the highest style of excellence. The principal entrance opens into a vestibule of very elegant proportions, with a domed ceiling, supported by four arches and fluted pilasters of the composite order, the apartment being 70 feet high, and 48 feet by 45 feet wide. It is separated from the large hall by a glass screen. In the centre of the vestibule stands a colossal statue in white marble of Queen Victoria, by Matthew Noble, Esq., of London, which stands upon a polished granite pedestal. The figure is 8 feet 6 inches high, and was presented to the corporation by the Mayor (Peter Fairbairn, Esq.) The floor is inlaid with encaustic tiles, from the works of Messrs. Minton, Hollings, and Co., of Stoke-upon-Trent. The great hall is entered from the vestibule, and whether viewed in relation to its size, the harmony of its proportions, or the extreme beauty of its decorations, it is one of the noblest public rooms in the country. Its dimensions are 161 feet long, by 72 feet wide, and 75 feet high. With the exception of a small balcony over the entrance, at the south end, the room is without galleries, and the general effect is considerably enhanced by the uninterrupted view thus obtained of the entire hall. It is enriched with ornament in relief and in colour in an almost lavish manner, every portion being more or less decorated. The sides of the hall are divided into five bays by composite Corinthian columns and pilasters, in imitation of Rosso Antico, with gilt bronze capitals and bases, standing upon a surbase, inlaid with precious and rare specimens of marbles, executed in the most finished style of painting. The inter-columns (or wall spaces between the columns) are of a pale green colour, bordered with a fret ornamental margin. The columns and pilasters support an enriched entablature, which, like the surbase, also run entirely round the hall. From this entablature springs the fine circular ceiling, which is divided into five bays, corresponding with the columns, each bay being subdivided into five compound panels, highly ornamented with conventional foliage, in relief and coloured. The hall is lighted by ten semicircular windows immediately above the entablature, and at the springing of the ceiling. They are of very large dimensions and are mixed with stained glass by Messrs. Edmundson and Son, of Manchester. Above the windows are appropriate figures and ornaments in full relief by Mr. John Thomas, of London. Projecting from the centres or key stones are ram's heads, from which are suspended ten magnificent cut glass chandeliers, made by Messrs. Osler, of Birmingham, specially for the hall. The north end of the hall is semicircular on plan, and coved at the top, the seats of the orchestra running across the front, — the organ, built by Messrs. Gray and Davidson, of London, from designs by Messrs. Smart and Spark, filling up the back. The case for this instrument from a design by Mr. Brodrick, has been made in Leeds by Messrs. Thorp and Atkinson. The ornamental portions are entirely of wood, and have been carved by Messrs. Matthews and Robinson, of Leeds. The pipes are burnished and diapered in gold, the woodwork being either gilded or of polished wainscot. On the top are four figures and the Leeds arms, standing in bold relief against the deep azure back ground of the cove, powdered with stars. The outward appearance of the organ is in strict "keeping" with the hall. Appropriate mottoes are inscribed in different parts of the hall. On the semicircular frieze at the north end are the words "Except the Lord build the house, they labour in vain that build it," and on the corresponding frieze at the opposite end, the text, "Except the Lord keep the city, the watchmen waketh but in vain." The other mottoes are placed on a level with the capitals of the columns, and run entirely round the hall:—"Honesty the best policy." — "Labor Omnia Vincit." — "Weave Truth with Trust." — "Magna Charta." — "Forward." — "Deo Regi, Patriæ." — "Trial by Jury." — "Auspicium Melioris Ævi." — "Good will towards men." — "Virtue the only Nobility." — "In Union is Strength." — "Glory to God in the highest." In the second recess of the large hall on the right, on entering, is the statue of the late Edward Baines, Esq., opposite which, is also the statue of the late Robert Hall, Esq., formerly M.P. for the borough. The whole of the coloured decorations in the large hall and vestibule were executed by John Crace, of London, at a cost of £1600. At each side of the large hall there are refreshment rooms, dressing rooms, retiring rooms, &c. The kitchen establishment connected with this portion of the building, is on the basement floor. There are also on the ground floor three Law Courts, and a Council Room for the meetings of the corporation. The two Law Courts at the north end of the building are each 55 feet long by 47 feet wide, and 45 feet in height. The Borough Court and Council Room are at the south end; the former being 55 feet long by 40 feet wide, and 40 feet high. These four apartments, situated at the four corners of the building, are of considerable architectural beauty, and are worthy neighbours to the grand hall. The rest of the ground floor is devoted to the town clerk's offices, borough surveyor's offices, rate office, judges', barristers', magistrates', jury, and waiting rooms; the whole being connected by a corridor, 10 feet in width, which runs entirely round the large hall, connecting the different entrances and vestibules together. The first or chamber floor is approached by four stone staircases, and contains the West-Riding magistrates' court, the mayor's reception rooms, and borough treasurer's offices. There is a large space all round the building, and the front, or south side, forms a good sized square, in the centre of which stands a bronze statue, on a polished granite pedestal, of the Duke of Wellington, by the Baron Marochetti. Equidistant from the statue are placed two handsome lamps, enclosed within a circle. The total cost of the building, including the interior fittings and decorations, and the organ, with the land, has been more than £100,000, raised by rates levied upon the inhabitants.

Bibliography

Aldrich, M. (ed.), *The Craces: royal decorators 1768-1899*, Brighton, 1990

Archer, J. H. G. (ed.), *Art and Architecture in Victorian Manchester*, Manchester, 1985

Archer, M., *Early Views of India*, London, 1980

Baroda, the Maharaja of, *The Palaces of India*, London, 1980

Bauer, G., Baudez, G., Roux, J.-M., *Banlieus de charme ou l'art des quartiers-jardins*, Aix-en-Provence, 1980

Beckwith, F., *Thomas Taylor, Regency Architect*, Leeds, 1949

Braham, A., *The Architecture of the French Enlightenment*, London, 1980

Briggs, A., *Victorian Cities*, London, 1963

The Builder (from 1842)

Building News (from 1856)

Burt, S., and Grady, K., *The Illustrated History of Leeds*, Derby, 1994

Casey, M., *et al.* (compilers and eds.), *Early Melbourne Architecture*, Melbourne, 1953

Crace, J. D., *The Art of Colour Decoration*, London, 1912

Crook, J. M., *William Burges and the High Victorian Dream*, London, 1981

Cunningham, C., *Victorian and Edwardian Town Halls*, London, 1981

Cunningham, C., and Waterhouse, P., *Alfred Waterhouse 1830-1905: biography of a practice*, Oxford, 1992

Davidson, R. (ed.), *Historic Public Buildings of Australia*, Melbourne, 1971

Deming, M. K., *La Halle au Blé de Paris 1762-1813*, Brussels, 1984

Dixon, R., and Muthesius, S., *Victorian Architecture*, London, 1978

Fergusson, J., *Picturesque Illustrations of Ancient Architecture of Hindostan*, London, 1847–48

Fergusson, J., *The Illustrated Handbook of Architecture*, 2 vols., London, 1855

Ferriday, P., *Lord Grimthorpe 1816-1905*, London, 1957

Gaito, D. N. K., 'Cuthbert Brodrick of Leeds: a Victorian architect', unpublished M.A. dissertation, University of Sheffield, 1976

Germann, G., *Gothic Revival in Europe and Britain: sources, influences and ideas*, London, 1972

Girouard, M., *Alfred Waterhouse and the Natural History Museum*, London, 1981

Goodhart-Rendel, H. S., 'Victorian Public Buildings', in P. Ferriday (ed.), *Victorian Architecture*, London, 1963

Hall, I. and E., *Historic Beverley*, York, 1973

Hall, I. and E., *Georgian Hull*, York, 1978/79

Hall, R. de Z., *Halifax Town Hall*, Halifax, 1963

Harbron, G. D., *Amphion; or, the Nineteenth Century*, London, 1930

Harbron, G. D., 'Cuthbert Brodrick: or Cabbages at Salona', *The Architectural Review*, 79 (1936), 33-35

Harper, R. H., *Victorian Architectural Competitions*, London, 1983

Hitchcock, H.-R., *Early Victorian Architecture in Britain*, 2 vols., London, 1954

Hitchcock, H.-R., *Architecture: nineteenth and twentieth centuries*, Harmondsworth, 1958

James, J., *Continuation and Additions to the History of Bradford and its Parish*, Bradford 1866

Leveson, C., 'The work of Cuthbert Brodrick 1844-1869', unpublished M.A. dissertation, De Montfort University, 1995.

Linstrum, D., 'Architecture of Cuthbert Brodrick', *Country Life*, 141 (1967), 1379-81

Linstrum, D., *Historic Architecture of Leeds*, Newcastle-upon-Tyne, 1969

Linstrum, D., 'Cuthbert Brodrick: an interpretation of a Victorian architect', *The Journal of the Royal Society of Arts*, 119 (January 1971), 72-88

Linstrum, D., *West Yorkshire Architects and Architecture*, London, 1978

Longmore, D., 'Cuthbert Brodrick's use of ornament', unpublished B.A. dissertation, University of Leeds, 1975

Loyer, F., *Paris, Nineteenth-Century Architecture and Urbanism*, New York, 1988

Mayhall, J., *The Annals of Yorkshire, ...*, 2nd edn., 3 vols., London, 1878

Middleton, R., and Watkin, D., *Neoclassical and 19th-Century Architecture*, New York, 1980

Mignot, C., *L'Architecture au XIXe siècle*, Fribourg, 1983

Milner, J., *The Studios of Paris*, New Haven and London, 1998

Moncan, P. de., *Les Jardins du Baron Haussmann*, Paris, 1992

Moncan, P. de., and Mahout, C., *Le Paris de Baron Haussmann*, Paris, 1991

Morgan, E. J. R., and Gilbert, S. H., *Early Adelaide Architecture*, Melbourne, 1969

Mosser, M., Rochebouët, B. de, Bruson, J. M. (eds.), *Le Catalogue de l'exposition Alexandre-Théodore Brongniart (1739-1813): architecture et décor*, Musée Carnavalet 22 avril –13 juillet 1986, Paris, 1986

Neave, D., *Lost Churches and Chapels of Hull*, Hull, 1991

Perrett, B., *A Sense of Style: being a brief history of the Grand Hotel, Scarborough*, Ormskirk, 1991

Pevsner, N., 'Victorian Prolegomena', in P. Ferriday (ed.), *Victorian Architecture*, London, 1963

Pevsner, N., *The Buildings of England: Yorkshire, the West Riding*, 2nd edn., Harmondsworth, 1967

Pevsner, N., and Neave, D., *The Buildings of England: York and the East Riding*, 2nd edn., London, 1995

Physick, J., and Darby, M., *Marble Halls*, London, 1973

Poisson, G., *La Curieuse Histoire du Vésinet*, le Vésinet, 1986

Port, M. H., *Imperial London: civil government building in London 1850-1915*, New Haven and London, 1995

Reid, T. W. (ed.), *A Memoir of John Deakin Heaton, M.D., of Leeds*, London, 1883

Robertson, A., *Atkinson Grimshaw*, Oxford, 1988

Rumsby, J. H., *The Hull Dock Offices, 1787-1976*, Hull, 1976

Saddy, P., *Henri Labrouste, architecte, 1801-75*, Paris, 1977

Scott, G. G., *Remarks on Secular and Domestic Architecture, Present and Future*, London, 1857

Scott, G. G., *Personal and Professional Recollections*, London, 1879; facsimile: Stamford, 1995, with introduction by G. Stamp

Sheahan, J. J., *General and Concise History and Description of the Town and Port of Kingston-upon-Hull*, London, 1864

Sheahan, J. J., *History of the Town and Port of Kingston-upon-Hull*, 2nd edn., Hull, 1866

Sheahan, J. J., and Whellan, T., *History and Topography of the City of York; the Ainsty Wapentake; and the East Riding of Yorkshire*, 2 vols., Beverley, 1855, 1856

Shuttleworth, J., *Shuttleworth's Guide Book to Ilkley and Vicinity*, Ilkley, 1863

Sitwell, O., *Before the Bombardment*, London, 1926

Stewart, C., *The Stones of Manchester*, London, 1956

Summerson, J., *Victorian Architecture: four studies in evaluation*, New York and London, 1970

Szambien, W., 'Durand and the continuity of tradition', in R. Middleton (ed.), *The Beaux-Arts and Nineteenth-Century Architecture*, London, 1982

Taylor, N., *Monuments of Commerce*, Feltham, 1968

Toplis, I., *The Foreign Office: an architectural history*, London and New York, 1987

Tyack, G., *Sir James Pennethorne and the Making of Victorian London*, Cambridge, 1992

Vidler, A., *Claude-Nicolas Ledoux*, Massachusetts, 1990

Villari, S., *J. N. L. Durand (1760-1834): art and science of architecture*, New York, 1990

Watkin, D., *The Life and Work of C. R. Cockerell*, London, 1974

Webster, C., *R. D. Chantrell: his life and work in Leeds 1818-1847*, Leeds, 1992

Webster, C., 'The architectural profession in Leeds 1800-50: a case-study in provincial practice', *Architectural History*, 38 (1995), 176-91

Wilson, T. B., *Two Leeds Architects*, Leeds, 1937

Zanten, D. van, 'Architectural composition at the École des Beaux-Arts from Charles Percier to Charles Garnier', in A. Drexler (ed.), *The Architecture of the École des Beaux-Arts*, London, 1977

159

Index

(Numerals in bold refer to illustrations)

161